Corpus Linguistics for '

Corpus Linguistics for Vocabulary provides a practical introduction to using corpus linguistics in vocabulary studies. Using freely available corpus tools, the author provides a step-by-step guide on how corpora can be used to explore key vocabulary-related research questions and topics such as:

- The frequency of English words and how to choose which ones should be taught to learners;
- How spoken vocabulary differs from written vocabulary, and how academic vocabulary differs from general vocabulary;
- How vocabulary contributes to the structure of discourse, and the pragmatic functions it fulfils.

Featuring case studies and tasks throughout, Corpus Linguistics for Vocabulary provides a clear and accessible guide and is essential reading for students and teachers wanting to understand, appreciate and conduct corpus-based research in vocabulary studies.

Paweł Szudarski is a Teaching Associate in the School of English at the University of Nottingham, UK.

Routledge Corpus Linguistics Guides

Routledge Corpus Linguistics Guides provide accessible and practical introductions to using corpus linguistic methods in key sub-fields within linguistics. Corpus linguistics is one of the most dynamic and rapidly developing areas in the field of language studies, and use of corpora is an important part of modern linguistic research. Books in this series provide the ideal guide for students and researchers using corpus data for research and study in a variety of subject areas.

SERIES CONSULTANT: RONALD CARTER
Ronald Carter is Research Professor of Modern English Language in the School of English at the University of Nottingham, UK. He is the co-series editor of the Routledge Applied Linguistics, Routledge Introductions to Applied Linguistics and Routledge English Language Introductions series.

SERIES CONSULTANT: MICHAEL McCARTHY
Michael McCarthy is Emeritus Professor of Applied Linguistics at the University of Nottingham, UK, Adjunct Professor of Applied Linguistics at the University of Limerick, Ireland and Visiting Professor in Applied Linguistics at Newcastle University, UK. He is co-editor of the Routledge Handbook of Corpus Linguistics and editor of the Routledge Domains of Discourse series.

OTHER TITLES IN THIS SERIES

Corpus Linguistics for ELT
Ivor Timmis

Corpus Linguistics for Translation and Contrastive Studies
Mikhail Mikhailov and Robert Cooper

More information about this series can be found at www.routledge.com/series/RCLG

Routledge
Taylor & Francis Group

Corpus Linguistics for Vocabulary

A Guide for Research

Paweł Szudarski

Routledge
Taylor & Francis Group

LONDON AND NEW YORK

First published 2018
by Routledge
2 Park Square, Milton Park, Abingdon, Oxon OX14 4RN

and by Routledge
711 Third Avenue, New York, NY 10017

Routledge is an imprint of the Taylor & Francis Group, an informa business

British Library Cataloguing-in-Publication Data
A catalogue record for this book is available from the British Library

Library of Congress Cataloging-in-Publication Data
A catalog record for this book has been requested

ISBN: 978-1-138-18721-4 (hbk)
ISBN: 978-1-138-18722-1 (pbk)
ISBN: 978-1-315-10776-9 (ebk)

Typeset in Times New Roman
by Swales & Willis Ltd, Exeter, Devon, UK

Contents

Figures

Tables

Acknowledgments

I would like to express my gratitude to Ronald Carter for introducing me to the world of corpora – without his encouragement and guidance, this book would not have been written. I would also like to thank Michael McCarthy for his comments on the initial book proposal and his useful ideas about the chapter on learner vocabulary.

I owe special thanks to Norbert Schmitt whose expertise in applied linguistics I have been able to draw on. His research group is a wonderful resource and regular discussions with its members have been instrumental in developing my own understanding of vocabulary and its use.

Many thanks are due to Hilde van Zeeland, Wipapan Ngampramuan, Matylda Weidner, Natalia Szygenda and Marion Fouan for their help as well as valuable comments on the early versions of the manuscript.

I am similarly grateful to my editorial team, Nadia Seemungal, Helen Tredget and Sally Evans-Darby, for their useful suggestions.

Finally, I would like to thank my family and friends for their patience and support throughout the process of writing this book.

Paweł Szudarski
June 2017, Nottingham

Introduction and aims of the book

Over the last thirty years corpus linguistics has evolved into "a healthy, vibrant discipline" (McCarthy and O'Keeffe 2010: 12), which relies on corpora as a means of studying language. In broad terms, corpora can be defined as large, principled and computer-readable collections of texts that allow analysis of **patterns** of language use across different **contexts**. As suggested by Sinclair (1991: 100), by collecting large amounts of data and looking at "a lot of it at once", corpus linguistics provides us with a new perspective on different aspects of real-life communication and offers "strong support for the view that language variation is systematic and can be described using empirical, quantitative methods" (Biber and Reppen 2015: 2).

Considering the fact that **corpus** techniques have become "an indispensable component of the methodological toolbox" (McEnery and Hardie 2012: 226) of modern applied linguists, the aim of this book is to introduce a range of corpus tools and procedures that are increasingly important for investigating patterns and intricacies within naturally occurring language. More specifically, *Corpus Linguistics for Vocabulary* has been written as a practical guide for students, teachers and language practitioners with little or no experience in corpus analysis. Having this particular audience in mind, the book presents corpus linguistics as a powerful methodology that can be employed to explore a wide variety of issues related to the use of vocabulary.

If you are new to corpus linguistics, you might be assuming that it is a highly technical area that is well beyond your capabilities. It is hoped that this book will help you overcome this assumption and equip you with all the necessary skills that are needed to engage in corpus research. The book offers many instances of corpus projects and exemplary studies focused on vocabulary, which will provide you with guidance and inspiration for your own empirical work in this area. This means that rather than being another general introduction to corpus linguistics, *Corpus Linguistics for Vocabulary* is more specific in its scope and covers the most important issues that pertain to vocabulary studies.

Given that corpus techniques can be employed to address different lines of vocabulary research, the subsequent chapters focus on a variety of topics and explain how your research can benefit from corpus-based analysis. Here is a list of some of the research questions we will discuss:

1   Which English **words** are the most frequent ones? Content or function words?
2   How is spoken vocabulary different from written vocabulary?
3   Why are collocations and other kinds of **multiword units** an important element of language?
4   How can I use corpus data in language teaching? How can corpus-based lists of vocabulary help me decide which words should be taught first?
5   What are the key features of learner vocabulary?
6   What is academic vocabulary? How is it different from general vocabulary?
7   How does vocabulary contribute to the structure of **discourse**?
8   What pragmatic functions does vocabulary fulfill?

All of these questions represent highly relevant issues to the study of vocabulary and by reading the book you will learn how corpora can assist you in finding answers to them.

Crucially, throughout the book you will find numerous practical activities and tasks (with answers and a commentary at the end) based on publicly available web-based interfaces. The aim of these activities is to familiarize you with different aspects of corpus analysis and, as you continue reading and make progress in your corpus journey, I encourage you to begin your own explorations of the highly patterned nature of vocabulary. Also, the book strives to highlight the fact that there is a lot of systematicity in the way words and longer lexical units are used, and corpora serve as a powerful tool to delve into such regularities. By reading *Corpus Linguistics for Vocabulary*, you will learn how to employ corpus techniques to carry out different types of lexical analysis. This will allow you to advance your research skills and improve your understanding of vocabulary and its use across different contexts.

The book is divided into ten chapters. Following this introduction, Chapter 1 provides a definition of corpora and outlines different types of such databases. It is followed by Chapter 2, which describes a range of corpus tools, tests and types of analysis that are commonly used by corpus linguists. Chapter 3 introduces the area of vocabulary studies and discusses terms such as '**type**', '**token**', '**lemma**' and '**word family**'. The understanding of these terms is crucial for conducting research in this area of linguistic study. Chapter 4 focuses on the role of frequency in corpus analysis. In Chapter 5 we turn our attention to **collocations**, **colligations** and other phraseological units, the importance of which has been highlighted by corpus research. Chapter 6 is devoted to direct and indirect applications of corpus linguistics in the process of teaching vocabulary. Chapter 7 centers on the usefulness of corpora for studying learner vocabulary. It is followed by Chapter 8, which is concerned with the use of specialized corpora. Chapter 9 deals with corpus-based analyses of vocabulary at the level of discourse and pragmatics. Chapter 10 serves as a summary of the book and offers a number of ideas for research projects to be undertaken by individual students and teachers.

Finally, when it comes to suggestions for how the book should be used, *Corpus Linguistics for Vocabulary* is a coherent guide that can be read in its entirety. However, depending on your needs and research interests, you can treat the individual chapters as separate units that can be used on their own. The book has been written in such a way that the first part (Chapters 1–2) provides a brief overview of corpus linguistics as a whole, while all the chapters in the second part (Chapters 3–10) introduce vocabulary studies and address more specific issues in this area. Each chapter ends with a list of references for further reading. There is also an index which should help you navigate through the discussed topics. Finally, the book contains a glossary that explains the most important concepts and terms from the field of corpus linguistics. All the items from the glossary are bolded throughout the chapters.

References

Biber, D. and Reppen, R. (2015). Introduction, in D. Biber and R. Reppen (eds.) *The Cambridge Handbook of English Corpus Linguistics*. Cambridge: Cambridge University Press, 1–8.

McCarthy, M. and O'Keeffe, A. (2010). Historical perspective: What are corpora and how have they evolved?, in A. O'Keeffe and M. McCarthy (eds.) *The Routledge Handbook of Corpus Linguistics*. London and New York: Routledge, 3–13.

McEnery, T. and Hardie, A. (2012). *Corpus Linguistics: Method, theory and practice.* Cambridge: Cambridge University Press.

McEnery, T., Xiao, R. and Tono, Y. (2006). *Corpus-based Language Studies: An advanced resources book.* London and New York: Routledge.

Reppen, R. (2010). *Using Corpora in the Language Classroom.* New York: Cambridge University Press.

Sinclair, J. (1991). *Corpus, Concordance, Collocation.* Oxford: Oxford University Press.

Tognini-Bonelli, E. (2001). *Corpus Linguistics at Work.* Amsterdam/Philadelphia: John Benjamins.

Chapter 1

What is corpus linguistics?

1.1 What is a corpus and corpus-based analysis?

In simple terms, corpus linguistics can be defined as the study of "the compilation and analysis of corpora" (Cheng 2012: 6), which are large collections of "naturally occurring language texts chosen to characterize a state or a variety of language" (Sinclair 1991: 171). According to Hunston (2002), even though corpus linguistics is a relatively new field, it has revolutionized language studies because it has provided new ways of analyzing and describing the use of language. The author emphasizes the fact that corpora consist of texts stored in an electronic format, which enables researchers to use special software (called concordancers) to conduct automatic searches and gain insights into the structure and regularity of naturally occurring language. Other important features of corpus-based analysis can be found in Biber et al. (1998: 4), who characterize it in the following way:

- it is empirical, analyzing the actual patterns of use in natural texts;
- it utilizes a large and principled collection of natural texts, known as a corpus, as the basis for analysis;
- it makes extensive use of computers for analysis, using both automatic and interactive techniques;
- it depends on both quantitative and qualitative analytical techniques.

At the same time, it should be stated that as in any discipline, also in corpus linguistics there are different approaches to how the actual analysis should be conducted and how its results should be interpreted. In a useful typology, Tognini-Bonelli (2001) distinguishes between corpus-based and corpus-driven approaches. In the former, corpus linguistics is perceived as a methodology (e.g. McEnery et al. 2003) in which corpus data are used to verify the existing theories of language. In contrast, corpus-driven approaches tend to view corpus linguistics as a theory which offers a new way of looking at the creation of meaning in a narrow sense and different aspects of the use of language in a broader sense (e.g. Stubbs 1993 or Teubert 2005). This demonstrates that the field of corpus linguistics is far from homogenous, with some authors regarding it is a theoretical approach which "may refine and define a range of theories of language" (McEnery and Hardie 2012: 1), while others (probably the majority of corpus linguists) use it as a methodology that enhances research into language use and variation (Biber and Reppen 2015). However, irrespective of which approach we adhere to, it needs to be acknowledged that corpus linguistics has the potential of changing one's perspective on the study of language as a whole and, by providing powerful tools of analysis, it opens up new avenues for linguistic research.

1.2 Corpus design

If we wish corpora to be principled collections of texts whose aim is to represent a specific kind of language, it is important to realize that they should be designed and created according to specific criteria. The following paragraphs aim to present the key criteria of corpus design and explain why corpus linguists treat them as guidelines for the development of corpora. This is particularly important if you consider compiling your own small-scale corpus, for all the methodological decisions related to the structure of your corpus will have an impact on the validity of your findings.

The first author to be discussed in relation to corpus design is John Sinclair, who is often referred to as the father of corpus linguistics. In 2005, Sinclair proposed a set of principles that should be considered with regard to the process of developing a corpus:

1   The contents of a corpus should be selected without regard for the language they contain, but according to their communicative function in the community in which they arise.
2   Corpus builders should strive to make their corpus as representative as possible of the language from which it is chosen.
3   Only those components of corpora which have been designed to be independently contrastive should be contrasted.
4   Criteria for determining the structure of a corpus should be small in number, clearly separate from each other and efficient as a group in delineating a corpus that is representative of the language variety under examination.
5   Any information about a text other than the alphanumeric string of its words and punctuation should be stored separately from the plain text and merged when required in applications.
6   Samples of language for a corpus should, wherever possible, consist of entire documents or transcriptions of complete speech events, or should get as close to this target as possible. This means that samples will differ substantially in size.
7   The design and composition of a corpus should be documented fully with information about the contents and arguments in justification of the decisions taken.
8   The corpus builder should retain, as target notions, representativeness and balance. While these are not precisely definable and attainable goals, they must be used to guide the design of a corpus and the selection of its components.

9   Any control of subject matter in a corpus should be imposed by the use of external, and not internal, criteria.
10 A corpus should aim for homogeneity in its components while maintaining adequate coverage, and rogue texts should be avoided.

It needs to be stated that these points are valuable not only in terms of practical advice on how to build a corpus, but also because they point to the importance of theoretical considerations that underpin this process. Naturally, there is no such a thing as an ideal corpus and consequently any attempt to create a corpus is "a compromise between the hoped for and the achievable" (Nelson 2010: 60). However, if you are planning to compile your own corpus, it is essential that you take the above principles into account and consider the impact of the structure and shape of your corpus on the quality of the information it will provide. The key decisions you are likely to make concern the size, representativeness and balance of the data within your corpus, and much of the corpus literature highlights the interrelatedness of these factors (see Hunston 2002 or McEnery and Hardie 2012 for details).

As far as the size of a corpus is concerned, it is largely dependent on the research question pursued. If you are interested in checking the occurrence of difficult, low-frequency words or phrases (e.g. 'foray'), then what you need is a large corpus so that you are able to find enough examples of how they are used in authentic texts. In turn, if your research focuses on frequent words such as 'make' or 'give', even small-sized corpora should provide sufficient empirical evidence for your analysis. Thus, establishing the right size for your corpus is an open question. It is fair to say that individual researchers and teachers working in the field of corpus linguistics make use of both multimillion corpora (e.g. the British National Corpus, BNC) and specialized, do-it-yourself collections of texts that are much smaller in size but suit the purposes of the local contexts in which they are created (see Chapter 8 for a discussion of general vs. specialized corpora). In addition, it is also important to state that written corpora predominate in the field of corpus linguistics and they are much larger than spoken corpora, which results from the difficulty of collecting and organizing spoken data (more details to follow).

Two other criteria that play a central role in corpus design are the representativeness and balance of corpus data. Biber (1993: 243) defines representativeness as "the extent to which a sample includes the full range of variability in a population". In other words, representativeness concerns the issue of how well a corpus represents a given language or variety that is under study. A related notion is balance because it refers to the structure and type of data used to build a corpus. As explained by Hunston (2002), a well-balanced corpus should consist of several subsections that represent different types (registers) of language use. Importantly, all of the sections ought to contain a roughly equal number of words. A good illustration of a well-balanced corpus is the Contemporary Corpus of American English or COCA (Davies 2011). It is a corpus of general English which consists of 520 million words divided into five sections. Each of the sections contains around 110 million words and represents a different register of use (spoken language, fiction, popular magazines, newspapers and academic language).

This design makes the corpus one of the biggest and best-developed corpora of contemporary English.

Another important aspect that needs to be discussed is annotation. This is an umbrella term that refers to procedures such as **tagging** and **parsing** which are carried out to add linguistic information to a corpus (Hunston 2002: 18). As Cheng (2012: 85) explains, the aim of annotation is to "enhance the corpus contents" in terms of the linguistic description of the data it contains. In their discussion of annotation, McEnery and Hardie (2012: 29) distinguish between three types of information that can accompany a corpus: metadata (details about a given text such as the name of the author), textual markup (information about the formatting of the text such as where italics starts and end or when a given speaker starts speaking) and linguistic annotation (assigning grammatical categories or tags to all the words within a corpus).

Crucially, the type and amount of information added to a corpus depend on the kind of analysis envisioned by its compilers. Referring to this issue, Cheng (2012) enumerates different levels or layers of annotation, the most important of which include: part-of-speech (PoS) tagging, syntactic (grammatical) parsing, error annotation, semantic annotation and phonetic annotation. It needs to be said that the level of annotation applied to a given corpus depends on the type of data collected and, even more importantly, what research purposes it will serve. For instance, if you wish to analyze the number of errors in a learner corpus composed of essays written by your students, it is essential that the corpus is error-tagged; that is, all the texts in the corpus need to be read to identify and flag up all examples of erroneous use. Or to use another example, it is rather obvious that phonetic annotation will be applied only to spoken data. However, irrespective of the kind of annotation applied, it is vital that this additional linguistic information is supplied in a removable form (i.e. separate files) and it cannot corrupt the original corpus data (Leech 2005).

Lastly, the process of annotating a corpus can be conducted in a number of ways. As explained by von Rooy (2015), annotation can be manual, computer-assisted (i.e. the output provided by a computer is subsequently edited by humans) or fully automatic. Automatic systems are the most efficient method and are often used for adding PoS tags (although their accuracy is not error free). A good example of an automatic tagger is CLAWS which was developed at Lancaster University (Garside and Smith 1997). Both the BNC and COCA have been annotated by means of this system and since a list of all the tags is publicly available, you can use them to search for specific examples of words or grammatical forms.

Task 1.1: Go to the following website: http://ucrel.lancs.ac.uk/claws7tags.html. Use some of the tags to search for specific examples of different word classes (e.g. plural or singular nouns, –ing or infinitive forms of verbs) in the BNCweb (http://bncweb.lancs.ac.uk/bncwebSignup/user/login.php). In case of difficulty, click on 'Simple query syntax help'.

1.3 Benefits of corpus analysis

Having presented the basics of corpus linguistics, it is vital to discuss what benefits we can accrue from conducting corpus research. As underlined by Sinclair (1991), looking at language all at once offers a new research perspective and provides valuable insights into naturally occurring discourse. Commenting on the value of corpora for studying language, both Hunston (2002) and McCarthy and O'Keeffe (2010) point out that corpus approaches can be applied to a number of areas of linguistic study: language teaching and learning, discourse analysis, translation studies, language for specific purposes, pragmatics, sociolinguistics, media discourse, literary linguistics and political linguistics. Thus, depending on your research interests, you can use corpus data to explore different aspects of language.

In her discussion of corpus linguistics, Flowerdew (2012) points to its two distinctive features. First, corpus-based linguistics is an inherently empirical methodology, and second, it follows a phraseological approach to language. As far as the former is concerned, corpus analyses are aimed at producing data-based descriptions of language and they help us explain the typical patterns and structure of language in use. It is also important to emphasize that corpus linguistics relies on automatic, computer-assisted searches of naturally occurring data, which provide us with information that is largely unavailable to linguistic intuition. As explained by Hunston (2002), given that much of speakers' linguistic experience "remains hidden from introspection", corpora are "a more reliable guide to language use than native speaker intuition" (Hunston 2002: 20). Thus, it can be said that corpus linguistics is a purely empirical approach which relies on frequency-based analyses as a way of studying the typical tendencies of naturally occurring language. Importantly, if we accept that native speakers' intuitions are not reliable when it comes to determining the most frequent elements in language, the very same task appears to be even more challenging for L2 users, whose exposure to authentic linguistic data is considerably smaller in comparison with expert users. In this context, then, corpora can be viewed as useful resources which provide new insights into language that may be unavailable to less proficient speakers.

Another key feature of corpus linguistics is that it focuses on the phraseological nature of language (Sinclair 1991). Corpus studies demonstrate that language exhibits a highly patterned structure and consists of different kinds of phraseological patterns. More specifically, detailed analyses of large amounts of data reveal that grammar and vocabulary are inextricably intertwined, and the notion of **lexico-grammar** becomes the focal point of corpus analyses (see Chapter 5 for a detailed discussion).

Finally, it is also essential to state that corpus investigations highlight different functions of language and demonstrate the central role of context in the analysis of linguistic behavior (Flowerdew 2012). Language use is dependent on factors such as **register**, purpose and form of communication, and, by exploring large amounts of data attested in corpora, we are able to investigate how these factors shape speakers' and writers' linguistic choices. As will be demonstrated in Chapter 8, thanks to specialized corpora, analyses of linguistic variation can be carried out across different contexts and communicative situations. This means therefore that corpus linguistics presents us with powerful tools for exploring the distribution of specific linguistic features (not only lexical but also grammatical and discoursal ones) across a wide range of domains of language use.

1.4 Limitations of corpus analysis

The above sections have demonstrated the benefits of using corpora. However, it is also important to acknowledge that corpus analyses are not without certain limitations, and they "cannot always be relied upon to tell us what is possible, acceptable, wellformed or pragmatically appropriate" (Flowerdew 2012: 34). As you embark on your corpus analysis, there are a number of issues you should bear in mind:

- A corpus can show us only what it contains.

As argued by Hunston (2002), corpus data cannot provide information about the features that are possible in language but are not recorded in a corpus. In other words, corpora contain only positive data (i.e. attested examples of natural language use). This suggests that there might be some features of language that you will not be able to find in your corpus (Flowerdew 2012: 32).

- A corpus may be too small.

It must be admitted that no corpus, no matter how big it is, can capture language as a whole. However, modern corpora are increasingly large collections of words and, because they contain millions of words, it can be argued that they are a good reflection of central tendencies that characterize natural language use. What is more, as mentioned above, the size of corpora is related to the notion of representativeness as a key aspect of corpus design. Therefore, there is no fixed number of words that need to be collected to build a corpus as its size depends on the purposes for which it will be used. As explained by Reppen (2010), if we compile a dictionary and seek to "capture all the sense of a particular word or set of words", then we need a large, multimillion-word corpus. However, if our aim is to describe the use of language in a particular **genre** or by a particular author, then a fit-for-purpose, small-scale corpus consisting of specialized data seems to be a better tool for our analysis; the fact that it is much smaller in comparison with general corpora should not pose any problems.

- A corpus presents language out of its context.

This criticism refers to the fact that corpora consist of decontextualized data and as a result do not provide any details or nuances that are embedded in the use of language in real-life communication. However, this can be remedied by corpus annotation which will provide additional information about the contents of a corpus. As already mentioned, part-of-speech (PoS) annotation describes all the words in a corpus in terms of the grammatical categories they belong to (e.g. verbs, nouns, prepositions). Error annotation, in turn, is usually applied to learner corpus data and gives insights into the types of errors found in a corpus. Finally, semantic annotation categorizes words on the basis of their different meaning-senses. It is worth noting that rapid changes in technology have encouraged linguists not only to rely on traditional, text-based analyses but also to make use of multimodal corpora, which contain text accompanied by video material (see Chapter 10 for more details). The advantage of having access to such data is that text-based insights can be supplemented with more context-based information such as speakers' gestures or body position, which in consequence leads to richer descriptions of language in use.

- A corpus cannot interpret data.

While computers are good at analyzing large amounts of data, they cannot explain why a given feature is used in a specific way. This is the responsibility of the researcher who delves into the data, analyzes them and tries to account for the patterns displayed by corpus software (see Chapter 2 for examples of corpus software packages). This means that the accuracy of corpus findings depends to a large extent on the analytical skills of the linguist. The role of the analyst is particularly relevant in the case of specialized corpora, as they are often compiled and analyzed by the same person. As emphasized by Flowerdew (2012), if the analyst knows a given context in which the data are collected, they are able to account for how contextual features such as the setting, text type and communicative purpose have a bearing on the use of specific linguistic features.

1.5 Types of corpora

1.5.1 General and specialized corpora

General corpora consist of a wide range of texts that represent natural language as it is used across a variety of contexts. As Hunston (2002) observes, a general corpus contains many types of texts that represent as wide a spread as possible. This means that general corpora are multimillion collections of words and are used as reference corpora or benchmarks against which smaller collections of words can be compared. The most commonly used general corpora are the BNC, with 100 million words (90% of the data are written and 10% spoken), and COCA, with 520 million words representing five different registers. Both of them can be accessed at http://corpus.byu.edu/, an open-access interface hosted by Brigham Young University (see Figure 1.1). We will make use of this interface throughout the rest of the book so it is recommended that you spend some time familiarizing

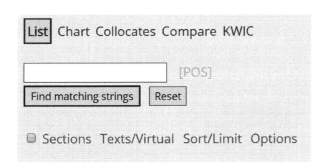

Figure 1.1 BYU-BNC interface

yourself with it. Additionally, the BNC can also be accessed via BNCweb hosted by Lancaster University: http://bncweb.lancs.ac.uk/bncwebSignup/user/login.php.

Specialized corpora, in contrast, "do not aim to comprehensively represent a language as a whole, but only specialized segments of it" (Lee 2010: 114). As Tognini-Bonelli (2010: 22) emphasizes, the selection of texts to be compiled is not meant to be representative of a language or variety in its natural use by ordinary speakers. Rather, texts for specialized corpora are chosen "for their extraordinariness" (Tognini-Bonelli 2010: 22). This means that such corpora are usually smaller in terms of their size and tend to be developed in specific contexts and for specific purposes such as exploring academic discourse (see Chapter 8 for details).

To illustrate, a good example of a specialized corpus is the Michigan Corpus of Academic Spoken English (MICASE), which consists of over 1,800,000 words taken from lectures, dissertation defenses, meetings and service encounters. It is publicly available and can be accessed via the following website: http://quod.lib.umich.edu/m/micase/. Other examples of specialized academic corpora are the British Academic Written English (BAWE) Corpus of proficient student writing (almost 7 million words) or the British Academic Spoken English (BASE) Corpus. The latter consists of data from 160 lectures and forty seminars (over 1,600,000 words plus video data). You can access both of these corpora by creating an account on a website called Sketch Engine: https://the. sketchengine.co.uk/bonito/run.cgi/first_form?corpname=preloaded/bawe2. It is also worth mentioning that specialized corpora can be built to represent the language of specific disciplines. An example of such a corpus is the Hong Kong Engineering Corpus (http://rcpce.engl.polyu.edu.hk/HKEC/), which comprises over 9 million words from the engineering sector of Hong Kong.

There are also a growing number of learner corpora which are specialized collections of language produced by second and foreign language learners (Granger 2002). Examples of such corpora are the International Corpus of Learner English (ICLE) and the International Corpus of Crosslinguistic Interlanguage. Chapter 7 provides a detailed discussion of how such corpora can be usefully employed in research on learner vocabulary.

A related kind of corpora are English as a **lingua franca** (ELF) corpora, which contain data representing the use of English as a global or contact language. According to Seidlhofer (2012), ELF refers to the use of English in contact situations in which speakers from different L1 backgrounds seek a common means of communication. Since ELF is a relatively new area of research, there are a small number of corpora which provide access to such data. The most well-known examples are the Vienna-Oxford International Corpus of English, VOICE (https://www.univie.ac.at/voice/), and the English as a Lingua Franca in Academic Settings Corpus, ELFA (http://www.helsinki.fi/englanti/elfa/elfacorpus). Both of them are 1 million-word collections of texts and they have been successfully employed for research purposes. Given that ELF research is concerned with the use of English as a specific form of contact language, it is perhaps unsurprising that both of these corpora represent spoken language. However, it is also vital to add that scholars from the University of Helsinki have recently completed a written corpus of academic ELF which they call the Corpus of Written English as a Lingua Franca in Academic Settings (WrELFA). The corpus consists of 1.5 million words and is expected to be made available to researchers interested in exploring this kind of language (see http://www.helsinki.fi/englanti/elfa/wrelfa.html for more information). A similar ELF corpus is the Asian Corpus of English (ACE) developed by Andy Kirkpatrick. The corpus can be accessed online via the following website: http://corpus.ied.edu.hk/ace/index.php?m=search&a=index.

Another recent development in the area of ELF is the European Corpus of Academic Talk (EuroCoAT). It consists of over 58,000 words collected from university consultations conducted during twenty-seven office hours in which English was used as an academic lingua franca. The corpus provides transcripts of academic conversations between undergraduate Erasmus students (L1 Spanish) and their lecturers at different host universities (Ireland, England, Sweden and the Netherlands). The data can be accessed by registered users via the following website: http://www.eurocoat.es/home.

Sociolinguistically oriented corpora are the last kind of specialized corpora to be mentioned. These are smaller-scale collections of data which are used for investigating the impact of sociolinguistic features (e.g. age and gender) on the use of language across different contexts and situations. More details of such analyses can be found in Chapter 8.

1.5.2 Written and spoken corpora

Another distinction that is often made concerns differences between written and spoken corpora. Even a brief overview of the literature reveals that the majority of corpora represent written language. This is because written texts are easier to collect and transform into an electronic format, unlike spoken texts which need to be recorded and transcribed before they can be collated as a corpus. As noted by McCarthy and Carter (1997), the compilation of spoken corpora is a long and tedious process which requires immense financial resources. The researchers made these observations in relation to the CANCODE (Cambridge and Nottingham Corpus of Discourse in English) Corpus developed in collaboration with Cambridge University Press. The corpus is a large (5 million words) collection of spoken British English and it has been used as a basis for a number of studies into the specific nature of spoken language (see O'Keeffe et al. 2007 for a useful overview).

Other examples of spoken corpora include the Santa Barbara Corpus of Spoken American English (http://www.linguistics.ucsb.edu/research/santa-barbara-corpus#access), the Hong Kong Corpus of Spoken English (http://rcpce.engl.polyu.edu.hk/HKCSE/default.htm) and the BASE Corpus, which was mentioned above. It is also worth remembering that both the BNC and COCA contain subsections of spoken data and given the overall size of these corpora, they can be used as a source of information about spoken language.

Crucially for the purposes of this book, it needs to be underlined that more and more large corpora of spoken and written language can be accessed free of charge via web-based interfaces (see Figure 1.1). This means that corpora as powerful databases of authentic language can be accessed by individual students, teachers and researchers who can use them to carry out various kinds of analyses related to natural language use. A good example of such an open-access corpus is a new spoken version of the BNC currently being developed. The corpus is called the spoken BNC2014 and it will be a collection of contemporary English spoken across the UK. As the developers of the corpus confirm, once all the data have been collected, the corpus will be made available free of charge. More details about the project can be found at: http://languageresearch.cambridge.org/index.php/spoken-british-national-corpus.

1.5.3 Historical (or diachronic) corpora

Historical (or diachronic) corpora are another type of databases available for corpus analysis. As the name suggests, such corpora represent data from specific historical periods and they are particularly useful if you are interested in the process of language change. For example, the Corpus of Historical American English, COHA, contains 300 million words taken from texts ranging from the early 1800s to the present day. As is the case with all the corpora hosted by

Brigham Young University, the COHA (http://corpus.byu.edu/coha/) is carefully divided into subgenres such as fiction, newspapers and academic prose, which is another benefit of the corpus.

Another useful example of a historical corpus is ARCHER, A Representative Corpus of Historical English Registers. It is a multi-genre corpus of British and American English comprising data from the period 1600–1999. The development of this corpus is an ongoing project run by a consortium of universities from seven countries and the coordinators of the project declare that all the data will be available for both members of the consortium and the general public. More details are available at: http://www.alc.manchester.ac.uk/subjects/lel/research/projects/archer/.

In the context of historical corpora, it is vital to mention monitor corpora, which are "designed to track current changes in a language" (Hunston 2002: 16). If such a corpus is to serve its purposes, it needs to be regularly updated; that is, new sets of data need to be added at regular intervals to keep track of the changing nature of a given language or variety. It is crucial that the types of texts added remain constant so that the sets of data from different periods of time are directly comparable with one another. These are important methodological conditions which must not be neglected, for, as we have already discussed, the way corpus data are collected has a profound effect on the results of the analyses that are based on them.

1.5.4 Parallel and comparable corpora

Parallel corpora are another type of corpora that you can use. They can be defined as "two (or more) corpora in different languages, each containing texts that have been translated from one language into the other" (Hunston 2002: 15). Such corpora are often employed by researchers working in the area of translation studies, who use them to make direct comparisons between the same texts written in different languages. The Oslo Multilingual Corpus (http://www.hf.uio.no/ilos/english/services/omc/) is an example of such a corpus. It is composed of German, French and Finnish source texts, and their respective translations, in all possible combinations. Another example worth mentioning is the Digital Corpus of the European Parliament. It contains a large amount of data (legal texts) written in different languages and can be downloaded from a special website of the European Commission (https://ec.europa.eu/jrc/en/language-technologies/dcep).

A similar type of corpora are comparable or multilingual corpora. These are databases that consist of texts written in different languages (e.g. French, Spanish and English) designed according to the same criteria or sampling frame. Such bi- or multilingual corpora are useful resources for carrying out cross-linguistic or comparative analyses because they can be used "to identify differences and equivalences in each language" (Hunston 2002: 15). An example of a comparable corpus is the Lancaster Corpus of Mandarin Chinese (http://www.lancaster.ac.uk/fass/projects/corpus/LCMC/), which was built according to the same criteria as the LOB Corpus of British English and the Brown Corpus of American English (McEnery et al. 2003).

1.5.5 Web as a corpus

Considering that the Internet is constantly growing and the number of websites is increasing, some linguists advocate the use of the web as a corpus (e.g. Kilgariff and Grefenstette 2003; Boulton 2015). As with any approach, it has advantages and disadvantages, and the aim of this section is to briefly discuss both.

According to McEnery and Hardie (2012), what is particularly useful about the web-as-corpus approach is the possibility of using a large amount of data. As a consequence, the crawling of data directly from the Internet can help us deal with issues such as size and representativeness. This means that a corpus based on web-based data can be regularly updated, which makes it very similar to monitor corpora. What is more, Boulton (2015) notes that the use of the Internet for corpus analyses is fast, flexible and free. Crucially, given that we are all used to search engines such as Google, the whole idea of web-as-corpus as a way of exploring language becomes ever more appealing.

However, there are also certain problems that are associated with this approach. If you decide to use data from the web, you have very little (if any) control over the quality of language that constitutes your corpus. As stated by McEnery and Hardie (2012: 7), "the material returned from a web search tends to be an undifferentiated mass" that is not controlled in terms of genre or register variation. This means that texts crawled from the Internet need to be sorted in a meaningful way before you start treating them as a corpus.

Other issues that are entailed by the use of web-based data are discussed by Boulton (2015). The author observes that the language crawled from the Internet is likely to contain many errors (e.g. inconsistency in spelling), endless reduplications and nonsense pages, all of which might become "unwelcome noise" in your data. In addition, due to the changing nature of the Internet, individual searches may not be easily replicable. However, according to Boulton (2015: 273), the same holds true for monitor corpora and therefore fluctuations in web-based corpora might be treated as "an advantage representing the state of the language". The author concludes that every corpus user is entitled to their own assessment of the web-as-corpus approach but irrespective of our perceptions of the Internet, "it contains data which can be useful for language learners" (Boulton 2015: 274). The WebCorp Linguist's Search Engine (http://wse1.webcorp.org.uk/) is an example of an interface that can be used to explore data found on the web. One of its assets is that it provides access to different types of language use (e.g. the Birmingham Blog Corpus or the Charles Dickens Corpus).

Another example of a corpus that can be accessed free of charge is Mark Davies's Google Books Advanced interface available at http://googlebooks.byu.edu/x.asp. The interface uses data from the American English portion of Google Books (https://books.google.com/ngrams) but it offers many more options in terms of the presentation and analysis of data. As Davies (2014: 403) explains, the Google Books Advanced (GB-Adv) website "allows for a wide range of research on lexical, phraseological, syntactic, and semantic changes in English". For instance, through the interface you can analyze patterns in the changing frequencies of vocabulary over time. The corpus contains 155 billion words spanning data from the 1810s to 2000s, which means that you can track and compare the use of specific words or phrases between different periods of time. Another advantage of the interface is the possibility of using wildcards to look for different forms of words. For example, * is a wildcard which stands for any missing word, so if you enter *ity, the computer will search for all the words ending with the suffix –ity.

The last example of a database composed of web-based data is the NOW Corpus (http://corpus.byu.edu/now/). The corpus was also created by Mark Davies and contains over 3.7 billion words from online magazines and newspapers. Crucially, it is composed of texts collected between 2010 and the present day in twenty different English-speaking countries. Furthermore, the interface is customizable in the sense that you can create your own virtual corpora of specific topics or time periods (e.g. a corpus of texts about US politics from November 2016). Such corpora can be saved on the interface and kept for future reference. For instance, you could compile two corpora of online texts from 2016, one from the UK and the other from the US, and search for the most commonly used words in both countries. Or you could identify the most salient words in these corpora by comparing them to a reference corpus (see Chapter 2 for details of keyword analysis). It is worth adding that the option of creating virtual corpora is also available in the Wikipedia Corpus (http://corpus.byu.edu/wiki/). See Chapter 10 for an example of a research project based on such data.

Task 1.2: Log into the NOW Corpus interface (http://corpus.byu.edu/now/) and look at sample searches suggested by Mark Davies and his team. Why are such searches useful? How can they contribute to a better understanding of the use and distribution of vocabulary?

1.5.6 Non-English corpora

Throughout this book we will focus on corpora that represent English because most research within corpus linguistics has been conducted on English texts. However, it is vital to remember that there exist corpora of other languages and some countries (e.g. Germany and the Czech Republic) have a long tradition in corpus-based research. If you are interested in reading about non-English databases, a useful survey of such corpora can be found at http://www.lancaster.ac.uk/fass/projects/corpus/cbls/corpora.asp or http://martinweisser.org/corpora_site/CBLLinks.html.

Summary

In this chapter we have introduced corpus linguistics as a methodology which relies on corpora, that is, large, principled and computer-readable collections of language data. In addition, we have discussed the usefulness of corpus-based analysis as well as its limitations. Finally, we have provided an overview of different types of corpora, focusing in particular on databases that can be accessed free of charge via web-based interfaces.

References

Aston, G. (1999). Corpus use and learning to translate. *Textus*, 12, 289–314.

Baker, P. (2010). *Sociolinguistics and Corpus Linguistics*. Edinburgh: Edinburgh University Press.

Barlow, M. (2000). *MonoConc Pro*. Houston, TX: Athelstan.

Biber, D. (1993). Representativeness in corpus design. *Literary and Linguistic Computing*, 8, 4, 243–257.

Biber, D. and Reppen, R. (2015). Introduction, in D. Biber and R. Reppen (eds.) *The Cambridge Handbook of English Corpus Linguistics*. Cambridge: Cambridge University Press, 1–8.

Biber, D., Conrad, S. and Reppen, R. (1998). *Corpus Linguistics: Investigating language structure and use*. Cambridge: Cambridge University Press.

Boulton, A. (2015). Applying data-driven learning to the web, in A. Leńko-Szymańska and A. Boulton (eds.) *Multiple Affordances of Language Corpora for Data-driven Learning*. Amsterdam/Philadelphia: John Benjamins, 267–295.

Cheng, W. (2012). *Exploring Corpus Linguistics: Language in action*. London and New York: Routledge.

Davies, M. (2011). *Corpus of Contemporary American English*. Retrieved from http://corpus.byu.edu/coca.

Davies, M. (2014). Making Google Books n-grams useful for a wide range of research on language change. *International Journal of Corpus Linguistics*, 19, 3, 401–416.

Flowerdew, L. (2012). *Corpora and Language Education*. London: Palgrave Macmillan.

Garside, R. and Smith, N. (1997). A hybrid grammatical tagger: CLAWS4, in R. Garside, G. Leech and T. McEnery (eds.) *Corpus Annotation: Linguistic information from computer text corpora*. London: Longman, 102–121.

Granger, S. (2002). A bird's eye view of learner corpus research, in S. Granger J. Hung and S. Petch-Tyson (eds.) *Computer Learner Corpora, Second Language Acquisition and Foreign Language Learning*. Amsterdam and Philadelphia: John Benjamins, 3–33.

Hunston, S. (2002). *Corpora in Applied Linguistics*. Cambridge: Cambridge University Press.

Jenkins, J. (2007). *English as a Lingua Franca: Attitude and identity*. Oxford: Oxford University Press.

Kilgariff, A. and Grefenstette, G. (2003). Web as corpus: Introduction. *Special Issue. Computational Linguistics*, 29, 3, 333–347.

Kirkpatrick, A. (2010). Researching English as a Lingua Franca in Asia: The Asian Corpus of English (ACE) project. *Asian Englishes*, 13, 1, 4–18.

Lee, D. Y. W. (2010). What corpora are available?, in A. O'Keeffe and M. McCarthy (eds.) *The Routledge Handbook of Corpus Linguistics*. London and New York: Routledge, 107–121.

Leech, G. (2005). Adding linguistic annotation, in M. Wynne (ed.) *Developing Linguistic Corpora: A guide to good practice*. Oxford: Oxbow Books, 17–29.

McCarthy, M. and Carter, R. (1997). Written and spoken vocabulary, in N. Schmitt and McCarthy, M. (eds.) *Vocabulary: Description, acquisition, pedagogy*. Cambridge: Cambridge University Press, 20–39.

McCarthy, M. and O'Keeffe, A. (2010). Historical perspective, in A. O'Keeffe and M. McCarthy (eds.) *The Routledge Handbook of Corpus Linguistics*. London and New York: Routledge, 3–13.

McEnery, T. and Hardie, A. (2012). *Corpus Linguistics*. Cambridge: Cambridge University Press.

McEnery, T., Xiao, R. Z. and Mo, L. (2003). Aspect marking in English and Chinese: Using the Lancaster Corpus of Mandarin Chinese for contrastive language study. *Literary and Linguistic Computing*, 18, 4, 361–378.

Nelson, M. (2010). Building a written corpus: What are the basics?, in A. O'Keeffe and M. McCarthy (eds.) *The Routledge Handbook of Corpus Linguistics*. London and New York: Routledge, 53–65.

O'Keeffe, A., McCarthy, M. and Carter, R. (2007). *From Corpus to Classroom*. Cambridge: Cambridge University Press.

Reppen R. (2010). Building a corpus: What are the key considerations?, in A. O'Keeffe and M. McCarthy (eds.) *The Routledge Handbook of Corpus Linguistics*. London and New York: Routledge, 31–37.

Scott, M. (2004). *WordSmith Tools Version 4.0*. Oxford: Oxford University Press.

Seidlhofer, B. (2012). Corpora and English as a Lingua Franca., in K. Hyland, M. H. Chau and M. Handford (eds.) *Corpus Applications in Applied Linguistics*. London and New York: Continuum, 135–149.

Sinclair, J. (1991). *Corpus, Concordance, Collocation: Describing English language*. Oxford: Oxford University Press.

Sinclair, J. (2005). Corpus and text: Basic principles, in M. Wynne (ed.) *Developing Linguistic Corpora: A guide to good practice*. Oxford: Oxbow Books, 1–16.

Stubbs, M. (1993). British traditions in text analysis: From Firth to Sinclair, in M. Baker, F. Francis and E. Tognini-Bonelli (eds.) *Text and Technology: In honour of John Sinclair*. Amsterdam: John Benjamins, 1–46.

Teubert, W. (2005). My version of corpus Linguistics. *International Journal of Corpus Linguistics*, 10, 1, 1–13.

Tognini-Bonelli, E. (2001). *Corpus Linguistics at Work*. Amsterdam and Philadelphia: John Benjamins.

Tognini-Bonelli, E. (2010). Theoretical overview of the evolution of corpus linguistics, in A. O'Keeffe and M. McCarthy (eds.) *The Routledge Handbook of Corpus Linguistics*. London and New York: Routledge, 14–27.

Von Rooy, B. (2015). Annotating learner corpora, in S. Granger, G. Gilquin and F. Meunier (eds.) *The Cambridge Handbook of Learner Corpus Research*. Cambridge: Cambridge University Press, 79–105.

Chapter 2

Corpus analysis
Tools and statistics

2.1 Corpus tools and types of analysis

As explained in Chapter 1, corpora are computer-readable collections of texts which enable linguistic analysis by means of special computer programs called concordancers. Some corpora such as the Corpus of Contemporary American English (COCA) or Michigan Corpus of Academic Spoken English (MICASE) are web-based interfaces, which means they can be explored by anybody who has access to the Internet. However, when you compile your own corpus (e.g. a collection of essays written by students), then you need to equip yourself with a concordancer which will allow you to carry out different kinds of searches. The most popular concordancers are WordSmith tools (Scott 1999), Sketch Engine (Kilgariff et al. 2004), MonoConc (Barlow 2000) and AntConc (Anthony 2014). For the purposes of this book, we will make use of AntConc which is a user-friendly program created by Laurence Anthony. Another important resource we will rely on is Lextutor (http://www.lextutor.ca/). This is a web-based platform developed by Tom Cobb that (2016) provides numerous tools for conducting corpus-based research.

What follows is a description of the most important types of corpus analysis which include frequency analysis and concordancing, **wordlists**, cluster (n-gram) analysis and keyword analysis. It is essential that you familiarize yourself with these procedures so that you can start using them in your own corpus analysis.

2.1.1 Frequency analysis and concordancing

The most basic type of corpus analysis is checking the frequency of occurrence of a given word or a phrase. We will demonstrate how to carry out such a search by means of a web-based interface developed by Mark Davies from Brigham Young University (http://corpus.byu.edu/bnc/). It is free of charge and once you create your own account, you can access data from the British National Corpus (BNC), COCA and several other large corpora.

To conduct a frequency search, you need to use a search box located on the left-hand side of the interface. This is where you type in a word or a phrase that you want to explore. Such a word is called a **node** and for the purposes of this demonstration the word 'computer' will be our node. Once you hit the enter button, you obtain information about the number of the occurrences of 'computer' in the whole corpus. As Figure 2.1 demonstrates, it occurs 13,446 times in the BNC. Note that when we search 'computer' as a lemma (you do it by putting square brackets around the target word as in [computer]), the frequency value goes up to 16,966 because the count includes both the singular and plural forms of 'computer' (see Chapter 3 for details on lemmas).

In the next phase of your analysis, you might be interested in exploring specific examples of sentences with the word 'computer'. To do this, you need to click on the word 'computer' and then the bottom part of the interface provides lines of texts which demonstrate how the word is used in context. These lines are called concordances and Figure 2.2 provides some examples. This is a standard format for displaying corpus data known as **Key Word In Context** (KWIC) and its main advantage is that you can easily analyze the co-text of the node; that is, all the words that precede and follow it (usually four words to the left and four words to the right). By analyzing the immediate company of words, you can explore patterns of co-occurrence between words and you can study how words tend to form various kinds of lexical, grammatical and lexico-grammatical combinations (see below for more details on collocation analysis).

It is also worth adding that the interface allows you to explore the frequency of words across different sections of the BNC, which represent different registers of use (e.g. spoken language or newspaper language). Such information is important because it shows us how the frequency of words changes depending on the type of discourse they are used in. To carry out such a search, instead of the default List option, select the Chart option. It will allow you to view all frequency values for the word 'computer' across the different portions of the corpus. As Figure 2.3 demonstrates, 'computer' occurs much less frequently in the language of fiction than in the language of magazines or newspapers.

There is, however, an important point that you need to bear in mind when it comes to comparing the frequencies of words across different datasets. Namely, it is essential that you use normalized frequency – that is, the frequency of a

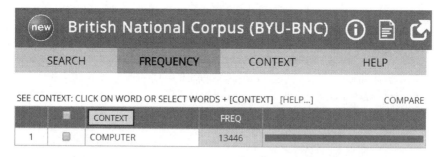

Figure 2.1 A search for the frequency of 'computer' through the BYU-BNC interface

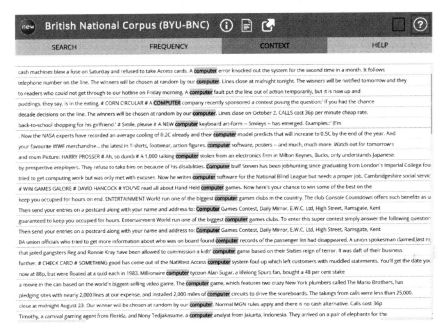

Figure 2.2 Examples of concordances for the word 'computer'

word per million words – when you compare the occurrence of words in different corpora. This is because corpora (or their different subsections) differ in terms of their size. For example, written corpora are much bigger than spoken corpora

SECTION (CLICK FOR SUB-SECTIONS) (SEE ALL SECTIONS AT ONCE)	FREQ	SIZE (M)	PER MIL	CLICK FOR CONTEXT (SEE ALL)	
SPOKEN	863	10.0	86.61		
FICTION	485	15.9	30.49		
MAGAZINE	969	7.3	133.43		
NEWSPAPER	1,114	10.5	106.44		
NON-ACAD	4,747	16.5	287.78		
ACADEMIC	2,305	15.3	150.34		
MISC	2,830	20.8	135.83		
TOTAL	13,313			SEE ALL TOKENS	

Figure 2.3 Frequency of 'computer' across different sections of the BNC

and as a result raw frequencies derived from them cannot be directly compared, as this would lead to inaccurate results. It is worth adding that when you use the chart option on the BYU interface, all the normalized frequencies are computed automatically and you can find them in the row called 'per mil'.

2.1.2 Wordlists

Information about the frequency of words obtained from corpora serves as a basis for the creation of wordlists. These are lists of words or phrases ranked according to their frequency or the number of their occurrences in a given corpus. For instance, Figure 2.4 demonstrates a wordlist of the most frequently occurring words derived from the COCA corpus. Such a wordlist can be easily obtained from a website called www.wordandphrase.info, a user-friendly resource developed by Mark Davies which accompanies the BYU interface. The website can be used for creating wordlists (the 'frequency lists' option) as well as analyzing texts in terms of the frequency of particular words they contain (the 'analyze texts' option).

As can be seen in Figure 2.4, the most frequent word in English is 'the', a finding that is rather unsurprising given the fact that articles are an inherent feature of English grammar and co-occur with nouns. What is more interesting perhaps is that the majority of the first twenty words from the list are functional (or grammatical) words such as prepositions ('of', 'to', 'for'), conjunctions ('and') or pronouns ('I', 'you', 'he'). It is also of note that 'be', 'have' and 'do' are among the most frequent words in English. This can be explained by the fact

WORD AND PHRASE . INFO   DAVIES | BYU | COCA

FREQUENCY LISTS · ANALYZE TEXTS | ALL GENRES · ACADEMIC   LOG IN HELP

WORD			RANK #	PoS	WORD	TOTAL	SPOKEN	FICTION	MAGAZINE	NEWSPAPER	ACADEMIC
			1	A	THE	23782115	4183469	4531786	4875815	4646517	5544528
LIST FROM #	1	(1-60,000)	2	V	BE	16711569	4873268	3173845	2989059	2926800	2748577
PART OF SPEECH	☑ NOUN ☑ VERB ☑ ADJ ☑ ADV		3	C	AND	11654439	2347151	2188166	2388111	2130798	2600213
			4	I	OF	11155504	1857279	1630728	2329089	2050072	3288336
INTERACTIVE HELP (1-2 MINUTES)			5	A	A	10999596	2110287	2125067	2496150	2331699	1936393
			6	I	IN	7557934	1385889	1117519	1580617	1600390	1873519
			7	T	TO	6868227	1666909	1259251	1390223	1308448	1253396
			8	V	HAVE	5335769	1369956	1275340	954391	1012197	723985
			9	I	TO	4176664	768794	791336	870507	803354	942673
			10	P	IT	4194790	1308873	1014229	742514	681594	447580
			11	P	I	4455521	1592284	1539597	638470	495517	189653
			12	C	THAT	3709830	1060065	483634	711691	627143	827297
			13	I	FOR	3564803	670859	535048	788184	799229	771483
			14	P	YOU	3354252	1532399	920083	538032	279422	84316
			15	P	HE	3138899	661647	1204627	475466	614726	182433
			16	I	WITH	2911620	514309	575927	662172	578339	580873
			17	I	ON	2703486	549302	545540	570032	553569	485243
			18	V	DO	2800961	1030761	692713	432729	403634	241124
			19	V	SAY	2077536	467020	514458	331793	682497	81768
			20	D	THIS	2047852	736448	308574	316993	275459	410376
			21	P	THEY	2014769	659475	391214	335742	361264	268074
			22	I	AT	1923946	335599	451667	402139	455463	279079

Figure 2.4 A wordlist of the most frequent words in English (based on COCA)

that except for being content words that express specific meanings, these verbs perform important grammatical roles; that is, they serve as auxiliaries which are used to form tenses in English. Thus, as can be seen, even a simple corpus analysis of the twenty most frequent words can lead you to some revealing findings about the structure of English.

It also needs to be pointed out that frequency-based wordlists have several important practical applications. First of all, if we assume that the most frequent words are also the most useful ones, language teachers and materials developers can use this information to decide which words should be addressed first in contexts where English is taught as a second/foreign language (see Chapter 6 on the role of corpora in language teaching). Moreover, wordlists are a powerful tool for making comparisons between corpora that represent different language uses. For instance, comparing wordlists extracted from spoken and written texts can yield valuable insights into how the use of vocabulary varies depending on the specific modes of communication (see Chapter 4 for more details). It is also worth adding that wordlists are usually accompanied by statistics such as the number of types (all unique words in a given corpus) and tokens (repetitions of the same words). Such information is valuable because by dividing the number of number of types by the number of tokens, we arrive at a type/token ratio which is used as a measure of lexical diversity (or richness) of texts (more details to follow).

2.1.3 Word combinations and n-gram analysis

Words tend to co-occur and form collocations, colligations and other examples of word combinations (also known as **chunks**, **n-grams** or **lexical bundles**), and exploring such tendencies is another type of corpus analysis that you can conduct. In fact, investigations into how words tend to co-occur and form various kinds of phraseological units constitute a major line of research within corpus linguistics, and therefore a thorough discussion of these issues is provided in Chapter 5. Here I only aim to present details of n-gram (or cluster) analysis, which is a corpus procedure that is used to identify recurrent sequences of words.

N-gram is a technical term used by corpus linguists to denote word combinations which consist of "two or more words that repeatedly occur consecutively in a corpus" (Cheng 2012: 72). As explained by O'Keeffe et al. (2007: 13), the process of identifying n-grams consists in using frequency information to identify recurrent strings of two, three, four or more words. This process is conducted automatically by means of corpus software such as AntConc or the n-gram Phrase Extractor available through Lextutor: http://lextutor.ca/n_gram/.

Task 2.1: Identify examples of the most frequent n-grams in the language of political speeches.

To complete this task, you will use AntConc, a free concordancer that can be downloaded from the following website: http://www.laurenceanthony.net/software.html. Unlike BYU-BNC, AntConc does not contain any data by itself, which means you are required to upload texts you want to analyze. Thus, since your aim is to identify the most frequent n-grams in the language of political speeches, you need to compile a corpus of texts that represent this specific kind of data. To do this, go to the following website: http://obamaspeeches.com/ and choose the first ten speeches made by Barack Obama. Copy all of them into a Word document which you will call the Obama Corpus. It is essential that you save it as a plain text document with .txt extension because other formats do not work on AntConc. Once your corpus is ready, you can upload it to AntConc (File > Open file).

Next, since the number of n-grams that can be found in corpora is very high, you should also set a minimum frequency threshold or a cut-off point for your analysis. According to Biber (2006: 134), at least forty occurrences per million words are needed for a sequence of words to be consider as a significant item. In turn, Greaves and Warren (2010) suggest the frequency of twenty occurrences per million words should be used as a threshold. As the Obama Corpus is small, the frequency threshold you will use is ten occurrences per million words. However, such a cut-off point can be raised or lowered depending on the size of your corpus and the type of n-grams you want to explore. In addition, it is also important that you indicate the length of sequences you aim to retrieve. For the purposes of this task, let us assume that you will focus only on 4-grams.

Once you have completed all these preparatory steps, you can run your analysis and you should be able to produce a list of n-grams similar to the one presented in Figure 2.5. It is worth adding that AntConc is accompanied by short video tutorials which explain how to use it (https://www.youtube.com/watch?v=O3ukHC3fy

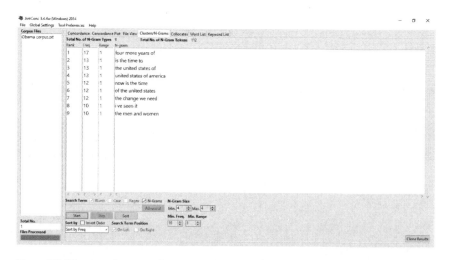

Figure 2.5 The most frequent 4-grams in a corpus of political speeches

uc&list=PLiRIDpYmiC0Ta0-Hdvc1D7hG6dmiS_TZj). Consult them in case you experience difficulty using the program.

As Figure 2.5 displays, the Obama Corpus contains nine examples of 4-grams which occur at least ten times. While some of these n-grams are whole chunks ('United States of America'), many examples of these sequences are incomplete units that are often called lexical bundles (e.g. 'is the time to' or 'now is the time'). This results from the fact that n-gram analysis is a purely frequency-driven approach which explores patterns of lexical co-occurrence without considering semantic and syntactic relationships between particular words. Crucially, there is a large body of corpus research that focuses on this specific type of word combinations and, as Biber et al. (2004: 398) point out, they "should be regarded as a basic linguistic construct with important functions for the construction of discourse" (see Chapter 5 for more details).

2.1.4 Keyness analysis and keywords

The last type of corpus analysis we will discuss in this section is keyword analysis, which allows you to identify keywords. As stated by Scott (1997: 236), a keyword "may be defined as a word which occurs with unusual frequency in a given text". Such words are useful because they provide information about the **keyness** or specificity of a given corpus in terms of what it is about (Cheng 2012). As Evison (2010: 127) explains, keywords are "those words which are identified by statistical comparison of a target corpus with another, larger corpus, which is referred to as the 'reference' or 'benchmark' corpus". To put it another way, keywords provide you with a window into the distinctiveness or uniqueness of data that are found in your target corpus. It is worth pointing out that keywords can be either positive (words which have much higher frequency in a target corpus in comparison with a reference corpus) or negative (words which have much lower frequency in a target corpus). Finally, it should be remembered that keywords are not absolute and need to be interpreted in relation to a given corpus that is used (Hunston 2012: 244). This means that your choice of a reference corpus is an important methodological decision because depending on which type of language you treat as a benchmark (e.g. written vs. spoken language), the analysis of keywords is likely to produce different results.

Task 2.2: Using the Obama Corpus, identify keywords which characterize the language of political speeches.

Similarly to the previous task, you will make use of the Obama Corpus and analyze these data by means of the Keywords tool which can be found on Lextutor (http://www.lextutor.ca/key/). The Keywords tool is already equipped with data

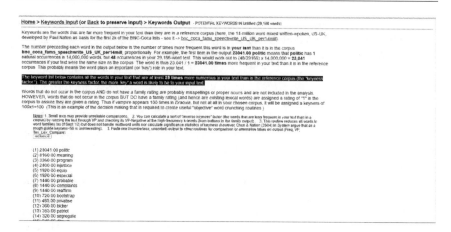

Figure 2.6 A list of keywords from the Obama Corpus

that can be used as a reference corpus. It contains 14 million words from both the BNC and COCA, assembled by Paul Nation: http://lextutor.ca/key/bnc_coca_fams_speechwrite_US_UK_per14mill.txt.

In the next stage of the analysis, you need to copy all the words from the Obama Corpus and paste them into the Keywords option in Lextutor. Once you click the Submit button, the software produces a list of keywords which are characteristic of the Obama Corpus. Figure 2.6 displays the computer output which lists all the keywords that have been identified.

It should be added that such a list of keywords might be a starting point for a more qualitative kind of analysis. For example, you could make a selection of several **concordance lines** from the Obama Corpus and investigate how the words 'political' and 'program' are used in some specific contexts (e.g. what is their typical collocational behavior?). Another option is to examine the use of these words in terms of their pragmatic importance because vocabulary plays a key role in fulfilling discourse functions (see Chapter 9 for more details). Owing to the fact that these aspects of language use cannot be captured by automatic computer searches, what is needed is "the insight and intuition of the observer" (Hunston 2002: 65). This shows that qualitative analyses conducted on smaller sets of corpus data can also be used as a source of valuable information about the use of vocabulary.

2.2 Corpus statistics

As a quantitative approach to linguistic analysis, corpus linguistics relies on a number of statistical tests which are used to find statistically significant differences between different sets of data. The aim of this section is to discuss the most important examples of such tests so that you know how to apply them to your own corpus analysis. First, we will explain how to use a log-likelihood test as a way of comparing frequency data from different corpora. Subsequently, we will present mutual information as an important statistical measure that is used for identifying collocations. Finally, we will introduce a type/token ratio as a simple test of the lexical diversity of texts.

2.2.1 Log-likelihood

Log-likelihood is a test which is used to compare differences in frequency values between different sets of data. In other words, a log-likelihood test helps you determine whether differences in the frequency of words are reflective of the actual variation in language or whether they result from chance occurrences. For instance, if you are interested in making comparisons between two subsections of the BNC which represent different registers of language use (e.g. academic language vs. spoken language), you can use a log-likelihood test as a quick way of verifying whether a difference in the occurrences of a given word has any statistical significance.

To illustrate how to use this test, we will compare the frequencies of the word 'discussion' which occurs 583 times in the spoken section of the BNC and 3,327 in the academic section. You can establish whether this difference is significant by using Rayson's online log-likelihood calculator (http://ucrel.lancs.ac.uk/llwizard. html). This is an automatic tool which computes the value of log-likelihood on the basis of the data you retrieve: the size of the two subcorpora you are comparing and the frequency of the word under study ('discussion' in this case) in both of the subsections. All these data are provided in Table 2.1 and all you need to do is to type them into the appropriate boxes of the online calculator. Note that the calculator operates in such a way that you cannot use commas or spaces as you enter all the information. As can be seen in the last column of the table, the log-likelihood is very high (1,124.57), which means that the difference in frequency is highly significant. Rayson and Garside (2000) explain that log-likelihood greater than 3.84 indicates a significant difference between the two sets of data. It is also important to add that the number is preceded by a minus sign, which suggests that 'discussion' is underused in the spoken subsection of the corpus in comparison with the academic section.

Other statistical measures you are likely to encounter in the corpus linguistics literature include a Chi-square test, dispersion plot analysis and factor analysis. These are helpful for pursuing more advanced research questions and consequently

Table 2.1 Frequency of 'discussion' in the spoken and academic BNC

	Frequency of word (no. of tokens)	Corpus size	Log-likelihood
Spoken BNC	583	9,963,663	−1124.57
Academic BNC	3,327	15,331,668	

it is beyond the scope of this book to explain how to use them (see McEnery et al. (2006) and Gries (2009) for useful overviews of advanced corpus statistics).

2.2.2 T-score and mutual information (MI)

T-score and **mutual information** (MI) tests are corpus statistics which are commonly used to identify collocations. Rather than relying on raw frequency which is "too unreliable a guide as to the strength of association between collocates" (Cheng 2012: 94), these tests inform us whether the co-occurrence of words has statistical significance, or whether it can be attributed to chance. MI scores higher than 3 and T-scores higher than 2 are customarily perceived as thresholds which indicate a significant association between two words (Hunston 2002). Importantly, modern corpus software such as WordSmith (Scott 1999) or ConcGram (Greaves 2009) and web-based corpus interfaces such as the BYU-BNC or BNCweb are equipped with built-in features which provide you with such statistical information.

By way of illustration, Figure 2.7 below presents a list of the most frequent adjectival collocates of the word 'school' as revealed by data from the BNC. The first five collocates are: 'primary', 'secondary', 'junior', 'comprehensive' and 'catholic'. Crucially, apart from showing the frequency values, the interface ranks all the collocates on the basis of their MI scores. As can be seen in the figure, all

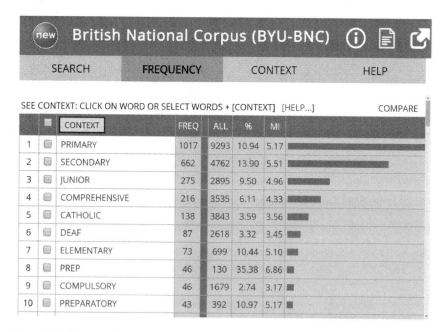

Figure 2.7 The most frequent adjectival collocates of 'school' in the BNC

of them have an MI score higher than 3, which means that they are strongly associated with the word 'school' (see Chapter 5 for more details on the use of corpus statistics for identifying collocations).

2.2.3 Type-token ratio and lexical richness

Another helpful corpus statistic is the **type-token ratio** (TTR) which can be treated as a measure of the lexical diversity or richness of texts. According to Cobb and Horst (2015: 189), **lexical richness** is "the level of development of a learner's lexicon" and a TTR is one of the most popular ways of tapping into this development. What is more, a TTR is used as a way of exploring vocabulary variation in different sets of data. You can calculate a TTR by dividing the number of types (all unique words) by the number of tokens (repetitions of the same words) in a given text or corpus and a percentage is the usual way of reporting it (i.e. a ratio multiplied by 100). For example, if a ratio is close to 100%, this means that the lexical diversity of a given text is high because it contains few repetitions of the same words.

However, it needs to be stated that one disadvantage of a TTR is that it "varies with the length of a text" (Cobb and Horst 2015: 192) and as a consequence only texts of a similar length should be compared by means of this measure. Referring to this problem, McEnery and Hardie (2012: 50) suggest that it can be overcome by using modified versions of the statistic. For instance, in the case of larger corpora, where a TTR is usually lower due to the high frequency of functional (or grammatical) words, many corpus linguists rely on a standardized type-token ratio (STTR), which is an average ratio across different sections of the corpus.

2.3 Combining quantitative and qualitative corpus analysis

So far we have presented corpus linguistics as a quantitative methodology that relies on computer-based calculations of numerical data. We have explained how counting frequencies of words and comparing them across different types of data (e.g. different varieties of English or groups of speakers) can yield new insights into the features of natural language use. However, many corpus linguists (e.g. O'Keeffe et al. 2007; McEnery and Hardie 2012) highlight the fact that both quantitative and qualitative forms of analysis are of equal importance when it comes to gaining a good understanding and producing an accurate description of naturally occurring language. To quote Teubert's (2007: 124–5) words, "without interpretation any study in corpus linguistics would be incomplete".

Referring to a synergy between quantitative and qualitative corpus approaches, Hunston (2012: 245) states that automatically derived wordlists can be a "starting point for a more detailed study of individual words and phrases". This means that qualitative corpus analyses can be treated as a follow-up to quantitative findings. Alternatively, preliminary observations resulting from a qualitative analysis carried out on a limited number of concordances can be explored further by statistical analyses conducted on larger amounts of data. In such cases, the quantitative phase of a study can either confirm or refute the initial qualitative findings.

As far as details of a qualitative analysis of corpus data are concerned, this usually involves selecting a sample of concordances retrieved for a specific linguistic feature (e.g. a word or collocation) and conducting a thorough investigation of its **co-text** of use, that is, the immediate textual environment both on the left and right side of the node or search item (Cheng 2012: 73). A good illustration of such a qualitative corpus analysis is O'Keeffe et al.'s (2007) study of the word 'abroad'. Using data from the Cambridge International Corpus, the authors demonstrate how a detailed reading and interpretation of concordance lines can lead to the creation of rich, data-based lexico-grammatical profiles. Such profiles provide valuable information about not only the most salient collocates of specific words but also other kinds of phraseological units that they form (e.g. idioms), syntactic and semantic tendencies and many other details that are relevant to the description of vocabulary in use. Here is a selection of insights reported by O'Keeffe et al. (2007: 15) who analyzed sixty random concordances for the word 'abroad':

- The most frequent collocates of 'abroad' are 'go' (different forms of the verb), 'trip' and 'work'.
- 'Home and abroad' is an example of a recurrent chunk that contains the word 'abroad'.
- In terms of its syntactic behavior, the authors emphasize that 'abroad' is used predominantly as an adverbial. What is more, when it comes to the grammatical partners of 'abroad', it does not require any prepositions when it co-occurs with verbs of motion such as 'travel' (e.g. 'to travel abroad') and nouns such as 'trip' (e.g. 'a trip abroad'). However, 'abroad' often co-occurs with the preposition 'from' when it is used in prepositional phrases (e.g. 'come from abroad').
- As far as semantics is concerned, the most frequent sense of 'abroad' is geographical or political. However, the analysis of concordances revealed that 'abroad' may also be used to convey the meaning of 'in the public domain' or 'out in the open'.

Commenting on the procedures that are used for creating corpus-based profiles of the lexico-grammatical patterning of words, O'Keeffe et al. (2007) note that ideally the analysis of the co-text (i.e. textual environment) of a given word ought to be carried out on both sides; that is, on the left and right of the search item. Fortunately, modern corpora are designed in such a way that with only one click, all the words that co-occur with your search item can be sorted either on the left or the right. Figure 2.8 displays an example of a left-sorted search for the word 'abroad' in the COCA corpus. To perform this kind of search, you need to click on the button 'KWIC'. Then the computer presents all the data in a color-coded format called '**key word in context**', which makes it very easy to analyze different kinds of lexical and lexico-grammatical patterning.

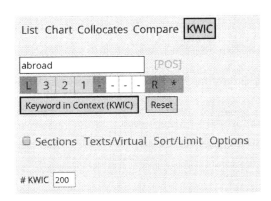

Figure 2.8 A left-sorted search for the word 'abroad' in COCA

Task 2.3: Using the KWIC option on the BYU-COCA interface, study a sample of concordances for the word 'abroad'. Make sure that you use left-screen sorting as you analyze the data. As O'Keeffe at al. (2007) report, this format produces the most visible patterning for the search word. Are your results similar to the ones described in this section? Would you add any new observations to the lexico-grammatical profile of 'abroad' produced by the authors?

Summary

In Chapter 2 we have presented a wide range of corpus tools and statistical tests that are commonly employed by corpus linguists. Our aim has been to show that the ability to use these tools is a necessary condition to undertake different types of corpus-based research. We have also emphasized the importance of combining quantitative and qualitative types of corpus analysis. In the following chapter, we will turn our attention to the area of vocabulary studies and present examples of vocabulary-related issues that can be explored by means of corpora.

References

Aijmer, K. (ed.). (2009). *Corpora and Language Teaching.* Amsterdam: John Benjamins.

Anthony, L. (2014). AntConc (Version 3.4.4) [computer software]. Tokyo: Waseda University.

Barlow, M. (2000). MonoConc Pro [computer software]. Available from http://www.athel.com/mono.html.

Biber, D. (2006). *University Language: A corpus-based study of spoken and written registers.* Amsterdam: John Benjamins.

Biber, D., Conrad, S. and Cortes, V. (2004). If you look at...: Lexical bundles in university teaching and textbooks. *Applied Linguistics,* 25, 3, 371–405.

Cheng, W. (2012). *Exploring Corpus Linguistics: Language in action.* London and New York: Routledge.

Cobb, T. (2016). *Compleat Lexical Tutor (LexTutor)* [online]. Available from www.lextutor.ca [20 June 2016].

Cobb, T. and Horst, M. (2015). Learner corpora and lexis, in S. Granger, G. Gilquin and F. Meunier (eds.) *The Cambridge Handbook of Learner Corpus Linguistics.* Cambridge: Cambridge University Press, 185–206.

Evison, J. (2010). What are the basics of analysing a corpus?, in A. O'Keeffe and M. McCarthy (eds.) *The Routledge Handbook of Corpus Linguistics.* London and New York: Routledge, 122–135.

Greaves, C. (2009). *ConcGram: A phraseological search engine.* Amsterdam/Philadelphia: John Benjamins.

Greaves, C. and Warren, M. (2010). What can a corpus tell us about multi-word units?, in A. O'Keeffe and M. McCarthy (eds.) *The Routledge Handbook of Corpus Linguistics.* London and New York: Routledge, 212–226.

Gries, S. (2009). *Quantitative Corpus Linguistics with R.* London and New York: Routledge.

Hunston, S. (2002). *Corpora in Applied Linguistics.* Cambridge: Cambridge University Press.

Hunston, S. (2012). Afterword: The problems of applied linguistics, in K. Hyland, M. H. Chau and M. Handford (eds.) *Corpus Applications in Applied Linguistics.* London: Continuum, 242–247.

Hyland, K., Chau, M. H. and Handford, M. (eds.) (2012). *Corpus Applications in Applied Linguistics.* London: Continuum.

Kilgariff, A., Rychly, P., Smrz, P. and Tugwell, D. (2004). *The Sketch Engine.* Lorient: Proc EURALEX., 105–116.

McEnery, T. and Hardie, A. (2012). *Corpus Linguistics.* Cambridge: Cambridge University Press.

McEnery, T., Xiao, R. and Tono, Y. (2006). *Corpus-based Language Studies: An Advanced resource book.* London: Routledge.

O'Keeffe, A., McCarthy, M. and Carter, R. (2007). *From Corpus to Classroom.* Cambridge: Cambridge University Press.

Rayson, P. (2015). Log-likelihood Calculator. [Online], Available: http://ucrel.lanc.ac.uk/llwizard.html [25 November 2015]

Rayson, P. and Garside, R. (2000). Comparing corpora using frequency profiling, in Proceedings of the workshop on comparing corpora, held in conjunction with the 38th annual meeting of the Association for Computational Linguistics. 1–8 October 2000, Hong Kong: Association for Computational Linguistics, 1–6.

Scott, M. (1997). PC analysis of key words – and key key words. *System*, 25, 2, 233–245.

Scott, M. (1999). *WordSmith Tools* [computer software]. Available from http://www. lexically.net.

Teubert, W. (2007). Natural and human right, work and property in the discourse of Catholic social doctrine, in M. Hoey, M. Mahlberg, M. Stubbs and W. Tuebert (eds.) *Text, Discourse and Corpora*. London: Continuum, 89–126.

Chapter 3

What is vocabulary?

Terminology, conceptualizations and research issues

3.1 Vocabulary as an important component of language use

Vocabulary is a core element of language use, and research exploring its relationships with other components of linguistic competence constitutes an important subfield of applied linguistics. Schmitt (2010) highlights the role of vocabulary and points to high correlations between measures of vocabulary and language proficiency. In a similar vein, Meara (1992: 6) claims that learners with bigger vocabularies are more proficient in a wide range of language skills than learners with smaller vocabularies. Thus it can be concluded that vocabulary knowledge is closely linked to overall language performance.

Evidence for the importance of vocabulary can be found in research on lexical coverage. Lexical coverage is often defined as the percentage of known words in a text (Laufer and Ravenhorst-Kalovski 2010; van Zeeland and Schmitt 2013). This means that the number of words we know influences how much text we are able to understand. For instance, Schmitt et al. (2011) found a linear relationship between the percentage of known vocabulary and reading comprehension, which suggests that the more words we know, the better comprehension scores we obtain. Naturally, the required number of known words is dependent on the level of comprehension desired. By way of illustration, if we aim at 60% reading comprehension, Schmitt et al. (2011) posit that 98% lexical coverage is needed, which translates into as many as 8–9,000 word families required to reach this level (Nation 2006). In turn, in a study exploring explored the relationship between vocabulary and listening, van Zeeland and Schmitt (2013) used a 95% threshold and suggested that adequate comprehension could be achieved with 2–3,000 word families. Irrespective of which figure we set as a threshold, it is clear that we need to know a large number of words to become successful language users.

Further arguments for the role of lexical knowledge in developing language proficiency are provided by research exploring the link between vocabulary and the four main language skills. Studies such as Milton et al. (2010) and Staehr

(2008) demonstrate that this relationship is strong and that vocabulary is an important factor contributing to overall language ability. More specifically, Milton et al. (2010) reported positive correlations between English as a second language (ESL) learners' vocabulary and their International English Language Testing System (IELTS) results, with the single variable of vocabulary size explaining between 40% and 60% variance in the learners' scores on the four main language skills. In a similar fashion, Staehr (2008) provided evidence in favor of the relevance of vocabulary to language proficiency. The author tested English as a foreign language (EFL) learners and found that their vocabulary size produced high correlations with reading, writing and, to a lesser extent, listening. Both of these studies thus suggest that lexical knowledge is a major contributor to successful language use, and as Milton (2013: 75) highlights, "developing learners' vocabulary knowledge appears to be an integral feature of developing their language performance generally". Interestingly, some participants in Staehr's (2008) study did not know the first 2,000 most frequent words and performed below average with regard to reading and writing, which shows that reaching the 2,000 vocabulary size level "is a crucial learning goal for low-level EFL learners" (Staehr 2008: 149).

At this point, it is vital to describe research which explores the amount of vocabulary known by L1 and L2 users. When it comes to the vocabulary size of educated native speakers, one of the most oft-cited figures is about 20,000 word families or 32,000 vocabulary items, excluding proper names (Goulden et al. 1990). Referring to this issue, Schmitt (2010) states that a range of 16–20,000 word families seems to be a fair estimate, even though the figure is likely to vary depending on the quality and amount of language use by individual speakers. Without a doubt, this is a very high number, and it would be unrealistic to expect non-native speakers to reach the same level considering they have much more limited exposure to authentic language input. Consequently, as far as the estimates of non-native speakers' vocabulary size are concerned, they tend to be lower and amount to around 8–9,000 word families. This is roughly half of what is expected of native speakers and results from research into the amount of vocabulary needed to perform different activities in a second (L2) language. In Nation's (2006) seminal study which was already mentioned, it was found that 8–9,000 word families (written language) and 6–7,000 word families (spoken language) provide enough lexical coverage to ensure a good understanding of L2 texts. Thus, these figures are often given as a reasonable goal for L2 learning (Schmitt 2010; Siyanova-Chanturia and Webb 2016).

To conclude, this section has highlighted the importance of vocabulary as a factor that influences general proficiency and constitutes a key element of becoming a mature language user. On the basis of the reviewed research, it can be stated that vocabulary plays a central role in general language performance; therefore, understanding how it is learned and used by individual speakers and writers is of paramount importance to the field of applied linguistics as a whole.

3.2 Terminology

'Words', 'vocabulary' and 'lexis' are examples of terms that are commonly used in the literature. A word can be defined as any sequence of letters bounded on either side by a space or punctuation mark (Carter 2004: 35), while 'vocabulary' and 'lexis' are terms that are often used interchangeably and subsume all lexical elements found in language. However, the term 'lexis' is probably more specific as it encompasses not only individual words but also different kinds of combinations between words (Scrivener 2005). Another alternative term is 'lexicon' which is understood as a collection of all words in a given language (Cheng 2012). A related notion is 'mental lexicon' which comes from psycholinguistics and refers to a 'private' dictionary of all the words stored in one's memory (see section 3.3.3 for more details).

When it comes to the terminology of corpus linguistics, once you engage in corpus analyses of vocabulary, you quickly realize that words occur in different forms and therefore the term '**word form**' is often used to refer to different realizations of one '**lexeme**'. According to Carter (2004: 38), a lexeme is an abstract unit which underlies different grammatical variants of a word. For example, the lexeme 'break' can be realized by different word forms such as 'broke', 'broken' and 'breaking', and such variation is captured by the term '**lemma**', which Francis and Kucera (1982: 1) define as "a set of lexical forms having the same stem and belonging to the same major word class, differing only in inflection and/or spelling". In other words, lemmas are base forms together with their inflected forms which represent the same grammatical class (e.g. all of them are nouns or verbs).

The term '**word family**' has an even broader meaning than a lemma as it encompasses a base form of a word together with its inflected forms and transparent derivatives (Bauer and Nation 1993; Coxhead 2000). Brezina and Gablasova (2015) use the word 'develop' to demonstrate this difference. A lemma includes all inflected forms of this verb ('develops', 'developed' and 'developing'), while a word family additionally includes representatives of other word classes such as adjectives ('undeveloped' and 'underdeveloped') and nouns ('development', 'developments', 'developer' and 'developers'). It should be added that some word families might have more members than others and consequently they might pose more difficulty for readers and listeners. Schmitt (2010) states that on average the most frequent word families have about six members and this number decreases to about four members for low-frequency vocabulary.

The last term to be introduced is a '**lexical item**', which, according to Sinclair (2004: 281), "consists of one or more words that together make up a unit of meaning". This notion emphasizes the fact that "most lexical meaning is associated with word patterns rather than with individual words" (Gardner 2007: 255) and therefore the meaning of an individual word is very much dependent on the meaning of its neighbors and the phraseological patterns it enters (see Chapter 5 for more information on phraseology).

This section has demonstrated that there is an abundance of terms we are likely to encounter in vocabulary studies, and it should be stressed that the use of specific terms and methodological considerations have important consequences for the validity of our empirical work. As Gardner (2007) convincingly argues, the way we conceptualize the construct of 'word' affects many aspects of vocabulary research, such as estimating the size of L2 learners' vocabulary and assessing their lexical competence. By way of example, if we state that a learner of English knows 5,000 words, we should consider whether this number refers to word forms, lemmas or word families. This is likely to be influenced by the way lexical knowledge is operationalized and measured by the research instruments used. That is why it is important to be precise in your use of terminology to avoid confusion and misinterpretation of the results of your research. Furthermore, it also needs to be acknowledged that what you select as a unit for analysis depends to a large extent on your research purposes and the specific design of your study (Anderson and Freebody 1981: 98). For example, Nation (2006: 67) notes that for productive purposes (speaking and writing) a lemma seems to be the largest sensible unit to use, because each lemma takes different collocates and different grammatical patterns. For clarity purposes, thus, in this book the term 'word' is used in the general sense mentioned above, unless there is a need for a more specific term such as 'lemma' or 'lexical item', in which cases it will be clearly marked.

3.3 Vocabulary knowledge as a complex construct

At the most elementary level of description, word knowledge can be conceptualized as a simple link between the form of a word and its meaning. However, many scholars (e.g. Nation 2013; Schmitt 2010; Milton and Fitzpatrick 2014) have pointed out that vocabulary knowledge is a multi-faceted construct that comprises several different aspects. The following paragraphs present three main approaches which have been most influential in the field.

3.3.1 The components approach

The most comprehensive description of what is involved in knowing a word has been proposed by Nation (2001, 2013). Continuing earlier work by Richards (1976), Nation follows a components approach to vocabulary which treats it as a multi-faceted construct that encompasses a number of different aspects. As the author (2013) explains, the knowledge of a word consists of a set of several different components grouped into three main categories: form, meaning and use. What is more, all of these components are considered at both a receptive (R) and productive (P) level of lexical mastery. As Melka (1997) observes, there are important differences between receptive and productive vocabulary (the former being much larger than the latter) and consequently lexical knowledge should be seen as a continuum or cline, with specific components (or degrees) being known at different levels.

Table 3.1 Aspects of knowing a word according to Nation (2001)

Form	spoken	R	What does the word sound like?
		P	How is the word pronounced?
	written	R	What does the word look like?
		P	How is the word written and spelled?
	word parts	R	What parts are recognizable in this word?
		P	What word parts are needed to express this meaning?
Meaning	form and meaning	R	What meaning does this word form signal?
		P	What word form can be used to express this meaning?
	concept and referents	R	What is included in the concept?
		P	What items can the concept refer to?
	associations	R	What other words does this make us think of?
		P	What other words could we use instead of this one?
Use	grammatical functions	R	In what patterns does the word occur?
		P	In what patterns must we use this word?
	collocations	R	What words or types of words occur with this one?
		P	What words or types of words must we use with this one?
	constraints on use (register, frequency ...)	R	Where, when and how often would we expect to meet this word?
		P	Where, when and how often can we use this word?

Another issue that should be highlighted is the fact that vocabulary learning is an incremental process (Schmitt 2008). This means that the learning of specific aspects of lexical knowledge takes place in small increments in a bit-by-bit manner. In addition, even though different aspects of lexical knowledge are learned simultaneously, gains are made at a different pace; that is, some aspects require more time and exposure to language to be learned than others. For instance, we first learn a word's meaning before we move on to its collocations or constraints on use. Furthermore, for very frequent words we are likely to acquire most or even all aspects of knowledge, while the full mastery of many infrequent words is rather unlikely (see Chapter 4 for a discussion of the role of frequency). To capture this process, vocabulary development is often viewed as a continuum or cline ranging from partial to precise knowledge (e.g. Schmitt 2010; Henriksen 1999; Melka 1997).

It needs to be stated that Nation's (2001) components approach has been developed with L2 learning in mind, in contexts where individual students progress from the most basic levels of knowledge such as form–meaning links to more advanced levels of competence such as collocations of a word or register awareness. However, the same patterns can be observed in the acquisition of L1 vocabulary, for vocabulary learning is an ongoing process which continues throughout our life.

3.3.2 Breadth and depth as dimensions of vocabulary knowledge

Another important aspect of conceptualizing lexical knowledge is making a distinction between vocabulary breadth and depth. Anderson and Freebody (1981) were the first authors to introduce these notions as two separate dimensions of the construct: vocabulary breadth (or size) is the number of words you know, while vocabulary depth refers to how well you know them. As observed by Schmitt (2014), vocabulary breadth is easier to operationalize and is usually assessed with tests that measure the total number of words known by an individual person. These include yes/no tests (Meara 1992), the Vocabulary Levels Test (Schmitt et al. 2001) and the Vocabulary Size Test (Nation and Beglar 2007).

Vocabulary depth, in turn, concerns those aspects of lexical knowledge "that go beyond the basic form-meaning mapping" (Gyllstad 2013: 14) and include elements such as the knowledge of collocations, associations and constraints on use. However, despite the popularity of tests such as Wesche and Paribakht's (1996) Vocabulary Knowledge Scale or Read's (1998) Word Associates Test, which have been used as measures of vocabulary depth, operationalizing depth and measuring it as a separate dimension of lexical knowledge remains a challenge. It appears that there are too many conceptualizations of this construct and it has been suggested that each test of depth is also to some extent a test of size (Schmitt 2014). Consequently, it can be concluded that while the general notion of vocabulary depth has been helpful in deepening our understanding of vocabulary knowledge, it is "far too vague and elusive" (Gyllstad 2013: 23) to be used for precise tasks such as theorizing, designing and interpreting research and assessments (Schmitt 2014: 942).

3.3.3 Vocabulary as lexical organization

Lexical organization is another approach to vocabulary knowledge. Rather than measuring different aspects of knowledge at the level of individual words, Meara (1997, 2010) suggests taking a more holistic perspective and perceiving vocabulary as a network of interconnected elements which make up our mental lexicon. Many scholars have approached the construct of vocabulary from the perspective of lexical networks in the speaker's mind. As Meara (2010) notes, "it has become a widely accepted convention to talk about vocabularies as if they are networks of connections between words".

To measure the network of one's vocabulary as a whole, Meara and Wolter (2004) developed a test called V_Links in which participants are asked to identify associations which are treated as links between words. While it seems a plausible way of measuring vocabulary knowledge, Fitzpatrick and Milton (2014: 11) note that "there are problems which emerge in deciding exactly what to include in the definition of a link". Similar difficulties may occur with reference to the notion of lexical fluency, which refers to "how readily and automatically a learner is able to use the words they know and the information they have on the use of these words" (Daller et al. 2007: 8).

It is of note that viewing vocabulary knowledge as a network allows us to tap into the structure of the mental lexicon as well as explore how lexical knowledge changes over time as individual speakers increase their proficiency. As Meara (1997) explains, lexical organization might help us account for the receptive-productive mastery, with items known at productive levels being more entrenched in the lexical system. At the same time, the author himself acknowledges that "vocabulary organization is not entirely independent of vocabulary size" (Meara 2010: 188) which seems to be of critical importance, particularly at the beginning of lexical development. During later stages of the learning process, however, its role decreases and this is when learners' ability to "exploit lexical structure to improve their performance" (Meara 2010: 188) becomes a dominant force. In short, lexical organization appears to be the most promising conceptualization of vocabulary knowledge with a lot of potential for capturing the complexity of the construct. However, more research using this approach is needed to "pursue this direction in a more tangible way" (Schmitt 2014: 943).

It needs to be added that the concept of vocabulary as lexical organization and the notion of the mental lexicon have been the object of a large number of studies within the field of psycholinguistics. In this context, the mental lexicon is perceived as all the lexical knowledge which each speaker is equipped with and, as Singleton (2000: 161) notes, it is the knowledge "upon which all use of any given language heavily depends". Considering the importance of psycholinguistics when it comes to understanding the structure of the mental lexicon, the following paragraphs seek to outline the most important findings from this area. It is hoped that our discussion of the main features that characterize the organization of lexical information as well as a brief description of one influential model of L2 lexicon will suffice to demonstrate that psycholinguistic research is of paramount importance when it comes to understanding issues such as the representation, access and processing of lexical information.

In a recent article reviewing empirical work on the nature of lexical knowledge available to L2 learners and highly skilled bilinguals, Kroll and Bogulski (2013) point to three main observations that have emerged from this psycholinguistic research:

- the L1 is active when L2 learners process words in the L2
- L1 activity persists even when L2 learners become highly proficient
- the parallel activation of words in the bilingual's two languages has the consequence that the native or dominant L1 changes so that the L2 comes to affect the L1.

As far as different models of the L2 lexicon are concerned, Kroll and Bogulski (2013) divide them into two classes: theories that explore mappings between the forms of words and their meanings, and theories that look at the activation of lexical knowledge during the process of word recognition. Discussing these theories is beyond the scope of this book (you are encouraged to consult Szubko-Sitarek (2015) or Singleton (2000) who provide thorough accounts of psycholinguistic research related to the mental lexicon) and therefore we will only refer to Kroll and Stewart's (1994) revised hierarchical model as one of the most influential examples of work in this area.

In broad terms, the model deals with conceptual and lexical links between learners' L1 and L2, and assumes that at the beginning of the learning process, because of their low proficiency, L2 learners rely on L1 translations as a way of accessing the meaning of L2 words. As they become more skilled language users and their proficiency grows, mediation via the L1 weakens and direct access to L2 meaning becomes possible. To test this hypothesis, Kroll and Stewart (1994) conducted an experiment in which L1-dominant Dutch-English bilinguals were asked to translate words from L1 to L2 and vice versa. The translation took the form of lists of words that were semantically blocked (i.e. words from one specific semantic area such as animals). Such semantic blocking is believed to reflect conceptual processing and by using it the authors were able to tap into differences in the processing of conceptual and lexical information. Their results revealed that only the translation from L1 to L2 was conceptually mediated, while in the L2 to L1 translation the learners were able to bypass conceptual processing and relied only on the lexical connections between the two languages. The model has attracted a lot of attention and since its publication, there have been studies both in favor and against the original claims by Kroll and Stewart. This only goes to show that the notion of the mental lexicon is a complex issue, in which various aspects of vocabulary knowledge can be explored from many different perspectives.

3.4 Usefulness of corpora for vocabulary studies

The previous sections have demonstrated that vocabulary studies is a rich area of linguistic research, with a large number of possible questions. Even though some aspects are more amenable to corpus analysis (e.g. dimensions of vocabulary knowledge related to its use) than others (e.g. processing of lexical information), it is fair to say that corpora can be usefully employed for both research and teaching purposes. What follows is a sample of issues related to vocabulary use and variation which can be studied via corpus-based analyses.

3.4.1 Polysemy of words

Polysemy of words is an example of a phenomenon that can be explored by means of corpus data. Carter (2004: 12) defines polysemy as "the existence of several meanings in an individual word" and states that there are a large number of polysemous words in English (e.g. 'bank' as a geographical term and 'bank' as a financial institution). Such polysemy of words is especially true for frequent items which are often characterized by multiple meaning-senses resulting from the use of language in different contexts. As McCarthy et al. (2010: 17) state, "the more frequent a word is, the more meanings it is likely to have". Given that corpora are large collections of natural language, they constitute a powerful tool for exploring how words take on different meanings when they are used across different real-life situations.

Task 3.1: Using data from the Corpus of Contemporary American English (COCA), explore the polysemy of the word 'bear' and look for examples of sentences which demonstrate its different meanings. Note that the completion of this task can be facilitated by the use of part-of-speech (PoS) tags, which allow you to carry out searches for specific word classes. For instance, if you wish to find examples of 'bear' as a verb, type in bear. [v*] into the search box (v* is a tag for verbs) and then your search will be limited only to this word class. Figure 3.1 presents a screenshot for this search in BYU-COCA.

Figure 3.1 A PoS search for 'bear' as a verb in COCA

3.4.2 Synonymy as a lexical relation

Relations between words constitute another aspect of vocabulary studies where corpora can provide valuable insights. Words do not exist in isolation and therefore their meanings can be studied by exploring the different lexical relations they have with one another. One example of a lexical relation is synonymy. According to Carter (2004: 20), it can be defined as a bilateral or symmetrical sense relation in which two or more linguistic forms have the same meaning. In light of this definition, the words 'issue' and 'problem' can be treated as synonyms which express the same meaning. However, as argued by Moon (2010), once we take a corpus perspective, it becomes clear that no two words can be considered perfect synonyms as corpus data reveal important differences in the phraseological patterns that tend to characterize the use of language in specific registers (formal vs. informal) or modes of communication (speech vs. writing).

Task 3.2: Look for synonyms of the words 'problem' and 'issue' using the following web-based interface: http://www.wordandphrase.info/analyzeText. asp. Do these synonyms express the same meanings? What are the most frequent collocations or word partnerships they form?

You will complete this task by using the 'Analyze texts' option available at www.wordandphrase.info. It is a useful resource which allows you to investigate different aspects of English vocabulary on the basis of data from COCA (see Figure 3.2). To find synonyms of the words 'problem' and 'issue', select the 'Analyze texts' option and type 'problem' and 'issue' into the text box. Once you hit search, you will see information about the frequency of the words (both of them are among the most frequent words). Next, when you click on 'problem', a window on the left-hand side of the interface will display a list of synonyms ranked according to their frequency of occurrence. Note that the interface provides different synonyms depending on which meaning of 'problem' is considered. Repeat the same procedure for the word 'issue' and compare the two sets of synonyms.

It is worth adding that the interface is constructed in such a way that it automatically lists examples of phrases or multiword units for the word that you explore. More specifically, when you click on the option 'multiword', you will be able to find examples of some frequent collocations that contain the search words: 'health problem' or 'problem solving' for the word 'problem' and 'at issue' or 'take issue' for the word 'issue'. After you have conducted this analysis, it should become clear that there are important differences between the words that tend to be perceived as synonyms and access to corpora provides us with an opportunity to explore such differences.

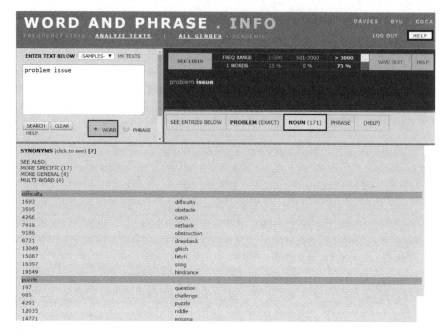

Figure 3.2 COCA-based interface www.wordandphrase.info

3.4.3 Metaphoricity and idiomaticity of words

Metaphoricity is another feature of vocabulary that can be studied through corpus-based analyses. As McCarthy et al. (2010: 75) explain, metaphoric meaning is a type of extended meaning when words "are used in an extended non-literal way to explain something in a comparative relationship". The authors point out that even though such non-literal meanings of words are usually associated with literary texts, the metaphoric use of language is pervasive across many different contexts. This is exemplified by the following sentences:

> She is also the **driving force** behind the New Georgia Project.
> The result is a surprisingly intense ethical struggle and a fresh **sea of tears.**
> But from out of a storm comes refreshing **winds of change**.

All of these examples have been taken from COCA, which demonstrates that large corpora as collections of real-life usage of words can serve as a helpful resource for identifying examples of the metaphorical use of language.

A special kind of non-literal language that attracts the attention of many researchers are idioms. In their account of idiomatic language, O'Keeffe at al. (2007: 80) state that both teachers and learners love idioms because they "offer a colorful relief" to the usual elements of the language learning process such as analyzing grammar rules, learning new words and preparing for tests. Items such as 'pulling one's leg' or 'burning the midnight oil' are examples of idioms which in broad terms can be defined as "expressions whose meaning is more than the sum of the meanings of the individual words" (McCarthy et al. 2010: 63). But even these two examples demonstrate differences in semantic transparency, that is, the extent to which the meaning of the whole idiom can be inferred by analyzing the meaning of the constituent parts. When you compare these two idioms, "burning the midnight oil" appears to be more transparent or easier to decode because in the past, when there was no electricity, burning oil was a popular way of lighting rooms.

Another feature of idioms that is worth emphasizing is that they are language- or culture-specific. This means that translating them word-by-word from one language into another should be avoided because it is likely to fail to yield the original meaning of the phrase. Such translational incongruence is probably one of the factors that make idioms so attractive from a pedagogical point of view, which results in the fact that many teaching materials target various kinds of idiomatic expressions. However, from a corpus linguistics perspective a slightly different picture emerges. As O'Keeffe et al. (2007) argue, corpora reveal that idioms are low-frequency items and in comparison with individual words their frequency is rather low. For instance, the authors report that idioms that occur ten times in the Cambridge and Nottingham Corpus of Discourse in English (CANCODE) would rank among the first 7,000 words if all the vocabulary from the corpus was presented as a lemmatized list of single-word items. Thus, one way in which corpora can assist research into idiomatic language is to check their frequency relative to the frequency of individual words and identify those items that occur most commonly and therefore should be included in teaching syllabuses. Naturally, there remains a question if high frequency can always be equated with pedagogical relevance, but these issues will be tackled in Chapter 6, which deals with corpora and teaching vocabulary.

Another example of how corpora can be used to study idioms is exploring the level of their fixedness. It is commonly believed that idioms are fixed in terms of their linguistic form and consequently learning such items by heart is often regarded as the best method of coping with them. However, Carter's (2004) corpus-based analysis of spoken language reveals a lot of examples of creativity in the use of idiomatic language and thus investigations into the frequency of such modifications, how they change the discourse that is created and what functions they fulfill are likely to produce important insights into the nature of authentic communication.

Task 3.3: In their discussion of non-literal language, McCarthy et al. (2010) state that some words are more idiom-prone than others; that is, they tend to occur in many metaphoric or idiomatic expressions. For instance, words that have to do with parts of the human body (e.g. hand, head, eye) are often used in a non-literal way. Using data from the British National Corpus (BNC) (http://corpus.byu.edu/bnc/), analyze concordances for the word 'hand' and look for examples of how it is used literally and metaphorically or idiomatically.

As Task 3.3 demonstrates, computers and concordancers are not yet able to identify idiomatic meanings of words and therefore automatic searches need to be combined with qualitative forms of analysis based on the reading of concordance lines. As a result, an important part of your responsibility as a corpus analyst is to develop analytic skills which will allow you to combine quantitative analysis of frequencies of words with more interpretative discourse-oriented examinations of how they are used in specific contexts (see Chapter 9 for details on the relationship between corpus linguistics and discourse analysis).

3.4.4 Register variation: jargon, slang and appropriateness

Another aspect of vocabulary studies where corpora can afford useful insights is the analysis of lexical variation that stems from the use of language in different contexts and social settings. The notion of register is of key importance here because it focuses on the varied use of language as dependent on factors such as communicative situation, formality level, the age and gender of language users and relationships between them (Gardner 2013; McCarthy et al. 2010). Thanks to the fact that modern corpora are carefully designed and sampled from a wide range of social and professional contexts, it is possible to explore how all of these factors impact on the nature of vocabulary and how its use varies depending on the purposes of specific writers and speakers.

Task 3.4: Go to the BYU-COCA interface and use the query presented in Figure 3.3. Your task is to look for examples of the most frequent nouns across different registers. For instance, compare the frequency of the noun 'things' in the spoken and academic sections of the corpus. What does this say about the nature of spoken and academic vocabulary?

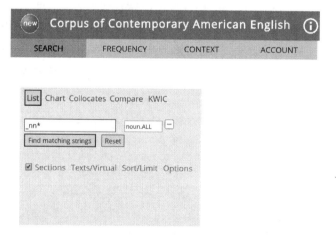

Figure 3.3 A search for the most frequent nouns in different sections of COCA

Answer

	Academic COCA	Frequency	Spoken COCA	Frequency
1	students	220,099	people	366,409
2	time	129,722	time	198,985
3	school	119,459	president	167,579
4	study	111,009	way	142,638
5	education	107,669	years	137,972
6	research	101,014	Mr	130,569
7	people	98,197	lot	119,493
8	children	96,838	things	113,870
9	years	89,302	thing	101,894
10	war	83,604	day	92,879

Figure 3.4 A list of the most frequent nouns in different sections of COCA

3.5 Examples of research questions

As the above sections have emphasized, corpus data can be used to address a number of different issues that are relevant to the study of vocabulary. Since this book is envisioned as an introduction to the use of corpora for exploring vocabulary, the following chapters provide numerous examples of how your research in this area can benefit from corpus-based analysis. Here is a list of some research questions that we will discuss:

1   Which English words are the most frequent ones? Content or function words?
2   How is spoken vocabulary different from written vocabulary?
3   Why are collocations and other kinds of multiword units an important element of language?
4   How can I use corpus data in language teaching? How can corpus-based lists of vocabulary help me decide which words should be taught first?
5   What are the key features of learner vocabulary?
6   What is academic vocabulary? How is it different from general vocabulary?
7   How does vocabulary contribute to the structure of discourse?
8   What pragmatic functions does vocabulary fulfill?

All of these questions represent highly relevant issues to the study of vocabulary, and by reading the subsequent chapters you will learn how corpora can assist you in finding answers to them.

Summary

This chapter has presented vocabulary as a crucial element of language and presented the key terminology used in the area of vocabulary studies. We have demonstrated that vocabulary is a multi-faceted construct that should be approached from different linguistic perspectives so that its complexity can be fully captured. As the aim of this book is to demonstrate the usefulness of corpora for investigating various aspects of the use of words, we have also considered examples of questions which can be explored by means of corpus techniques.

References

Aitchison, J. (2003). *Words in the Mind: An introduction to the mental lexicon.* Third edition. Oxford: Blackwell Publishing.

Anderson, R. C. and Freebody, P. (1981). Vocabulary knowledge, in J. T. Guthrie (ed.) *Comprehension and Teaching: Research reviews.* Newark, NJ: International Reading Association, 77–117.

Bauer, L. and Nation, I. S. P. (1993). Word families. *International Journal of Lexicography,* 6, 4, 253–279.

Brezina, V. and Gablasova, D. (2015). Is there a core general vocabulary? Introducing the New General Service List. *Applied Linguistics,* 36, 1, 1–22.

Carter, R. (2004). *Language and Creativity: The art of common talk.* London: Routledge.

Cheng, W. (2012). *Exploring Corpus Linguistics: Language in action.* London and New York: Routledge.

Coxhead, A. (2000). A new academic word list. *TESOL Quarterly,* 34, 2, 213–238.

Daller, H., Milton, J. and Treffers-Daller, J. (2007). Editors' introduction: Conventions, terminology and an overview of the book, in H. Daller, J. Milton and J. Teffers-Daller (eds.) *Modelling and Assessing Vocabulary Knowledge.* Cambridge: Cambridge University Press, 1–32.

Fitzpatrick, T. and Milton, J. (2014). Introduction: Deconstructing vocabulary knowledge, in J. Milton and T. Fitzpatrick (eds.) *Dimensions of Vocabulary Knowledge.* Basingstoke: Palgrave Macmillan, 1–12.

Francis, N. and Kucera, H. (1982). *Frequency Analysis of English Usage: Lexicon and grammar.* Boston, MA: Houghton Mifflin.

Gardner, D. (2007). Validating the construct of word in applied corpus-based vocabulary research: A critical survey. *Applied Linguistics,* 28, 2, 241–265.

Gardner, D. (2013). *Exploring Vocabulary: Language in action.* London and New York: Routledge.

Goulden, R., Nation, I. S. P. and Read, J. (1990). How large can a receptive vocabulary be? *Applied Linguistics,* 11, 4, 341–363.

Gyllstad, H. (2013). Looking at L2 vocabulary knowledge dimensions from an assessment perspectives: Challenges and potential solutions, in C. Bardel, C. Lindqvist and B. Laufer (eds.) *L2 Vocabulary Acquisition, Knowledge and Use: New perspectives on assessment and corpus analysis.* Amsterdam: Eurosla, 11–28.

Hanks, P. (2013). *Lexical Analysis: Norms and exploitations.* Cambridge, MA and London: The MIT Press.

Henriksen, B. (1999). Three dimensions of vocabulary knowledge. *Studies in Second Language Acquisition*, 21, 2, 303–317.

Hu, M. and Nation, P. (2000). Vocabulary density and reading comprehension. *Reading in a Foreign Language*, 23, 1, 403–430.

Kroll, J. F. and Bogulski, C. A. (2013). Organization of the second language lexicon, in C. A. Chapelle (ed.) *The Encyclopedia of Applied Linguistics*. Oxford: Blackwell Publishing.

Kroll, J. F. and Stewart, E. (1994). Category interference in translation and picture naming: Evidence for asymmetric connections between bilingual memory representations. *Journal of Memory and Language*, 33, 149–174.

Laufer, B. and Ravenhorst-Kalovski, G. C. (2010). Lexical threshold revisited: Lexical text coverage, learners' vocabulary size and reading comprehension. *Reading in a Foreign Language*, 22, 1, 15–30.

McCarthy, M., O'Keeffe, A. and Walsh, S. (2010). *Vocabulary Matrix: Understanding, learning and teaching*. Andover: Heinle Cengage Learning.

Meara, P. (1992). *EFL Vocabulary Tests*. Swansea: Centre for Applied Language Studies, University College Swansea.

Meara, P. (1997). Towards a new approach to modeling vocabulary acquisition, in N. Schmitt and M. McCarthy (eds.) *Vocabulary: Description, acquisition and pedagogy*. Cambridge: Cambridge University Press, 109–121.

Meara, P. (2010). The relationship between L2 vocabulary knowledge and L2 vocabulary, in E. Macaro (ed.) *The Bloomsbury companion to second language acquisition*. London: Bloomsbury Academic, 179–193.

Meara, P. and Wolter, B. (2004). V_Links: Beyond vocabulary depth, in D. Albrechtsen, K. Haastrup and B. Henriksen (eds.) *Angles on the English-speaking World 4*. Copenhagen: Museum Tusculanum Press, 85–96.

Melka, F. (1997). Receptive vs. productive aspects of vocabulary, in N. Schmitt and M. McCarthy (eds.) *Vocabulary: Description, acquisition and pedagogy*. Cambridge: Cambridge University Press, 84–102.

Milton, J. (2013). Measuring the contribution of vocabulary knowledge to proficiency in the four skills, in C. Bardel, C. Lindqvist and B. Laufer (eds.) *L2 Vocabulary Acquisition, Knowledge and Use: New perspectives on assessment and corpus analysis*. Amsterdam: Eurosla, 57–78.

Milton, J. and Fitzpatrick, T. (eds.) (2014). *Dimensions of Vocabulary Knowledge*. Basingstoke: Palgrave Macmillan.

Milton, J., Wade, J. and Hopkins, N. (2010). Aural word recognition and oral competence in a foreign language, in R. Chacon-Beltran, C. Abello-Contesse and M. del Mar Torreblanca-Lopez (eds.) *Insights into Non-native Vocabulary Teaching and Learning*. Bristol: Multilingual Matters, 88–98.

Moon, R. (2010). What can a corpus tell us about lexis? in A. O'Keeffe and M. McCarthy (eds.) *The Routledge Handbook of Corpus Linguistics*. London and New York: Routledge, 197–211.

Nation, I. S. P. (2001). *Learning Vocabulary in Another Language*. 1st edition. Cambridge: Cambridge University Press.

Nation, I. S. P. (2006). How large a vocabulary is needed for reading and listening? *Canadian Modern Language Review*, 63, 1, 59–81.

Nation, I. S. P. (2013). *Learning Vocabulary in Another Language*. 2nd edition. Cambridge: Cambridge University Press.

Nation, I. S. P. and Beglar, D. (2007). A vocabulary size test. *The Language Teacher*, 31, 7, 9–13.

O'Keeffe, A., McCarthy, M. and Carter, R. (2007). *From Corpus to Classroom*. Cambridge: Cambridge University Press.

Read, J. (1998). Validating a test to measure depth of vocabulary knowledge, in A. Kunnan (ed.) *Validation in Language Assessment*. Mahwah, NJ: Lawrence Erlbaum, 41–60.

Read, J. (2013). Assessment of vocabulary, in C. A. Chapelle (ed.) *The Encyclopedia of Applied Linguistics*. Oxford: Blackwell Publishing.

Richards, J. C. (1976). The role of vocabulary teaching. *TESOL Quarterly*, 10, 1, 77–89.

Schmitt, N. (2008). Instructed second language vocabulary learning. *Language Teaching Research*, 12, 3, 329–363.

Schmitt, N. (2010). *Researching Vocabulary: A research manual*. Basingstoke: Palgrave Macmillan.

Schmitt, N. (2014). Size and depth of vocabulary knowledge: What the research shows. *Language Learning*, 64, 4, 913–951.

Schmitt, N. and Schmitt, D. (2014). A reassessment of frequency and vocabulary size in L2 vocabulary teaching, *Language Teaching*, 47, 4, 484–503.

Schmitt, N., Jiang, X. and Grabe, W. (2011). The percentage of words known in a text and reading comprehension. *Modern Language Journal*, 95, 1, 26–43.

Schmitt, N., Schmitt, D. and Clapham, C. (2001). Developing and exploring the behavior of two versions of the Vocabulary Levels Test. *Language Testing*, 18, 1, 55–88.

Scrivener, J. (2005). *Learning Teaching: A guidebook for English language teachers*. Basingstoke: Macmillan.

Sinclair, J. (2004). *Trust the Text*. London: Routledge.

Singleton, D. (2000). *Language and the Lexicon: An introduction*. London: Arnold.

Siyanova-Chanturia, A. and Webb, S. (2016). Teaching vocabulary in the EFL context, in W. A. Renandya and H. P. Widodo (eds.) *English Language Teaching Today: Linking theory and practice*. New York: Springer, 227–239.

Staehr, L. S. (2008). Vocabulary size and the skills of listening, reading and writing. *Language Learning Journal*, 36, 2, 139–152.

Szubko-Sitarek, W. (2015). *Multilingual Lexical Recognition in the Mental Lexicon of Third Language Users*. New York: Springer.

Van Zeeland, H. and Schmitt, N. (2013). Lexical coverage in L1 and L2 listening comprehension: The same or different from reading comprehension? *Applied Linguistics*, 34, 3, 457–479.

Wesche, M. and Paribakht, T. S. (1996). Assessing L2 vocabulary knowledge: Depth versus breadth. *The Canadian Modern Language Review*, 53, 1, 13–40.

Chapter 4

Frequency and vocabulary

4.1 The importance of frequency in corpus analysis

One of the most basic applications of corpora is ranking words on the basis of their frequency of occurrence. As highlighted by Tognini-Bonelli (2010: 19), frequency "takes pride of place" in corpus investigations because it underlies all kinds of analyses. In fact, sorting words according to how frequent they are is one of the main reasons why we invest considerable resources in compiling corpora of naturally occurring language. This is because analyzing texts together as one body of data (rather than looking at them individually) gives us new insights into the complexity of language use. As O'Keeffe et al. (2007: 31) observe, by analyzing corpora that represent data from different speakers and contexts of use, "we can make fairly reliable statements about how many words are 'in circulation' in everyday communication". What is more, such empirically derived statements about tendencies in language are more accurate than those based on speakers' intuitions. Specifically, research demonstrates that intuitions of both native and non-native speakers are often unreliable, in particular when it comes to judging lower-frequency vocabulary (e.g. Siyanova-Chanturia and Spina 2015; McCrostie 2007).

> Task 4.1: Order these five words according to their frequency of occurrence starting with the most frequent one. Then check the accuracy of your predictions by exploring the frequency of these words in the BYU-COCA corpus.
>
> wall, harmonize, chimney, favorably, outlook

4.1.1 Frequency of spoken and written vocabulary

Information about the frequency of words obtained from corpora can be applied to explore the use of language in specific contexts. For instance, a frequency-based analysis can be employed to make comparisons between the use of vocabulary in speech and writing. As explained by Cheng (2012), these are two separate modes of communication and they are characterized by different sets of features. Speech is more interactive, spontaneous and dynamic, whereas written language is more planned, detached and takes more time to be produced. Access to corpora provides you with an opportunity to explore these differences and juxtapose the use of language in the two modes. Crucially, such comparisons are useful for research (e.g. when you aim to design study materials that should reflect either written or spoken language) as well as pedagogical purposes (e.g. corpora can help you select the target vocabulary for a specific group of learners who wish to improve their communicative skills in one of the two modes).

As noted in Chapter 1, because of the difficulty of collecting and transcribing spoken data, most corpus analyses have tended to focus on written language. According to McCarthy and Carter (1997: 20), the dominance of written corpora has shaped "our view of not only of which words are the most important ones, but also of how words are used in acts of communication". However, the number of large databases of spoken language is rising and more and more studies explore the frequency of words in speech. Examples of spoken corpora that you can consider exploring include the Hong Kong Corpus of Spoken English (http://rcpce.engl.polyu.edu.hk/HKCSE/), the Michigan Corpus of Academic Spoken English (MICASE) (http://quod.lib.umich.edu/m/micase/) and the British Academic Spoken English Corpus (BASE) (https://the.sketchengine.co.uk/bonito/run.cgi/first_form?corpname=preloaded/base).

A convincing demonstration of corpus-based research into differences between speech and writing is Carter and McCarthy's work on spoken grammar (Carter and McCarthy 1995; McCarthy and Carter 1997; Carter and McCarthy 2017). On the basis of comparisons between spoken and written texts, the authors have found that spoken English is distinctly different from written English. For example, since spoken communication tends to be more personal, it contains a higher number of personal pronouns (e.g. 'you' and 'I'), response tokens (e.g. 'right') and organizational **discourse markers** (e.g. 'now' used at the beginning of sentences). These items play a key role in building the structure of spoken discourse and by exploring patterns of their occurrence in corpora, you can gain useful insights into the nature of spoken communication.

Task 4.2: Using the chart option of the BYU-BNC interface, compare the frequency of 'you', 'right' and 'now' in the spoken and academic sections of the British National Corpus (BNC).

Another aspect that characterizes spoken language is the prevalence of lexical chunks such as 'you know' or 'I see' (O'Keeffe et al. 2007). As the authors

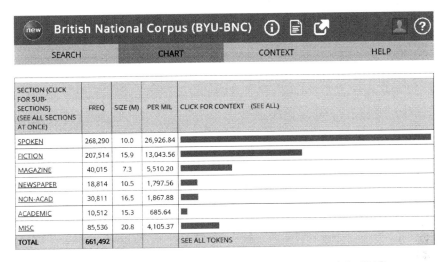

SECTION (CLICK FOR SUB-SECTIONS) (SEE ALL SECTIONS AT ONCE)	FREQ	SIZE (M)	PER MIL	CLICK FOR CONTEXT (SEE ALL)
SPOKEN	268,290	10.0	26,926.84	
FICTION	207,514	15.9	13,043.56	
MAGAZINE	40,015	7.3	5,510.20	
NEWSPAPER	18,814	10.5	1,797.56	
NON-ACAD	30,811	16.5	1,867.88	
ACADEMIC	10,512	15.3	685.64	
MISC	85,536	20.8	4,105.37	
TOTAL	**661,492**			SEE ALL TOKENS

Figure 4.1 A search for the frequency of 'you' in different sections of the BNC

underline, some of the chunks are so common that their frequency is higher than that of individual words (e.g. check the frequency of 'you know'). This can be attributed to the fact that phraseological chunks are a key element of language and they help speakers perform a number of discourse functions such as maintaining relationships (see Chapter 5 for the importance of phraseology).

Task 4.3: Check the frequency of 'you know' and 'I see' in the Corpus of Contemporary American English (COCA) and compare it with the frequency of the most commonly occurring words from the following list: http://www.wordfrequency.info/free.asp.

Other features of spoken vocabulary are described in McCarthy and Carter (1997) who explore issues such as lexical repetition (repeating the same words or phrases by a speaker and/or their interlocutors across longer stretches of language), relexicalization (expressing the same meaning by means of different lexical forms) and the use of vague terms (expressing imprecision, uncertainty and generalization). However, since the authors have explored these issues by combining corpus analysis with discourse-analytical approaches (using individual texts and concordances rather than frequency information from the whole corpus), we will discuss them in a more detailed way in Chapter 9, which is devoted to the study of vocabulary at the level of discourse.

4.1.2 Frequency of function vs. content words

Another example of useful insights into the nature of vocabulary can be obtained by comparing the frequency of function and content words. Table 4.1 presents a sample wordlist which displays the most frequent words in English. The list was created on the basis of data from COCA (note that the first 5,000 most frequent words can be downloaded free of charge from the following website: http://www.wordfrequency.info/free.asp).

What is striking about the list is that the majority of the words it contains are function words such as prepositions ('of', 'for', 'with') or articles ('the' and 'a'). The highest-ranked content word (i.e. a word carrying meaning) is 'say'. 'Have' is ranked higher than 'say' but it is important to remember that 'have' can be used as both a content and grammatical word and an automatic frequency search does not distinguish between these uses. These observations highlight the relevance of function words as they account for a large portion of English texts across all types of language use. For instance, Davies and Gardner (2010) report that as few as fifty function words account for 60% of spoken English. This means that regardless of what text you analyze, the top of your frequency list is likely to contain many function words.

Table 4.1 Twenty most frequent words in American English (based on COCA)

	Word	Part of speech	Raw frequency
1	The	Det	22,038,615
2	Be	V	12,545,825
3	And	Conj	10,741,073
4	Of	Prep	10,343,885
5	A	Det	10,144,200
6	In	Prep	6,996,437
7	To	Inf	6,332,195
8	Have	V	4,303,955
9	To	Prep	3,856,916
10	It	Pron	3,872,477
11	I	Prep	3,978,265
12	That	Conj	3,430,996
13	For	Prep	3,281,454
14	You	Pron	3,081,151
15	He	Pron	2,909,254
16	With	Prep	2,683,014
17	On	Prep	2,485,306
18	Do	V	2,573,587
19	Say	V	1,915,138
20	This	Det	1,885,366

4.1.3 Frequency and Zipf's law

Our discussion of frequency-based categorizations of vocabulary would not be complete without a reference to Zipf's law. By analyzing the occurrence of words in different texts, Zipf (1935) observed that there is an inverse relationship between the frequency of words and their rank in frequency lists. More specifically, if words from a text are ranked in a descending order, it can be discerned that the first most frequent word occurs roughly twice as often as the second most frequent word and three times as often as the third one. Crucially, this pattern continues as you go down the frequency list, which reveals the extent of regularity in natural language. What is more, Zipf's law points to the importance of high-frequency words which play a key role in providing the lexical coverage of large proportions of texts (Nation 2016). For instance, high-frequency words such as 'the' or 'of' occur in almost every sentence in English and consequently they account for large portions of any text. Nation (2016: 4–5) points to three generalizations that follow from Zipf's law:

- there is a relatively small number of words that have a high frequency
- there is a very large number of words that have a low frequency
- the frequency of words on a wordlist drop very quickly and "about halfway down the list the words from there on have a frequency of only one occurrence in the text".

These are useful observations that constitute the essence of corpus linguistic research into vocabulary. Importantly, a Zipfian distribution characterizes not only the occurrence of words but also other aspects of language such as multiword units (Ellis 2012). This shows there is a lot of systematicity in the distribution of vocabulary and language as a whole and through corpus-based analyses we are able to delve into details of these phenomena.

4.1.4 Frequency, lexical coverage and bands of vocabulary

Dividing vocabulary into categories such as high-, mid- and low-frequency is another example of the usefulness of frequency analysis. It is generally agreed that high-frequency English vocabulary consists of 2,000 of the most frequent word families (although see below for Schmitt and Schmitt's (2014) call for treating the first 3,000 word families as high-frequency vocabulary). Since the most frequent words are used to create different texts and they play a key role in successful language use, many scholars treat them as core vocabulary that needs to be acquired as quickly as possible. As explained by Nation (2011: 531), high-frequency words are "a relatively small, very useful group of words that are important no matter what use is made of the language".

The significance of high-frequency words is corroborated by research on lexical coverage. As signaled in Chapter 3, lexical coverage is usually defined as the percentage of words that are known in a given piece of discourse (Laufer and Ravenhorst-Kalovski 2010; Adolphs and Schmitt 2003). It is an important notion because it allows us to estimate how many words are needed for successful comprehension of written and spoken texts and making such calculations is greatly facilitated by corpus analyses. As contended by O'Keeffe et al. (2007: 48), corpus evidence can be used to assess how many words a reader/listener needs to know to understand a given proportion of any written or spoken text.

Crucially, words differ in terms of how much coverage they provide, with high-frequency vocabulary accounting for the largest amount of text (Nation 2006). As O'Keeffe et al. (2007: 32) observe, "the first 2,000 or so word-forms do most of the work" and cover "more than 80% of all of the words in spoken and written texts". In a similar vein, Dang and Webb (2016a: 133) state that high-frequency vocabulary offers learners "a good return for their learning effort" as this relatively small group of words cover large amounts of different kinds of texts. Words at lower frequency levels, in turn, provide a progressively smaller coverage by dint of their decreasing frequency of occurrence. Referring to this issue, Schmitt and Schmitt (2014: 488) point out that beyond the 2–3,000 frequency levels the frequency of occurrence drops off to low levels and this is consistently confirmed by data from a range of different corpora. In this light, high-frequency vocabulary can be defined as that which occurs before the coverage percentages become small. In fact, this is one of the main reasons why Schmitt and Schmitt propose that rather than using the traditional figure of the first 2,000 word families as the upper boundary of high-frequency vocabulary, the threshold should be moved and include the first 3,000 word families. According to the authors, this figure is more valid pedagogically and given the importance of such high-frequency vocabulary, learning it should be treated as a milestone in language development.

Interestingly, Nation and Anthony's (2013) recent article follows this idea and the 3,000 band is used as a threshold for high-frequency vocabulary. Look at Table 4.2 and compare how much coverage is provided by the different types of vocabulary as attested by data from the BNC. It is worth noting that the figure includes the category of mid-frequency vocabulary, the new construct proposed by Schmitt and Schmitt (2014) as a way of reassessing the traditional frequency-based bands.

Table 4.2 Coverage levels for different types of vocabulary (Nation and Anthony 2013)

Type of vocabulary (word family frequency level)	Coverage (%)
High-frequency (1st–3rd 1,000)	90
Mid-frequency (4th–9th 1,000)	5
Low-frequency (10th 1,000 onwards)	1–2
Other (e.g. proper nouns or abbreviations)	3–4
Total	100

According to Schmitt and Schmitt (2014), the introduction of this new category is pedagogically motivated and mid-frequency words deserve the attention of both teachers and learners. The authors estimate that mid-frequency vocabulary consists of around 6,000 word families that lie between the first 3,000 (a threshold for high-frequency vocabulary) and 9,000 (a threshold for low-frequency vocabulary) most frequent words in English. Dang and Webb (2016a) rightly observe that reaching these levels of lexical competence is rather unlikely for many L2 learners, as they often struggle with learning even the most frequent items (e.g. Webb and Chang 2012). Consequently, the authors suggest that perhaps the first 1,000 words should be treated as a 'general service' list and prioritized in L2 programs, as learning this high-frequency vocabulary seems like "a more attainable objective in the EFL/ESL context" (Dang and Webb 2016a: 151). Of course learning these words might still take a long time but knowing them is an essential condition of successful L2 use and can open up new possibilities (e.g. more efficient and enjoyable reading or accessing a wider range of texts).

Low-frequency vocabulary is perceived as words that are beyond the 9,000 frequency threshold, often regarded as "restricted to certain subject areas" (Nation 2011: 531). This 9,000 threshold is taken from Nation's (2006) study in which the author found that L2 learners need a receptive lexical knowledge of 8–9,000 word families to reach a 98% coverage. As the author calculates, with this level of coverage, forty-nine out of every fifty words in a text should be known, which allows a pleasurable engagement with and understanding of authentic texts (e.g. novels or newspapers). As stated by Schmitt and Schmitt (2014: 494), "if 8–9,000 word families is enough to enable both listening to and reading a wide range of texts . . ., then the low-frequency/utility vocabulary can plausibly be defined as anything beyond this frequency level".

Moreover, low-frequency vocabulary is frequently defined as specialized and technical words which are important for understanding specialized texts. In practical terms this means that low-frequency vocabulary consists of words of a limited range which are specific to a particular subject area. Very often, such words are identified by comparing wordlists from general and specialized corpora. That is, technical words tend to be more frequent in a specialized corpus while in large general corpora, which represent language as a whole, such words come up as low-frequency items. Thus, by relying on frequency as a key factor that organizes the classification of vocabulary, you can identify different types of technical vocabulary (e.g. words that are characteristic of specific topics or fields of study).

It is vital to add that frequency is also helpful when it comes to identifying academic words. These are words that are common in academic texts (Schmitt 2010), and corpora which are built of academic texts can be used to create lists of such words. The best-known example of a frequency-based list of academic vocabulary is Coxhead's (2000) Academic Word List (AWL); details of how it was developed can be found in Chapter 8, which deals with different types of specialized vocabulary.

To sum up, this section has demonstrated that frequency plays a central role in analyzing and describing the use of vocabulary. By exploring the occurrence of words in authentic texts, corpus linguists have been able to establish different types of vocabulary representing specific frequency bands (high-, mid- and low-frequency words). At the same time, however, it should be stated that to some extent these divisions are arbitrary and boundaries between them can be fuzzy. As Dang and Webb (2016a: 149) point out, "there is no perfect way of comparing word lists" and drawing lines between specific types of vocabulary remains a challenge. Similarly, Nation (2015: 581) states that "there is no ultimate wordlist" because "the best wordlist is the one which is most suited to the purpose for which it is being used". Also, our decisions as to how we view high- vs. low-frequency words are likely to be dependent on factors such as the unit of counting (e.g. a word family vs. a lemma), the context in which we function and perhaps most importantly the purposes for which we intend to use our frequency-based lists of vocabulary. For instance, if you teach beginners in an English as a foreign language (EFL) context, Dang and Webb's (2016b) Essential Word List of the most frequent items can serve as a general service list, whereas for more advanced learners the bar can go higher and Schmitt and Schmitt's (2014) 3,000 most frequent word families can be viewed as a more ambitious and appropriate goal. Given that research on wordlists is thriving (see section 4.3), this discussion is likely to continue. However, regardless of where we set our cut-off points, it is fair to say that corpus-based analyses have enhanced our understanding of the use of vocabulary and its role in building discourse.

4.1.5 Basic (core) and advanced vocabulary

Another frequency-based account of vocabulary has been described by O'Keeffe et al. (2007). Drawing heavily on corpus data, the authors make a distinction between basic and advanced vocabulary. With regard to the former, it refers to the first 2,000 most frequent or core words that are a key element of everyday language use and consequently need to be acquired during the initial stages of lexical development. On the basis of their corpus analyses (both written and spoken data), O'Keeffe et al. point out that the core vocabulary consists of several broad categories such as basic verbs (including modal and delexical verbs), basic nouns, stance words, general deixis, basic adjectives and adverbs, discourse markers and basic chunks. According to the authors, such categories hold a lot of potential for an organized pedagogy in which the core vocabulary is viewed as "an important index of what should be included in a basic syllabus" for L2 learners (O'Keeffe et al. 2007: 36).

Defining advanced vocabulary appears to be more problematic and establishing the boundaries of this category is likely to involve some level of arbitrariness. To avoid this problem, O'Keeffe et al. (2007) turn to corpus-based estimates of lexical coverage as a benchmark and use a frequency-based criterion for advanced vocabulary. Relying on findings on the relationship between vocabulary and reading comprehension, the authors argue that a receptive mastery of 5–6,000 words seems to be a border between the intermediate and advanced level of proficiency. In other words, once an L2 learner has acquired the first 5–6,000 words, he or she has reached a point at which they are ready to embark on advanced-level vocabulary learning.

Further details of advanced vocabulary have been provided by McCarthy (1997). The author contends that at the advanced level of proficiency, vocabulary acquisition is a special kind of lexical development that pertains to several issues. These include, among others, learning frequent and metaphorical senses of words, increasing the knowledge of phraseological relationships that exist between words, focusing on differences between spoken and written vocabulary, becoming more aware of connotative meanings (positive or negative associations) invoked by specific words and paying attention to register- and genre-specific distinctions found in naturally occurring lexis. In addition, McCarthy observes that achieving advanced proficiency involves not only gains in vocabulary size but also qualitative improvement related to deepening one's lexical knowledge. As discussed in Chapter 3, vocabulary depth encompasses the knowledge of different aspects of individual words such as register restrictions, collocations or grammatical functions and it has been acknowledged by many vocabulary specialists (e.g. Schmitt 2010; Nation 2012) that these elements of lexical competence require a lot of exposure before they can be mastered. Lastly, McCarthy (1997) highlights the importance of learners' autonomy and agency in achieving advanced lexical proficiency. In light of the sheer volume of words that have to be acquired at this level, it is impossible to address all of them through explicit instruction; consequently, advanced learners themselves need to take responsibility for the learning process and become more proactive when it comes to making lexical gains. For instance, they should increase their awareness of different learning strategies, make a selection and start employing those that meet their needs and foster their lexical development.

Task 4.4: Using the BYU-BNC interface, check the frequency of the following items and decide whether they belong to basic- or advanced-level vocabulary. Which pedagogical criteria will you take into account?

As well, shuffle, motorway, in spite of, debate, as usual

So far in this section we have focused on the advantages of using frequency as a method of identifying the core or most useful vocabulary. However, there are certain challenges that are entailed in compiling frequency-based lists of vocabulary.

In an insightful discussion of factors that contribute to the coreness of words, Gardner (2013: 36) points out that except for the frequency of occurrence, which is "a primary determination of whether words make a core list of general English vocabulary", issues such as polysemy (different meaning-senses of words) and register (different subject areas and domains tend to have their own core vocabulary as reflected in context-specific frequency distributions) are equally important and therefore ought to be considered while creating frequency-based bands of vocabulary.

What is more, Gardner (2013) also stresses the importance of the ever-changing nature of vocabulary. Generally speaking, English, as any other language, is in a constant state of flux and, as time goes by, some words fall out of use and become dated (e.g. 'telegraph'), while others enter the lexicon as a result of changes in social life (e.g. 'email' or 'smartphone'). To address this in determining the notion of coreness, Gardner introduces the concept of a stable and unstable core of English vocabulary. According to the author, the stable core consists of high-frequency words, which are important because of their role in language at large and consequently should be prioritized in the process of language learning and teaching. As Gardner (2013: 58) emphasizes, these words "represent the best starting point for dealing with the general high frequency words of English". Importantly, this vocabulary contains not only function words (e.g. 'the' or 'of') but also commonly occurring content words such as 'go' or 'time'. For instance, if we explore the frequency of the word 'time' in the Corpus of Historical American English (COHA), which consists of data from the 1810s–2000s, we can clearly see that it is a core word characterized by a fairly stable frequency pattern across longer periods of time. What is more, Gardner (2013: 52) also points out that the core vocabulary needs to include "more specific or specialized content words that hang around for a while" and occur with a fairly high frequency over relatively long periods of time. Examples of such words which have entered the English language relatively recently are 'Internet' and 'online'.

As far as the unstable core is concerned, Gardner uses this notion to highlight the variable nature of vocabulary. According to the author, vocabulary at this level of coreness encompasses words that are "more frequent in general than most content words of the language [as a whole] but they are normally less frequent than content words in the stable core" (Gardner 2013: 52). To put it another way, these are less versatile words whose occurrence is less consistent across samples of texts from various periods of time but they still need to be considered as important because they provide a large amount of coverage of the language encountered by L2 learners. Examples of such words are 'download' or 'terrorism', which are a fairly new additions to the English lexicon.

What transpires from this discussion yet again is that there is some arbitrariness in setting boundaries for core vocabulary as "no absolute distinctions can be made between stable and unstable core words" (Gardner 2013: 55). Except for important theoretical considerations, this also shows the difficulty of producing reliable, research-based lists of vocabulary that remain pedagogically relevant. However, Gardner's approach to coreness is a welcome addition to the field and it aptly illustrates how frequency information obtained from corpora can be usefully applied to categorize vocabulary into pedagogically friendly bands (see below for a discussion of Gardner's list of vocabulary).

In short, as the above paragraphs have presented, frequency information plays an essential role in defining vocabulary and dividing it into different types. Such divisions are especially relevant to L2 learners, who face the challenge of developing an L2 lexicon. Given the massive number of words in English L2 learners are likely to seek research-based guidance from their teachers and materials developers with respect to what vocabulary they should tackle first (see section 4.4 for a discussion of the role of frequency in language pedagogy).

4.2 Frequency-based analysis of vocabulary load

Having explained how frequency information can be used to categorize words on the basis of their occurrence, we need to discuss details of how such an analysis can be conducted. The procedure is called lexical frequency profiling (LFP) and Laufer and Nation (1995) were the first authors to use it as a measure of the lexical richness or sophistication of texts. The rationale behind the LFP was that more proficient language users should produce more lexically rich or sophisticated texts, such that they contain more infrequent words in comparison with less sophisticated texts produced by learners at lower proficiency levels. The results of Laufer and Nation's study confirmed this and suggested that L2 learners' ability to use infrequent vocabulary is an effective way of distinguishing between different proficiency levels.

The LFP can be carried out by means of a corpus program called VocabProfile. The program is available on Tom Cobb's (2015) Lextutor and you can access it via this link: http://www.lextutor.ca/vp/comp/. The classic version of the program operates in such a way that it creates a lexical profile of a text that interests you (e.g. an essay written by a student or an article that you want to use for teaching purposes). More specifically, VocabProfile classifies all words from a given text into four frequency levels: the first 1,000 most frequent word families (1K band), the second 1,000 most frequent word families (2K band), academic vocabulary (identified on the basis of Coxhead's (2000) Academic Word List) and an off-list which contains all the remaining vocabulary. However, since its original publication, VocabProfile has been revised and updated several times and the most recent version of the program, BNC-COCA-25, analyzes texts at twenty-five levels of frequency. These levels are based on twenty-five 1,000-word bands created by Paul Nation (details of the lists can be found at http://www.lextutor.ca/vp/comp/coca.html). Figure 4.2 presents a sample output that has been generated by VocabProfile.

Note that except for dividing words into the twenty-five frequency levels, the program also provides other types of frequency information such as tokens, types, cumulative tokens and a type-token ratio. You can learn how to use VocabProfile by completing the following task.

Home > VocabProfilers > VP-Compleat Input > **Output** (Use 'Back' to preserve previous inputs)

Freq. Level	Families (%)	Types (%)	Tokens (%)	Cumul. token %
K-1 Words :	60 (61.86)	67 (54.92)	129 (63.86)	63.86
K-2 Words :	16 (16.49)	18 (14.75)	20 (9.90)	73.76
K-3 Words :	16 (16.49)	17 (13.93)	22 (10.89)	84.65
K-4 Words :	1 (1.03)	1 (0.82)	1 (0.50)	85.15
K-5 Words :	1 (1.03)	1 (0.82)	2 (0.99)	86.14
K-6 Words :	1 (1.03)	1 (0.82)	1 (0.50)	86.64
K-7 Words :				
K-8 Words :	1 (1.03)	1 (0.82)	1 (0.50)	87.14
K-9 Words :				
K-10 Words : ·				
K-11 Words :	1 (1.03)	1 (0.82)	2 (0.99)	88.13
K-12 Words :				
K-13 Words :				
K-14 Words :				

Figure 4.2 An example of output from VocabProfile available at Lextutor

Task 4.5: Choose an article from an online version of your favorite newspaper and create its lexical profile using the VocabProfile program.

As a first step, choose the BNC-COCA-25 option on Lextutor (http://www.lextutor.ca/vp/comp/). Next, copy all the words from any article that you wish to analyze and paste them into the input box. Once you click the button 'submit', you will see an output window similar to the one in Figure 4.2. It will show you which words from your article represent the first 1K most frequent vocabulary, followed by a list of the words from the second 2K band and so on. According to Cobb and Horst (2015: 190), "a typical profile for written English texts is 70% items from the most frequent 1,000 word families, 10% from the second, and the remainder from less frequent zones". However, it is important to remember that these frequency distributions might vary depending on the type of texts that are chosen. For instance, academic texts are likely to contain a higher degree of lower-frequency vocabulary than informal texts.

Another tool we will discuss in this section is RANGE (Nation and Heatley 2002) which is used to analyze the distribution of words across different texts or sections of corpora. It is a free program which can be downloaded from Paul Nation's website (http://www.victoria.ac.nz/lals/about/staff/paul-nation) or accessed online via Lextutor (http://www.lextutor.ca/range/). The program is particularly useful when you wish to compare a series of texts (e.g. from a textbook or graded reader) because it allows you to determine "how much the vocabulary is repeated in different texts" (Nation 2001: 38). RANGE operates in such a way that it creates the lexical profiles of texts that are uploaded and compares them with reference wordlists derived from large corpora (i.e. the same lists as the ones used in VocabProfile). Through this procedure, you can obtain detailed information about the analyzed texts in terms of the number of tokens, types and word families they contain. What is more, the program can also be used to explore the number of repetitions of individual words throughout the text under study. Such information is valuable because it helps you determine whether the text provides enough repetition of vocabulary for incidental learning to occur. In simple terms, this process can be defined as unintentional uptake of lexical knowledge that results from reading or listening (Hulstijn 2003; Webb and Nation 2013).

It should be added that similar analyses can be conducted by means of AntWordProfiler (Anthony 2014). This is also a free piece of software which can be downloaded from Laurence Anthony's website (http://www.laurenceanthony.net/software/antwordprofiler/). Yet another tool worth exploring in relation to vocabulary profiling is the AnalyzeText option available at http://www.wordandphrase.info/analyzeText.asp. The tool has been created by Mark Davies and it allows you to analyze different texts on the basis of frequency information from COCA.

Task 4.6: Create a lexical profile of the same newspaper article from the previous task but this time use the AnalyzeText option available at http://www.wordandphrase.info/analyzeText.asp. Which vocabulary profiler do you find more helpful?

4.3 Frequency-based lists of useful vocabulary

As shown in the previous section, ranking vocabulary on the basis of its occurrence in corpora is a fairly simple procedure that leads to valuable insights. It is not surprising, therefore, that for decades researchers have been working on lists of vocabulary with a view to using them as additional resources for both research and teaching.

One of the earliest examples is Basic English which dates back to the 1920s. Ogden (1930) and Richards (1943) are two names that are usually associated with this list. In their conceptualization, Basic English consisted of a list of 850 words treated as the core of English vocabulary. To put it another way, these words were treated as the first step in one's linguistic development and therefore they needed to be acquired by language learners during the initial stages of the learning process. 'Air', 'come' and 'able' are examples of such words, and the whole list can be viewed on this website: http://ogden.basic-english.org/.

However, as Nation (2016) points out, Basic English was not based on frequency but rather on the subjective judgment of its authors, who believed that the words from their list were essential to cover the most important ideas in language. Furthermore, Carter (1998) notes Ogden and Richards did not stipulate how learners should go about moving from the basic level of 850 words to more complicated aspects of lexical knowledge which are required to use English at more advanced levels. Lastly, some of the words that constitute Basic English are polysemous (e.g. 'head' or 'bear') and consequently a question arises of whether learners should learn only the most frequent meaning-sense or focus also on less frequent ones. Thus, these limitations of Basic English show that creating word-lists is not a straightforward procedure as selecting the most useful vocabulary is influenced by a range of factors. As Gardner (2013: 53) rightly states, "the task of producing a valid and reliable core list is extremely difficult".

Another list that should be mentioned is West's (1953) General Service List of English Words (GSL). The list consists of 2,000 word families and information about their frequency, different meaning-senses, grammatical classes to which they belong and lexical phrases in which they occur. The whole list can be found on Lextutor (http://www.lextutor.ca/freq/lists_download/) or on John Bauman's website: http://jbauman.com/aboutgsl.html. However, even though the GSL has had a profound influence on vocabulary studies, West has been criticized for making subjective judgments in terms of the selection of the target words and, even more importantly, the list has become outdated (Schmitt 2010; Nation 1990).

It should be stated that the issues associated with the GSL have been recently addressed by Brezina and Gablasova (2015). The authors have made an attempt to produce a New General Service List (new-GSL), which can be viewed at http://corpora.lancs.ac.uk/vocab/browse.php. The new-GSL consists of 2,494 lemmas which were identified on the basis of the frequency analysis of 12 billion words taken from four corpora: the Lancaster-Oslo-Bergen (LOB) Corpus, the BNC, the BE06 Corpus of British English and EnTenTen12 (which consists of over 21 million texts collected from the Internet). While the LOB and BNC are older corpora, the latter two corpora were included to take into consideration the current use of English (e.g. the words 'mobile' and 'Internet' are new additions to the English lexicon reflecting technological advances in the twentieth century). Another important methodological aspect of the new-GSL is that it lists lemmas (a headword plus its inflectional variants) rather than word families (a headword plus inflections as well as derivatives). Brezina and Gablasova (2015) question the rationale behind the use of a word family as it assumes that once a speaker knows a headword, they also know the meanings of other words that are derived from it. The authors believe that an ability to infer the meaning of words within a specific word family depends on the morphological competence of individual language users, which tends to vary.

Thus, in short, the new-GSL is an exemplification of cutting-edge research which demonstrates the role of frequency analysis in studying vocabulary. It can be predicted that as an updated and improved version of West's GSL, Brezina and Gablasova's list will be widely used by researchers, teachers and language specialists. It is important to mention that the new-GSL list is accompanied by a web-based interface called English vocabulary tool (http://corpora.lancs.ac.uk/vocab/analyse.php). Similarly to the VocabProfile program, you can use this interface to explore texts in terms of their frequency profiles.

> Task 4.7: To familiarize yourself with the English vocabulary tool, create a lexical profile of the same article you used in Task 4.6. How many words from the new-GSL list does it contain? Which levels of frequency do they represent?

Another example of a corpus-based list is Gardner's (2013) Common Core List or CCL (http://routledgetextbooks.com/textbooks/_author/rial/vocabulary.php). The list is proposed "as a bridge from the GSL and AWL approach to a more contemporary view of English core vocabulary" (Gardner 2013: 53) and it attempts to address the criticisms leveled at the earlier lists of vocabulary. The CCL prioritizes high-frequency vocabulary and consists of the most frequent items shared by the BNC and COCA. As Gardner explains, the list is compiled in such a way that the top 1,000 words receive a higher priority than the second 1,000 words. The list is also divided into three sublists which form a cline of stability spanning from the most (Sublist A) to the least (Sublist C) stable vocabulary. However, it needs to be acknowledged that no absolute distinctions between these different types of vocabulary can be made as the use of English is a dynamic process and words constantly fall in and out of use.

In total, the CCL consists of 2,857 items: 150 function words (Sublist A), 999 content words (Sublist A), 821 words (Sublist B) and 887 words (Sublist C). Sublist A comprises both function words and content words because all of these, according to Gardner, represent the stable core of English vocabulary. What is more, academic words from Coxhead's (2000) AWL are distributed across the three sublists. For instance, Sublist A of CCL contains 118 AWL word families such as 'area', 'authority' and 'community'. This shows that academic vocabulary should not be treated as a separate category that L2 learners master after the first most frequent 2,000 words have been learned. Rather, many words from the AWL are so frequent that they belong to the core English vocabulary and therefore should be acquired as soon as possible (see Chapter 8 for a detailed discussion of academic vocabulary).

Importantly, Gardner (2013) himself acknowledges that his CCL has certain limitations. Namely, it does not take into consideration the importance of multiword units (see Chapter 5 for a detailed discussion) or the polysemy of many words, both of which are key factors that should have an impact on the shape of a frequency-based list of vocabulary. As pointed out by Schmitt (2010: 117), vocabulary "has a tendency to occur in multiple word phraseological units" and corpus-based analyses are instrumental in revealing the occurrence of various kinds of chunks and multiword lexico-grammatical units. In fact, a growing body of empirical work is focused on the identification of multiword units and comparisons between the frequency of individual words and longer phraseological chunks constitute a major line of corpus research. Examples of such frequency-based lists of phraseological units are presented in Chapter 5, which deals with the relevance of corpora to the study of phraseology.

4.4 Frequency and language pedagogy

Throughout this chapter, we have stressed the significance of corpus analyses in relation to various aspects of lexical research. Not only do these analyses lead to a better understanding and description of vocabulary use, but they also have many practical implications which are highly relevant to education practitioners working on different language programs. For instance, frequency-based analyses can inform teachers' and materials developers' decisions in terms of prioritizing what vocabulary should be targeted in language instruction and make up the lexical content of textbooks. The same holds true for lexicographers, who can rely on frequency data as a valuable source of insights that feed into the development of contemporary dictionaries (see Chapter 6 for more details).

What is more, frequency information can also be used by language teachers to organize the teaching process around those words or chunks that represent the high-frequency levels and/or enable learners to achieve specific communicative goals such as comprehending spoken language or producing register-specific texts. Given the magnitude of words that need to be learned in an L2, we are bound to be selective and focus only on sets of the most useful vocabulary. By using corpus findings, teachers and language practitioners can ensure that the limited classroom teaching time is devoted to the promotion of those lexical items that provide a good return for the learning effort. Importantly, this applies to both individual words and longer multiword units (see Chapter 6 for a discussion of a lexical syllabus). On the one hand, these will be the most frequent items that provide a large lexical coverage but, on the other, a research-led vocabulary teaching course should also address problematic items such as collocations, as they are known to pose challenges for L2 language learners (see Chapter 7 for a discussion of learner vocabulary).

This brings us to the question of whether the frequency of occurrence is the only factor that determines the usefulness of vocabulary in the context of language pedagogy. It turns out that while frequency serves as a good starting point for identifying the key vocabulary that should be taught, there are several other criteria that are likely to play a role in the process of language instruction (Kennedy 1998). To follow Granger's (2011: 135) arguments, frequency needs to be considered alongside other factors that are pedagogically relevant and these are, among others, the learnability and teachability of specific items (e.g. some items are easier to learn than others), learner variables (e.g. age or learning styles) and specific purposes for which the vocabulary is studied. Similar arguments are put forward by Leech (2001), who notes that for many teachers the communicative needs of learners will be the overriding criterion in selecting the target vocabulary. Needless to say, a syllabus of a business English course for professionals will differ considerably from one aimed at teenagers enrolled on a general English course. This thus highlights the importance of needs analysis, which should be conducted by individual teachers and materials writers as a way of ensuring that corpus findings are merged with pedagogical decisions. As will be highlighted in the subsequent chapters of this book, a closer cooperation between corpus linguists and language teaching practitioners is a necessary condition to create optimal conditions for learning and teaching vocabulary (see Chapters 5, 6 and 7 for details).

4.5 Exemplary study: Nation and Anthony (2013) on mid-frequency readers

The last section of this chapter presents a detailed description of Nation and Anthony's (2013) research into mid-frequency graded readers. As the authors explain, the area of vocabulary studies suffers from a lack of resources for learning the mid-frequency words of English and therefore this study can be treated as an exemplary application of frequency-based analysis that fills this gap.

As already discussed in the earlier sections, mid-frequency vocabulary refers to a band of around 6,000 word families that lie between the end point of high-frequency vocabulary (the 3,000 level) and the starting point of low-frequency vocabulary (the 9,000 level). Schmitt and Schmitt (2014) argue that such vocabulary is an important element of L2 lexical development, for reaching the vocabulary size of 8–9,000 word families allows learners to comprehend a wide variety of authentic texts. As a result, mid-frequency vocabulary becomes a major learning goal for learners who are already familiar with the first 3,000 most frequent word families.

Unfortunately, learning mid-frequency vocabulary is no mean feat as it requires a lot of exposure to L2 input. Considering the fact that classroom time is limited, vocabulary specialists (e.g. Nation 2012; Schmitt 2010) suggest that such exposure can be increased through extensive reading. So far, however, research in this area has focused mainly on the creation of graded readers that promote high-frequency vocabulary, while theoretical discussions of the importance of mid-frequency words have not yet been translated into the design of appropriate teaching materials. Seeking to resolve this issue, Nation and Anthony (2013) conducted a corpus analysis which illustrates the usefulness of frequency information for the development of graded readers. The main outcome of the study is a series of mid-frequency readers, envisioned as free resources and aimed at advanced learners of English who face the task of learning mid-frequency vocabulary. Table 4.3 displays some examples of mid-frequency words that were identified by Nation and Anthony.

In terms of the methodology that was used to create the readers, Nation and Anthony (2013) relied on twenty-five 1,000-word bands of vocabulary derived from the BNC and COCA (Nation 2012). As argued by Nation (2012), these lists represent cutting-edge corpus research and can be applied in numerous ways for both research and teaching purposes. To control the vocabulary of the graded readers, Nation and Anthony adapted and simplified a number of original books taken from Project Gutenberg (https://www.gutenberg.org/). Thanks to the AntWordProfiler program, the texts were modified in such a way that if a given book contained words beyond the specified 1,000-word family level, they were replaced by higher-frequency and therefore easier vocabulary. By using this procedure, the authors made sure that the readers were more accessible and made for interesting reading for L2 learners. Examples of the readers can be downloaded from Paul Nation's website (http://www.victoria.ac.nz/lals/about/staff/paul-nation) and, at the time of writing, there are nine different titles.

In addition, to cater to the needs of different students, each of the readers is available at three levels of difficulty: the 4,000 level (for learners who know the first 4,000 word families and aim to learn words at the 5th 1,000 level), the 6,000 level (for learners who know the first 6,000 word families and aim to learn words at the 7th and 8th 1,000 levels) and the 8,000 level (for learners who know the first 8,000 word families and aim to learn words at the 9th and 10th 1,000 levels). At each level, words unknown to learners are repeated ten or more times, which is in line with vocabulary research into incidental learning. For instance, Schmitt (2010) suggests that multiple encounters with new vocabulary are needed before any lexical gains are made.

As Nation and Anthony (2013: 10) explain, the mid-frequency readers "can be used in extensive reading programs or for individual study and enjoyment" and ideally they will be read electronically (i.e. on a computer or tablet). This should ensure that as learners read the readers, they can use different multimedia, look

Table 4.3 Examples of mid-frequency families (adapted from Nation and Anthony 2013)

Frequency level	Examples of word families
4th 1,000	ballet, balloon, ballot
5th 1,000	badge, bail, bait
6th 1,000	babe, bachelor, baffle
7th 1,000	badger, bale, ballad
8th 1,000	babble, backfire, baggy
9th 1,000	backlog, bailiff, bandwagon

up the meaning of unknown words and even listen to a spoken version of the texts (e.g. via speech recognition software such as Dragon Naturally Speaking). Of course, the idea of using such readers will require some promotion among teachers and publishers and, perhaps more importantly, L2 readers themselves need to be motivated to do a lot of self-directed reading. Cobb (2016) rightly states that in some contexts this might be a tall order (e.g. in some EFL countries three classes of English each week is all the L2 input learners are exposed to). However, Nation and Anthony (2013) seem to be aware of these challenges and consequently call for more empirical work in this area so that we are able to assess the actual effectiveness of the mid-frequency graded readers as a way of increasing L2 lexical knowledge.

Summary

The chapter has underlined the importance of frequency for corpus research. We have explained how frequency-based analyses of word occurrences reveal differences between spoken and written vocabulary. We have also discussed the usefulness of frequency when it comes to categorizing vocabulary and creating lexical profiles of individual texts. Finally, we have presented how information about the occurrence of words can be usefully employed by language teachers and materials developers.

References

Adolphs, S. and Schmitt, N. (2003). Lexical coverage of spoken discourse. *Applied Linguistics*, 24, 4, 425–438.

Anthony, L. (2014). *AntWordProfiler* (Version 1.4.1) [computer software]. Tokyo: Waseda University. Available from http://www.laurenceanthony.net/.

Brezina, V. and Gablasova, D. (2015). Is there a core general vocabulary? Introducing the New General Service List. *Applied Linguistics*, 36, 1, 1–22.

Carter, R. (1998). *Vocabulary: Applied linguistic perspectives*. 2nd edition. London and New York: Routledge.

Carter, R. and McCarthy, M. (1995). Grammar and the spoken language. *Applied Linguistics*, 16, 2, 141–158.

Carter, R. and McCarthy, M. (2017). Spoken grammar: Where are we and where are we going? *Applied Linguistics*, 38, 1, 1–20.

Cheng, W. (2012). *Exploring Corpus Linguistics: Language in action*. London and New York: Routledge.

Cobb, T. (2015). *Compleat Lexical Tutor (LexTutor)* [online]. Available: www.lextutor.ca [20 December 2015].

Cobb, T. (2016). Numbers or numerology? A response to Nation (2014) and McQuillan (2016). *Reading in a Foreign Language*, 28, 2, 229–304.

Cobb, T. and Horst, M. (2015). Learner corpora and lexis, in S. Granger, G. Gilquin and F. Meunier (eds.) *The Cambridge Handbook of Learner Corpus Linguistics*. Cambridge: Cambridge University Press, 185–206.

Coxhead, A. (2000). A new academic word list. *TESOL Quarterly*, 34, 2, 213–238.

Dang, T. N. Y. and Webb, S. (2016a). Evaluating lists of high-frequency words. *International Journal of Applied Linguistics*, 167, 2, 132–158.

Dang, T. N. Y. and Webb, S. (2016b). Making an essential word list for beginners, in I. S. P. Nation (ed.) *Making and Using Word Lists for Language Learning and Testing*. Amsterdam: John Benjamins, 153–167.

Davies, M. and Gardner, D. (2010). *A Frequency Dictionary of Contemporary American English: Word sketches, collocates and thematic lists*. London and New York: Routledge.

Ellis, N. (2012). Formulaic language and second language acquisition: Zipf and the phrasal teddy bear. *Annual Review of Applied Linguistics*, 32, 17–44.

Gardner, D. (2013). *Exploring Vocabulary: Language in action*. London and New York: Routledge.

Granger, S. (2011). From phraseology to pedagogy: Challenges and prospects, in T. Herbst, S. Faulhaber and P. Uhrig (eds.) *The Phraseological View of Language: A tribute to John Sinclair*. Berlin: De Gruyter Mouton, 123–146.

Hulstijn, J. (2003). Incidental and intentional learning, in C. J. Doughty and M. H. Long (eds.) *The Handbook of Second Language Acquisition*. Oxford: Blackwell, 349–381.

Hwang, K. and Nation, P. (1995). Where would general service vocabulary stop and special purposes vocabulary begin? *System*, 23, 1, 35–41.

Kennedy, G. D. (1998). *An Introduction to Corpus Linguistics*. London: Longman.

Laufer, B. and Nation, P. (1995). Vocabulary size and use: Lexical richness in L2 written production. *Applied Linguistics*, 16, 3, 307–322.

Laufer, B. and Ravenhorst-Kalovski, G. C. (2010). Lexical threshold revisited: Lexical text coverage, learners' vocabulary size and reading comprehension. *Reading in a Foreign Language*, 22, 1, 15–30.

Leech, G. (2001). The role of frequency in ELT: New corpus evidence brings a re-appraisal, in W. Hu (ed.) *ELT in China 2001: Papers presented at the 3rd International Symposium on ELT in China*. Beijing: Foreign Language Teaching and Research Press, 1–23.

Martinez, R. and Schmitt, N. (2012). A Phrasal Expressions List. *Applied Linguistics*, 33, 3, 299–320.

McCarthy, M. and Carter, R. (1994). *Language as Discourse: Perspectives for language teaching*. London and New York: Routledge.

McCarthy, M. and Carter, R. (1997). Written and spoken vocabulary, in N. Schmitt and M. McCarthy (eds.) *Vocabulary: Description, acquisition, pedagogy*. Cambridge: Cambridge University Press, 20–39.

McCrostie, J. (2007). Investigating the accuracy of teachers' word frequency intuitions. *RELC Journal*, 38, 1, 53–66.

Nation, I. S. P. (1990). *Teaching and Learning Vocabulary*. New York: Newbury House.

Nation, I. S. P. (2001). *Learning Vocabulary in Another Language*. 1st edition. Cambridge: Cambridge University Press.

Nation, I. S. P. (2006). How large a vocabulary is needed for reading and listening? *Canadian Modern Language Review*, 63, 1, 59–81.

Nation, I. S. P. (2011). Research into practice: Vocabulary. *Language Teaching*, 44, 4, 529–539.

Nation, I. S. P. (2012). The BNC/COCA word family lists. Retrieved 20 May 2016 from http://www.victoria.ac.nz/lals/about/staff/publications/paul-nation/Information-on-the-BNC_COCA-word-family-lists.pdf.

Nation, I. S. P. (2015). Which words do you need?, in J. R. Taylor (ed.) *The Oxford Handbook of the Word*. Oxford: Oxford University Press, 568–581.

Nation, I. S. P. (2016). Word lists, in I. S. P. Nation (ed.) *Making and Using Word Lists for Language Learning and Testing*. Amsterdam/Philadelphia: John Benjamins, 3–13.

Nation, I. S. P. and Heatley, A. (2002). RANGE: A program for the analysis of vocabulary in texts [online]. Available: http://www.victoria.ac.nz/lals/about/staff/paul-nation [20 August 2016].

Nation, I. S. P. and Anthony, A. (2013). Mid-frequency readers. *Journal of Extensive Reading*, 1, 1, 5–16.

Ogden, C. K. (1930). *Basic English: A general introduction*. London: Kegan Paul, Trench & Trubner.

O'Keeffe, A., McCarthy, M. and Carter, R. (2007). *From Corpus to Classroom*. Cambridge: Cambridge University Press.

Richards, I. A. (1943). *Basic English and Its Uses*. London: Kegan Paul.

Schmitt, N. (2010). *Researching Vocabulary: A research manual*. Basingstoke: Palgrave Macmillan.

Schmitt, N. and Schmitt, D. (2014). A reassessment of frequency and vocabulary size in L2 vocabulary teaching, *Language Teaching*, 47, 4, 484–503.

Shin, D. and Nation, P. (2008). Beyond single words: The most frequent collocations in spoken English. *ELT Journal*, 62, 4, 339–348.

Siyanova-Chanturia, A. and Spina, S. (2015). Investigation of native speaker and second language learner intuition of collocation frequency. *Language Learning*, 65, 3, 533–562.

Tognini-Bonelli, E. (2010). Theoretical overview of the evolution of corpus linguistics, in A. O'Keeffe and M. McCarthy (eds.) *The Routledge Handbook of Corpus Linguistics*. London and New York: Routledge, 14–27.

Webb, S. and Chang, A. C.-S. (2012). Second language vocabulary growth. *RELC Journal*, 43, 1, 113–126.

Webb, S. and Nation, I. S. P. (2013). Computer-assisted vocabulary load analysis, in C. A. Chapelle (ed.) *The Encyclopedia of Applied Linguistics*. New York: Blackwell Publishing.

Zipf, G. K. (1935). *The Psycho-biology of Language: An introduction to dynamic philology*. Cambridge, MA: MIT Press.

Chapter 5

Corpora, phraseology and formulaic language

5.1 Corpus linguistics, phraseology and lexical priming

In the previous chapters, we have discussed the usefulness of corpus tools for analyzing the occurrence of individual words. However, it is vital to state that corpora have also been instrumental in demonstrating that a large part of language consists of units longer than single words. More specifically, once we start exploring large amounts of naturally occurring data, we quickly discover that words have a tendency to cluster with one another and form lexical combinations. As Sinclair (1991: 108) notes, "most everyday words do not have an independent meaning, or meanings, but are components of a rich repertoire of multi-word patterns that make up a text". Similarly, Tognini-Bonelli (2010) highlights the fact that the patterns of lexical repetition and co-selection are an important aspect of language use and Stubbs (2002: 59) notes "the pervasive occurrence of phrase-like units of idiomatic language". Analyzing the structure and occurrence of such multiword units is the domain of phraseology and it constitutes a major line of research within corpus linguistics.

An influential manifestation of empirical work in this area is Hunston and Francis's (2000) pattern grammar. This is an innovative type of lexical grammar built around the most commonly occurring patterns defined as "all the words and structures which are regularly associated with the word and which contribute to its meaning" (Hunston and Francis 2000: 37). An example of a simple pattern is a head noun followed by a to-infinitive which complements it ('a decision to do something' or 'an intention to buy something'). According to Hunston and Francis (2000), there are important associations between patterns and meanings and they can be observed at two levels: different meanings of a word tend to be associated with different patterns but also different words with the same patterns often share some aspects of the same meaning. As McEnery and Hardie (2012: 81) explain, pattern grammar is a model "where language is built up of a series of linked sequences of fuzzy structures" which influence both structural coherence and meaning.

Another proposal informed by corpus analysis is Hoey's (2005) theory of **lexical priming**. The theory links corpus-based research into phraseology with psycholinguistic views on the mental lexicon. Hoey argues (2005: 8) that "we can only account for collocations if we assume that every word is mentally primed for collocational use", which is linked the fact that all language users are primed to use vocabulary in specific phraseological configurations created and reinforced by their everyday use of language. As listeners/readers and speakers/writers, we are constantly exposed to different types of word co-occurrences (e.g. **collocations**, **colligations** and any other kind of lexical patterning) and all this information is cumulatively stored as associative links in our mental lexicons. This in turn exerts influence on the type and quality of the language that we produce or, to put it another way, we are psychologically primed to use vocabulary in specific collocational patterns. As aptly stated by Stubbs (1996), our language experience determines the lexical selections we make.

It needs to be pointed out that there is a growing body of psycholinguistic research which confirms Hoey's (2005) theory and demonstrates the importance of frequency and statistical learning in the processing and storage of lexical information. It is now firmly established that words and lexical items that occur more frequently in language cause less of a cognitive burden and enjoy processing advantages in comparison with less frequent items (see Conklin and Schmitt 2012 for a useful overview). Importantly, while these frequency effects have been demonstrated for both L1 and L2 contexts, L2 speakers seem to benefit less from such processing advantages, which supports Hoey's claim that the strength of lexical priming is dependent on the amount of exposure to natural language.

Thus, to recap, both pattern grammar and lexical priming highlight the importance of phraseology and point to the contributions of corpora to the study of vocabulary. As will be discussed throughout this chapter, a substantial part of meaning in naturally occurring discourse is conveyed by means of multiword units and, as a result, phraseological tendencies have become a pivotal topic in linguistic considerations. That is, after years of research in which single words were the predominant focus of analysis, **formulaic language** has now come to the fore and, as Schmitt (2013) contends, it is likely to be one of the most relevant topics in applied linguistics as a whole.

However, before we move on to discussing different aspects of corpus research into formulaicity, we need to address the issue of terminological abundance that characterizes this area of inquiry. As Granger (2009: 63) observes, the terminological chaos "besets theoretical phraseological studies", which leads to a myriad of terms in the corpus and phraseological literature. Some of the most common ones include: **formulaic sequences**, chunks, multiword units, idiomatic expressions, prefabricated routines, n-grams, lexical bundles, clusters, collostructions and many more. While all of these types of phraseological units can be subsumed under the label of formulaicity in language, it is important to point out that there are essential differences between them in terms of what kind of phraseological units they denote. For instance, lexical bundles are defined as combinations of words "that are repeated without change for a set number of times in a particular corpus" (Byrd and Coxhead 2010: 32), while collostructions refer to lexical elements which are strongly attracted or repelled by specific grammatical constructions (Stefanowitsch and Gries 2003). Yet, despite numerous differences between the various types of multiword units, there is one element that all of them seem to have in common. Namely, formulaic sequences are an essential feature of naturally occurring language and they constitute important building blocks of both spoken and written discourse (Schmitt 2013). Crucially, such sequences fulfill important textual, functional and communicative roles and consequently formulaic language is perceived as a key feature of successful language use, which contributes to native-like fluency and facilitates communication (Pawley and Syder 1983).

5.2 Definition of formulaic language

The notion of 'formulaic language' as an umbrella term embraces all types of phraseological units and it is often attributed to Alison Wray (2002). The author introduced the term in her seminal book devoted to the role of phraseology in language. Another key publication in this area was Schmitt's (2004) edited volume which explored the nature of formulaic language from various standpoints. Both of these books highlighted the importance of formulaic sequences defined by Wray (2002: 9) as:

> a sequence, continuous or discontinuous, of words or other elements, which is, or appears to be, prefabricated, that is, stored and retrieved whole from memory at the time of use, rather than being subject to generation or analysis by the language grammar.

Without getting into much detail, this definition offers a psycholinguistic view on formulaic material and the efficiency with which it is processed.

However, there are also other approaches to formulaic sequences which have been studied from the perspective of their syntactic and semantic structure. For example, Moon (1997: 43) defines a multiword unit as "a vocabulary item which consists of a sequence of two or more words which semantically and/or syntactically forms a meaningful unit". Yet other scholars (e.g. Howarth 1998) tend to view formulaic language as a continuum of multiword units, which span from fixed items such as idioms ('blow your own trumpet'), through restricted collocations ('blow a fuse') to free combinations ('blow a trumpet'). Given that the present book prioritizes corpus methodologies in the study of language, we will follow a frequency-based approach to formulaicity and adhere to corpus techniques as a way of identifying various kinds of lexical combinations and patterns of co-occurrence. What is more, to stay in line with a broad and inclusive understanding of formulaic language, we will treat terms such as 'chunks', 'multiword units' and 'lexical items' as synonyms and use them interchangeably throughout the following paragraphs. Finally, we will seek to recognize the importance of formulaic language as an essential element of proficient language use (Crossley, Salsbury and McNamara 2015;

Kremmel, Brunfaut and Alderson 2015) and will highlight its pervasiveness across different contexts and domains of language use.

5.3 The idiom principle and lexico-grammar

Arguably a lot of corpus research into phraseology has been influenced by John Sinclair's approach to language. Sinclair was one of the first scholars who advocated the use of corpora for describing language and gaining insights into the intricacies of natural communication. As evidenced by his pioneering work on the COBUILD corpus and the resultant COBUILD Dictionary published in the 1980s, corpora have shed new light on the process of investigating language use, with phraseological patterning being placed at the heart of linguistic analysis. As Sinclair himself acknowledges, it has become clear that to produce an accurate description of language in use, we need to "take the 'unrandomness' in the distribution of words into account" (Sinclair 1991: 10).

To cope with this unrandomness of natural language, Sinclair (1991) suggested that it operated on two principles: the **open-choice principle** and the **idiom principle**. The open-choice principle refers to language users' unrestricted choices, in which words are treated as single elements selected item-by-item to construct grammatically correct sentences (the slot-and-filler approach). The idiom principle, in contrast, stipulates that instead of constructing new sentences in a piecemeal manner, speakers and writers make extensive use of ready-made phrases or chunks, which consist of specific patterns and recurring lexico-grammatical elements.

This brings us to the concept of lexico-grammar, which occupies a central position within corpus-based investigations of phraseology. As stated by Römer (2009: 160), corpus research on the idiom principle has revealed "the inseparability of lexis and grammar", two aspects of language traditionally seen as separate levels of linguistic description. However, once we adopt a corpus perspective, this dichotomy is no longer tenable because lexico-grammar, a notion which emphasizes the pervasiveness of various kinds of phraseological units, becomes the focal point of analysis. The term was first coined by Halliday (1961) and it came into widespread use after the advent of large corpora, which have enabled automatic analyses of the occurrence of various kinds of lexico-grammatical sequences. The aim of the following sections is to present examples of such sequences and explain how they can be studied by means of corpus techniques.

5.4 Types of multiword units

Having underlined the importance of phraseology in the previous section, we can now turn our attention to different types of multiword units. Using Sinclair's (2004) model of phraseology, we will introduce the notions of collocation, colligation, **semantic preference** and **semantic prosody** as examples of how words tend to cluster with one another and form extended units of meaning. All of these notions emphasize the fact that meaning is not only conveyed through the use of invariable core meanings of individual words but it is also "created across co-selected words in the lexical item" (Cheng 2012: 114). By looking at specific examples of word co-occurrences, we seek to discuss how to use corpus data to search for different kinds of lexical and lexico-grammatical units and consequently gain a better understanding of phraseological patterning within language.

5.4.1 Collocations

In general terms, collocations can be defined as pairs of words that are commonly found together. The term is usually attributed to Firth (1957), who was one of the first scholars to pay heed to lexical partnerships. The author observed that the meaning of a word depended not only on what it possessed in itself but also on how it combined with other items; to paraphrase a famous quote, words should be known by the company they keep. By way of illustration, we will mention the phrase 'dark night', which demonstrates that "one of the meanings of night is its collocability with dark, and of dark, of course, collocation with night" (Firth 1957: 196).

Halliday (1966) was another scholar who did pioneering work in the study of word partnerships. Defining collocations as syntagmatic relations between words whose probability of occurrence can be objectively measured, the author called for the use of large samples of data and argued that they were the only way to provide evidence that co-occurrences of words "are sufficiently regular to constitute a pattern" (Halliday 1966: 159). This shows that as early as the 1960s corpora were seen as a powerful tool for examining lexical relationships and the ways in which words tend to co-occur and form various kinds of lexical associations.

To demonstrate how to conduct a simple collocational analysis, we will use the BYU-BNC interface and search for collocations of the verb 'take' (see Figure 5.1 which presents a screenshot of this search). 'Take' will be treated as a node (a search word that you analyze) and your task will be to try to identify its collocates, that is, "any word that occurs in the specified environment of a node" (Sinclair 1991: 115).

As a first step, you need to type [take] in the word/phrase box. Putting 'take' in square brackets indicates that you treat it as a lemma and therefore the computer will search for collocates around all the grammatical forms of 'take' (e.g. 'taking', 'took', 'taken'). This lemma search will simplify your analysis. However, it is important to remember that various grammatical forms of words can attract different collocational partners. This is aptly demonstrated by Stubbs's (2002) analysis of the collocational patterning of different forms within the lemma of [consume]. The analysis showed that the words 'costly', 'difficult' and 'expensive' were frequent collocates of the adjective 'time-consuming' but none of them were found to collocate with 'consume' or 'consumed', which also belong to the same lemma. Thus, it is vital to note that different lexical forms "can have different co-selections

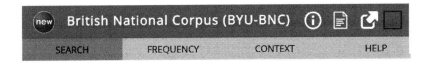

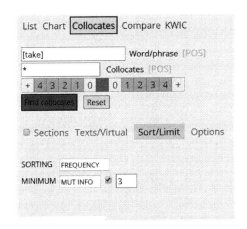

Figure 5.1 A BYU-BNC search for collocates of the verb [take]

and so be part of different extended units of meaning, with, of course, different meanings" (Cheng 2012: 126), and potential phraseological variation should be taken into consideration as you search for specific examples of collocations.

To continue your analysis, put an asterisk in the collocates box. This is a symbol that stands for any missing word and therefore the computer will look for any possible collocate of [take]. What is more, you should also specify the size of the window (or **span**) of your collocational search. In other words, you need to indicate how many words around the node (both to the left and right) should be analyzed by the computer. The standard span to be recommended is +/− 4 words (Sinclair 1991), as it allows you to identify both significant collocates that occur immediately next to the node and those that occupy more distant positions (on either side). The BYU-BNC interface has a special box with numbers which allows you to determine the size of the collocational span for your search. Select 4 both on the left and right and click on the button 'Find collocates'. Your results should be similar to the ones presented in Table 5.1.

Note that except for the frequency of all the collocates, the output also provides information about their mutual information (MI) scores. As mentioned in Chapter 2, MI is one of the most popular statistical tests that corpus linguists use to explore collocations. However, it should be pointed out that the identification of collocations via different statistical measures is likely to lead to different results.

Table 5.1 Examples of the most frequent collocates of [take] in the BNC

	Collocate	Frequency	Mutual information (MI)
1	place	11,810	4.13
2	account	4,413	4.27
3	action	2,844	3.21
4	advantage	2,077	4.35
5	steps	1,637	4.12
6	seriously	1,532	4.29
7	step	1,175	3.29
8	granted	992	3.95
9	breath	741	3.45
10	photographs	425	3.24

I aim to illustrate this by showing data from the BNC (see Figures 5.2 and 5.3). Using the BNCweb interface, I have identified collocates of the word 'nice', first on the basis of T-scores and next on the basis of MI scores.

As can be seen, these are two very different sets of results, with only several collocates featuring on both lists ('very nice', 'really nice', 'look nice'). For instance, note that the list produced on the basis of MI contains many examples of adverbs as

Figure 5.2 Collocates of 'nice' identified on the basis of T-scores (span +/– 1)

Collocation parameters:

Information:	collocations ▼	Statistics:	Mutual information ▼
Collocation window span:	1 Left ▼ - 1 Left ▼	Basis:	whole BNC ▼
Freq(node, collocate) at least:	5 ▼	Freq(collocate) at least:	5 ▼
Filter results by:	Specific collocate [ ]	and/or tag: no restrictions ▼	Submit changed parameters ▼ Go!

There are 5978 different types in your collocation database for "[word="nice"%c]". (Your query "nice" returned 12723 hits in 1820 different texts)

No.	Word	Total No. in whole BNC	Expected collocate frequency	Observed collocate frequency	In No. of texts	Mutual information value
1	awfully	375	0.040	11	10	8.086
2	smells	743	0.080	16	14	7.6401
3	jolly	865	0.093	15	14	7.3276
4	looks	11,225	1.212	154	78	6.9896
5	very	119,400	12.890	1418	589	6.7815
6	mister	542	0.059	5	3	6.4171
7	terribly	1,163	0.126	10	9	6.3156
8	really	46,363	5.005	384	171	6.2616
9	quite	39,839	4.301	328	164	6.2529
10	exceptionally	898	0.097	7	7	6.1741
11	tastes	976	0.105	7	5	6.0539
12	somewhere	6,643	0.717	21	19	4.872
13	sounds	5,775	0.623	18	16	4.8516
14	thoroughly	2,045	0.221	5	5	4.5013
15	look	51,972	5.611	124	89	4.466
16	sounded	2,697	0.291	6	5	4.3651
17	rather	41,741	4.506	91	75	4.3359
18	real	22,611	2.441	47	20	4.2671
19	smell	3,508	0.379	7	7	4.2082
20	extremely	6,682	0.721	13	10	4.1717
21	re	80,640	8.705	153	85	4.1355

Figure 5.3 Collocates of 'nice' identified on the basis of MI scores (span +/– 1)

collocates of 'nice' (e.g. 'awfully', 'exceptionally', 'terribly', 'thoroughly'), whereas they are largely absent from the list based on T-scores. These differences demonstrate thus that the choice of statistical tests influences the kinds of collocations that are retrieved from a corpus. Usually, combinations with high T-scores have a higher frequency and consist of words (very often function words) which collocate with many other items. In turn, collocations with high MI scores often consist of less frequent words, which tend to have a restricted number of collocates and therefore form much stronger or tightly bound pairs of words. As Hunston (2002: 72) explains, "if a word occurs rarely but most of its few occurrences appear in the proximity of another word, the collocation between those words will obtain a high MI score". However, one limitation of MI is that it tends to give prominence to infrequent collocates "that are rare occurrences" (Cheng 2012: 94). Thus, even though some collocations have high MI scores, they might not be the most representative examples as their total number of occurrences in a corpus will be very low.

In practical terms, this means that, as you carry out searches for collocations, it is advisable that you consider which type of combinations you are interested in and which measure you should use to select them. As argued by Schmitt (2010), the optimal way of identifying collocations appears to be combing both types of measures: T-scores as a source of information about the frequency of occurrence and MI as a test of the strength of co-occurrence between specific words.

Differences in the types of collocational partners are also highlighted by Sinclair's (1991) notion of upward and downward collocations. In the former, collocates have a higher frequency than a given node, whereas in the latter the pattern is reversed and collocates have a lower frequency than the node. As Sinclair (1991: 116) explains, in statistical terms upward collocations are weaker patterns and they "tend to be elements of grammatical frames or superordinates". In turn, downward collocations are mainly content words, which provide us with "a semantic analysis of words" (Sinclair 1991: 116). To illustrate this difference, Sinclair analyzed collocations of the word 'back' and found the following examples. Prepositions (e.g. 'at', 'from', 'into'), pronouns (e.g. 'her' or 'him') and verbs (e.g. 'get' and 'go') often collocated with 'back' in phrases such as 'get back to work' or 'go back to the same nest', and were among the examples of upward collocates, while content words such as 'arrive', 'bring', 'again', 'normal', 'camp' or 'flat' represented downward collocates.

Task 5.1: Explore the most frequent collocations of the word 'back' in the Corpus of Contemporary American English (COCA). Treat 'back' as a node and try to find examples of upward or downward collocates. Do your results confirm Sinclair's (1991) findings?

5.4.2 Colligations

In the previous section, we have elaborated on collocations as examples of lexical partnerships. The notion of colligation deals with similar forms of linguistic patterning but it focuses on the co-occurrence of grammatical elements. Very often, making a distinction between collocations and colligations depends on the specific aim of your analysis. As explained by Carter (1987: 47–8), in the case of collocations, even though syntax is not ignored, more prominence is given to lexical elements and ways in which they co-occur across specific contexts, whereas colligations highlight syntactic dependencies between words. Similarly, Cheng (2012: 82) observes that analyzing colligations "requires the analyst to operate at a level of abstraction" because it is concerned with exploring patterns of co-occurring words in relation to grammatical categories and structural relationships.

Access to corpus data allows you to study a number of aspects related to the notion of colligation. For instance, Nattinger and DeCarrico (1992) explored colligations of perception (sense) verbs such as 'hear', 'notice', 'see' and 'watch' and found distinct types of grammatical patterns. Their analysis revealed that the sense verbs are followed by patterns which are either bare infinitives (e.g. 'hear + somebody + verb-infinitive') or –ing gerund forms (e.g. 'hear + somebody + verb-ing').

Task 5.2: Use the BYU-BNC interface to compare the frequency of two colligational patterns around the verb 'hear': 'hear + pronoun + bare infinitive' and 'hear + pronoun + gerund'. Which pattern is more frequent? Is there a difference in the meaning that is conveyed depending on which colligation is chosen?

Figures 5.4 and 5.5 show screenshots with appropriate tags that you should use to complete this task: [hear] indicates that you treat 'hear' as a lemma and want to include all of its grammatical forms (e.g. 'hearing' or 'heard') in your search, [p*] is a tag for pronouns (e.g. him, her, it, them), [vvi] is a tag for the infinitive forms of verbs and [vvg] is a tag for the gerund ('ing') forms of verbs.

Another option that is worth considering is the analysis of colligations in terms of what tenses they co-occur with as well as what position within a sentence they occupy. For example, you can search for the phrase 'so far' as a feature associated with the present perfect tense and check whether it tends to occur at the beginning or end of sentences (see Task 5.3). Information about the different positions of colligations within specific parts of texts is valuable because it can help you gain a better understanding of the structure of discourse, in particular if you compare how the use of combinations and patterns changes across different registers and linguistic domains (see Chapter 8 for a discussion of specialized corpora).

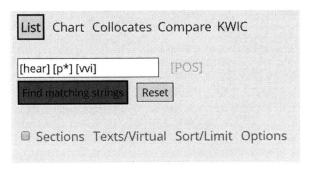

Figure 5.4 A search for [hear] + pronoun + verb-infinitive

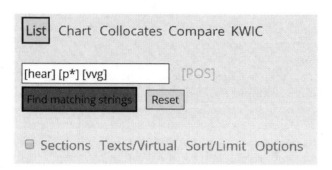

Figure 5.5 A search for [hear] + pronoun + verb-ing

Task 5.3: Look at the sample of concordances from COCA displayed in Figure 5.6 and explore the colligational behavior of the phrase 'so far'. What grammatical tenses does it occur with?

No of concordance	KWIC
46	the flipped classroom (Lage, Platt, & Teglia, 2000). **So far**, however, both scholars and practitioners have demonstrated conservatism with regard to educational media
47	Universities, " 2015, para. 4). Others have gone **so far** as to make the bold claim that " brick and mortar " educational institutions will
48	The comments of one parent illustrated this point: " The education system is **so far** behind and underfunded. He only got speech for 15 minutes, once a month
49	Six issues of this popular interactive ebook series have been published **so far** and six more are under development. The first issue is free, while other

50	credit information, in order to clarify the copyright status of all images reproduced **so far** as possible, for the benefit of readers, researchers, and subsequent users of
51	attacks, but also engendered legal and political attacks in the international arena. **So far**, the 2014 military operation has achieved the same results, but no one can
52	every semester and that's pretty much all the guidance that I have gotten **so far**. # Many of the student borrowers described watching the counseling videos and taking the
53	reconstructing of experience. It has all the time an immediate end, and **so far** as activity is educative, it reaches that endthe direct transformation of the quality of
54	credit information, in order to clarify the copyright status of all images reproduced **so far** as possible, for the benefit of readers, researchers, and subsequent users of
55	one of a woman with a professional career and ambitions. # The examples **so far** have mostly revolved around the ideal of a rational parent, but the last citation
56	that Prince's narrative also mediates Moodie's. Although I would not go **so far** as George Elliott Clarke, who argues that Moodie's memoir is " really— audaciously—a displaced
57	and more generous in payment, than any literary outfit I've run across **so far** " (Newlove, Letter to Barbara Kilvert).2 # But the poets'
58	the Thailand-Cambodia border and subsequently reported in neighboring countries, although not in Africa **so far** (3, 4).
59	and Limits of Molecular Diagnostics # The diagnosis of resistance to antimicrobial drugs has **so far** relied on culture techniques performed in reference centers;
60	himself, and had to find himself, in contradiction to his today. **So far** all these extraordinary furtherers of man whom one calls philosophers? have found their task

Figure 5.6 Sample concordance lines for the phrase 'so far'

In addition, colligational analysis can also focus on frequent patterns around function words such as prepositions, auxiliary verbs (e.g. 'be' or 'have') and words expressing grammatical notions such as negation, possession and modality. When it comes to prepositions (e.g. 'for', 'about', 'on'), they constitute a closed group of grammatical words which play a key role in showing relationships between specific elements of English sentences. This results from the fact that English syntax does not allow flexibility in word order and prepositions are required to link different parts of sentences. The consequence of this is that prepositions rank among the most commonly occurring words across all types of English texts. Moreover, prepositions are an important constituent element of multiword units such as phrasal verbs (e.g. 'pass out') and prepositional phrases (e.g. 'in the storm'). It is worth stressing that corpus searches for such items can be easily conducted by means of Part of Speech (PoS) tags, which are a standard feature of most modern concordancers. Such tags allow you to look for colligations built around specific word classes such as nouns, verbs and adjectives. For instance, Figure 5.7 demonstrates how you can search for the most frequent verbs around the preposition 'for'.

> **Task 5.4:** Using the BYU-COCA interface, search for examples of colligations (verbs, nouns and adjectives) around the preposition 'for'.

To sum up, this section has shown that corpora provide us with an opportunity to study colligations, which can be treated as a window into the grammatical behavior of words. We have shown that from the perspective of corpus linguistics, language is seen as a highly patterned system, in which lexico-grammatical interdependencies become the focal point of linguistic analysis. In the subsequent sections we will continue this discussion by focusing on the issues of semantic preference and semantic prosody as further aspects of phraseological patterning within language.

(new) Corpus of Contemporary American English

| SEARCH | FREQUENCY | CONTEXT | HELP |

List Chart Collocates Compare KWIC

| for | | Word/phrase [POS] |
| _v* | Collocates | verb.ALL | [⋯] |

| + | 4 | 3 | 2 | 1 | 0 | | 0 | 1 | 2 | 3 | 4 | + |

| Find collocates | Reset |

☐ Sections Texts/Virtual Sort/Limit Options

Figure 5.7 A BYU-COCA search for verbal colligations of 'for'

5.4.3 Semantic preference

Semantic preference is another level of lexical patterning which demonstrates tendencies of words to cluster with one another and become extended units of meaning. According to Sinclair (2004: 142), semantic preference is the restriction of the co-occurrence of words "to items which share a semantic feature". In a similar vein, Cheng (2012: 114) notes that semantic preference refers to "the tendency for lexical items to be restricted to identifiable semantic fields". This suggests that semantic preference can be understood as a semantic environment in which words are typically used and, as McEnery and Hardie (2012) contend, it can be used to group lexical elements on the basis of their semantic similarity. To put it another way, analyzing semantic preference can help us group words and lexical items according to their semantic similarities (e.g. words associated with a given topic such as medicine or sport or sets of lexical items used to describe specific phenomena such as change).

An example of a corpus-based study into semantic preference is Partington's (1998) examination of the intensifying adjective 'sheer'. Using concordance lines from academic and newspaper corpora, the author explored the phraseological patterning of this adjective and his analysis revealed that 'sheer' collocated with words which represented four different semantic sets:

- words expressing magnitude, weight or volume, e.g. 'the sheer volume of reliable information' or 'the sheer size of the stadium'
- items expressing force, strength or energy, e.g. 'the sheer force'
- words expressing persistence, e.g. 'sometimes through sheer insistence'
- nouns expressing strong emotion, e.g. 'sheer joy in life'.

It is worth adding that Partington wanted to validate his observations about 'sheer' and explored the patterning of 'complete', 'pure' and 'absolute', all of which can be considered as near-synonyms that express meanings similar to 'sheer'. Interestingly, none of these adjectives shared the same patterns with respect to their semantic preferences. This shows that even synonymous words which are close in meaning can differ in terms of the phraseological patterning they exhibit and, more importantly, such differences can affect the shades of meaning that are conveyed.

Task 5.5: Explore collocates of the word 'sheer' in the BYU-BNC corpus. Can you find any examples that confirm Partington's findings?

5.4.4 Semantic prosody

The most abstract level of corpus-based analysis of word combinations concerns their semantic prosody (sometimes also called discourse prosody). According to

Sinclair (2004), semantic prosody is of key importance to the study of phraseology because it integrates a given word with its neighbors. The term is attributed to Louw (1993: 157), who defines it as "a consistent aura of meaning with which a form is imbued by its collocates". In other words, semantic prosody concerns attitudinal or evaluative meanings which result from a word's co-occurrence with specific collocations.

It needs to be pointed out that such evaluative meanings are "much less evident to the naked eye" (Partington 2004: 131–2) and speakers' intuition is notoriously unreliable when it comes to predicting the attitudinal features of vocabulary use (Hunston 2002). That is the reason why semantic prosody is yet another example of how corpus techniques contribute to and support research into naturally occurring language. As summarized by Hunston (2002: 142), "semantic prosody can be observed only by looking at a large number of instances of a word or phrase, because it relies on the typical use of a word or a phrase". This suggests that the semantic prosody of a given word or phrase comes to light only when we are presented with large amounts of authentic data, which allows us to explore different patterns and configurations of lexical and lexico-grammatical units.

It is also of note that the notion of semantic prosody is the subject of many discourse-oriented investigations which explore the pragmatic role of vocabulary. As Greaves and Warren (2010: 218) explain, "it is the selection of semantic prosody by the speaker that leads to the selection of the core and the other co-selections of a lexical item". In a similar fashion, Stubbs (2013) emphasizes the fact that the ways in which words tend to co-occur and form extended units of meaning (e.g. chunks with a positive or negative semantic prosody) are fundamentally determined by the pragmatic or communicative functions that language users wish to fulfill. A more detailed discussion of the pragmatic role of semantic prosody is provided in Chapter 9, which deals with the pragmatics of vocabulary use.

An oft-cited example of corpus work into semantic prosody is Stubbs's (1996) analysis of the words 'cause' and 'provide'. By means of corpus analysis, the author showed that there are marked differences in the collocational patterns of these verbs: the former tends to collocate with negative words (e.g. 'accident'), while the latter tends to collocate with positive ones (e.g. 'care'). In a recent overview of corpus work in this area, Partington, Duguid and Taylor (2013) discuss further examples of words and chunks that exhibit interesting patterns in relation to semantic prosody; 'fraught with', 'sit in' and 'potentially' are given as examples of items with a negative attitudinal tendency, whereas 'make a difference', 'brimming with' and 'my place' represent a semantic prosody with positive connotations.

However, one caveat needs to be made. As Partington (2004: 153) rightly notes, the quality and strength of the semantic prosody of many vocabulary items might differ from genre to genre or from domain to domain. This means that insights into the semantic prosody of words are likely to be dependent on the type of language that is analyzed (e.g. academic vs. general English). Such potential variation, therefore, needs to be taken into account as you carry out your corpus analysis.

> **Task 5.5:** Choose one of the words or phrases from the section above and explore their semantic prosody in COCA.

In short, corpus-based investigations into semantic prosody are an excellent illustration of how vocabulary can be studied from the perspective of its pragmatic force. All the examples presented above demonstrate that the analysis of phraseological patterning around specific words can lead to valuable observations on the context-dependent aspects of language use such as the functional meaning of vocabulary.

5.5 Phraseology and register variation

Another aspect of phraseological research that is studied via corpora is register variation. As the notion of register is discussed in detail in Chapter 8, here we will only state that it refers to specific types or varieties of language related to its use in social contexts (Cheng 2012). To illustrate, the use of English in academic settings is one of the most studied registers and, with the growing number of different kinds of specialized corpora of academic language, the field is developing a better understanding of this type of language and differences in the frequency of linguistic features that result from the use of language in academic texts. Phraseology is no exception in this regard and, as Greaves and Warren (2010) note, corpora provide a lot of evidence of register specificity and the distribution of multiword units.

Most studies into register-specific variation in the use of phraseology have focused on lexical bundles or sequences of three or more words which occur repeatedly in a given register (Cortes 2004). This is largely caused by the relative ease with which such units can be identified via automatic, corpus-driven techniques. As Gray and Biber (2015: 128) explain, what characterizes corpus-driven studies of phraseological patterns is that "they do not begin with a pre-selected list of phraseological patterns" but rather the corpus is analyzed inductively and, using frequency as the main criterion, the computer identifies "the lexical phrases that are especially noteworthy".

A good illustration of such work is Biber, Conrad and Cortes's (2004) study into the distribution of lexical bundles across four registers: spoken language, classroom teaching, university textbooks and academic research writing. The study revealed higher numbers of lexical bundles in speech than in writing, both in terms of tokens and types. Interestingly, in comparison with conversation, classroom language was found to make more extensive use of lexical bundles that marked stance (e.g. 'and I think that') and organized discourse (e.g. 'if you look at'). This suggests that the use of lexical bundles can also vary in terms of the functions that they perform in different types of discourse; similar comparisons can be found in Carter and McCarthy's (2006) corpus-informed description of English. Demonstrating the importance of register specificity, the authors provide examples of chunks which are typical of spoken and written language. The former is characterized by phrases that express interpersonal meanings ('you know', 'I know what you mean') or vagueness ('kind of' or 'sort of'), while the latter relies on chunks (or clusters) that describe time and place (e.g. 'in the middle of the night'), express possession, agency and purpose (e.g. 'of a/the', 'to the', 'with a/the') and are used as linking devices (e.g. 'as a result'). This highlights the pragmatic importance of chunks which become lexical tokens that realize a wide range of discourse functions.

Lastly, there is also a substantial body of corpus research investigating the role of discipline-specific phraseology. For instance, Hyland (2008) explored variation in the use of four-word lexical bundles across four disciplines. The author reported that biology and electrical engineering ('hard science' fields) relied more on research-oriented bundles (chunks which are used to structure and describe research activities and procedures such as 'in the present study' or 'one of the most'), whereas business and applied linguistics ('soft science' fields) relied more on participant-oriented chunks (items focused on the reader or writer of the text such as 'as can be seen' or 'it should be noted that') and text-oriented bundles (chunks that have to do with the organization of the text such as 'on the other hand' or 'these results suggest that'). In a more recent study, Durrant (2015) investigated disciplinary variation in the use of four-word lexical bundles in university students' writing. Using data from the British Academic Written English Corpus (BAWE), the author found distinctive patterns of reliance on such phrases in hard (science/technology) and soft (humanities/social sciences) disciplines, with life sciences and commerce being treated as 'borderland' cases exhibiting more variation.

In case you are interested in exploring the occurrence of lexical bundles, the BYU-COCA interface allows you to view the frequency of different phrases across a number of disciplines. First, use the 'Chart' option to see the frequency of a given lexical bundle across the different sections of COCA. Next, if you click on the word 'academic', you get a more detailed breakdown with information about the distribution of phrases across different disciplines.

Task 5.6: Using the academic section of the BYU-COCA corpus, check the frequency of the following ten lexical bundles taken from Durrant's (2015) study. Are there any interesting patterns in the way they are distributed across different academic disciplines?

the form of the
the presence of a
of the concept of
the presence of the
the fact that it
on the surface of
the shape of the
at the bottom of
the existence of a
the existence of the

5.6 Corpus-informed lists of phraseology

Throughout this chapter we have been emphasizing the fact that phraseology is a vital aspect of language, and thanks to the increasing availability of corpora, the field of vocabulary studies has recently experienced an upsurge of interest in a wide variety of phraseological issues. One area that has been particularly prolific is research into the development of corpus-informed lists of phraseological units, as is confirmed by the constantly growing number of such lists (see Martinez and Schmitt 2012 for a useful review). A lot of this research has been practically motivated, in the sense that it has tried to address the question of which phrases are the most useful ones and how they should be tackled in language instruction. Consequently, most of the work conducted in this area spans the boundaries of corpus linguistics, second language acquisition and language pedagogy, and has direct implications for teachers and materials writers. Thus, this section is a short overview of the most important issues that pertain to the process of compiling corpus-based lists of phraseology followed by a description of Martinez and Schmitt's (2012) Phrasal Expressions List as an exemplary study in this area.

In a new volume devoted to the creation of wordlists, Nation (2016) enumerates several issues that have a direct impact on the process of identifying and selecting useful vocabulary:

- the focus of the list and the kind of vocabulary it aims to promote
- a distinction between receptive and productive knowledge
- the main unit of counting that the list is based on needs to represent the kind of knowledge that is needed by its users
- differences between spoken and written language
- the nature and variety of texts that comprise a corpus
- the age of the users of the list.

While Nation poses these issues with reference to lists of individual words, all of them are equally relevant to the study of phraseology and the creation of listings of phraseological units. What is of key importance to corpus linguistics is the question about the nature of a corpus that a given list is derived from, for the decision as to which data should inform the selection of useful phraseology has fundamental consequences for the quality of the list. However, apart from the factors that are related to the design of a corpus (e.g. the range of texts that enter a corpus), the creation of corpus-informed lists of vocabulary is also dependent on issues such as the difficulty of phrases or their pedagogical relevance. As Shin and Nation (2008: 345–6) argue, even though frequency is a key criterion, "it is only one of several important criteria" and other factors such as learner needs, range of use (spoken vs. written language), teachability and suitability for learners also need to be taken into account. In this context, it is worth mentioning Diane Schmitt's (2016) recent call for a thorough assessment of the research that underpins the development of such lists. The author notes that in recent years the field of vocabulary studies has been bombarded with a proliferation of wordlists, without ever validating them in terms of what purposes they serve and how they address the needs of teachers and language learners, the end-users of these lists. Consequently, Schmitt argues that it is time that both corpus linguists and language practitioners paid closer attention to the methodologies that are used to compile new lists of words and phraseological units with a view to ensuring they fulfill the purposes for which they created. This is a valid point that should serve as a stark reminder that if vocabulary list research is to lead to successful learning of vocabulary, it should always start with the analysis of the actual needs of L2 learners.

The good news is that the importance of numerous criteria has been recognized by some authors whose work focuses on corpus-based lists of phraseological units. As already signaled, research on phraseological units is thriving and therefore there is a large number of such lists. The most influential examples include Shin and Nation's (2008) list of spoken collocations, Simpson-Vlach and Ellis's (2010) Academic Formulas List (see Chapter 8 for details) and Garnier and Schmitt's (2015) PHaVE list of phrasal verbs. However, presenting all of these lists is beyond the scope of this book and our discussion will be confined to Martinez and Schmitt's (2012) PHRASE List as a prime example of a comprehensive approach to identifying useful phraseology.

5.7 Exemplary study: Phrasal Expressions List by Martinez and Schmitt (2012)

Martinez and Schmitt's (2012) PHRASE List (accessible through Norbert Schmitt's website http://www.norbertschmitt.co.uk/#untitled41) is a corpus-derived list of phraseology which consists of non-transparent phrasal expressions. As the authors emphasize, considering the vast number of phrases in English, the list is not exhaustive. Rather, it seeks to point to the most common expressions that might cause difficulty for L2 learners. For instance, one of the chunks that are found on the list is 'look after'. While learners are likely to know the meaning of these two individual words, some of them, especially those at the beginner's level, may not know the meaning of 'look after' as a phrase. Using that rationale, Martinez and Schmitt identified 505 non-transparent phrases and ranked them according to their frequency of occurrence in the BNC.

Being aware of the potential pitfalls that are associated with identifying the most problematic phraseology, Martinez and Schmitt relied on a number of criteria that guided their selection. These included, among others, high frequency, meaningfulness (potential usefulness to learners and teachers) and lack of semantic transparency. As far as the latter is concerned, the user's guide that accompanies the PHRASE List states that the list is intended for receptive use and contains phrases that are difficult to decode when read word-for-word. In other words, the researchers sought to include those phrases whose meanings and/or discourse functions could not be easily derived from the meaning of their constituent elements. For instance, 'at this time' is semantically transparent and even if a language learner has never encountered this phrase before, they should have no difficulty understanding the meaning of the whole phrase. As a result, chunks such as 'at this time' are not found on the list.

Perhaps the most innovative aspect of the PHRASE List is the fact that it presents all the phrases in the form of the Integrated List Rank, with the frequency of chunks being integrated with the frequency of individual words. Using data from the BNC, Martinez and Schmitt were able to match the frequency of the phrases from their list with the frequency of the first 5,000 most frequent words in English. As a consequence, the PHRASE List makes it easy to compare the rates of occurrence of lexical chunks and individual words. This should help both teachers and students develop awareness that chunks constitute an important element of discourse and many of them occur with a high frequency comparable to the frequency of individual words.

It is also worth stating that Martinez and Schmitt's list provides useful information about register variation. More specifically, the list shows the frequency of chunks in three different kinds of discourse: spoken general, written general and written academic. To mark differences in the distribution of specific phrases, the authors have used stars, with three stars denoting a high frequency and the symbol 'x' indicating very few or no occurrences in the corpus. This is commendable because we know that each type of register is characterized by its own specific phraseology, and the fact that the PHRASE List takes this into account is its valuable asset (see Chapter 8 for more details on register variation).

Finally, as far as the applicability of the PHRASE List is concerned, Martinez and Schmitt (2012: 316) state that the list should lead to the development of pedagogical materials such as textbooks, graded readers and language tests, which will highlight the importance of multiword units. For instance, language testers can use the list as a source of items to develop measures of phraseological knowledge (see Kremmel, Brunfaut and Alderson 2015 for an example). When it comes to language teaching, the PHRASE List is a good starting point for teachers and materials developers, who face the task of selecting vocabulary for teaching purposes. Since there is so much phrasal vocabulary that needs to be learned in a second language, perhaps prioritizing those chunks that are potentially confusing due to their semantic opacity is the most pedagogically viable solution. Finally, in light of the importance of phraseology, the PHRASE List can be applied as a research tool. For instance, the developers of the English Vocabulary Profile (http://www.englishprofile.org/wordlists) and Text Inspector (http://www.text inspector.com/), web-based interfaces that enable the user to analyze texts in terms of their difficulty and lexical content, have used the PHRASE List as a proxy of phraseological vocabulary. While still new tools that require further validation, both of them look promising and hold a lot of potential for both teaching and research (see Chapter 7 for details on learner vocabulary).

Task 5.7: Go to Norbert Schmitt's website and explore examples of chunks from the PHRASE List. How would you go about teaching these phrases to a group of intermediate learners on a general English course? What would be your focus/main criterion when it comes to selecting the target items?

Summary

The aim of this chapter has been to introduce phraseology, the study of word combinations, and underline the usefulness of corpora for exploring the nature of formulaic language. We have demonstrated how corpus-based analyses can be employed to identify and classify various kinds of lexico-grammatical phraseological units as important elements of naturally occurring discourse. We have shown how corpora are instrumental in studying phraseological patterning and the way meaning is created and conveyed by means of multiword units.

References

Ädel, A. and Erman, B. (2012). Recurrent word combinations in academic writing by native and non-native speakers of English: A lexical bundles approach. *English for Specific Purposes*, 31, 2, 81–92.

Biber, D., Conrad, S. and Cortes, V. (2004). If you look at …: Lexical bundles in university teaching and textbooks. *Applied Linguistics*, 25, 3, 371–405.

Byrd, P. and Coxhead, A. (2010). On the other hand: Lexical bundles in academic writing and in the teaching of EAP. *University Of Sydney Papers in TESOL*, 5, 31–64.

Carter, R. (1987). *Vocabulary: Applied linguistic perspectives*. London: Allen and Unwin.

Carter, R. and McCarthy, M. (2006). *Cambridge Grammar of English*. Cambridge: Cambridge University Press.

Chen, Y.-H and Baker, P. (2010). Lexical bundles in L1 and L2 academic writing. *Language Learning and Technology*, 14, 2, 30–49.

Cheng, W. (2012). *Exploring Corpus Linguistics: Language in action*. London and New York: Routledge.

Conklin, K. and Schmitt, N. (2012). The processing of formulaic language. *Annual Review of Applied Linguistics*, 32, 45–61.

Cortes, V. (2004). Lexical bundles in published and student disciplinary writing: Examples from history and biology. *English for Specific Purposes*, 23, 4, 397–423.

Crossley, A. S., Salsbury, T. and McNamara, D. S. (2015). Assessing lexical proficiency using analytic ratings: A case for collocation accuracy. *Applied Linguistics*, 36, 5, 570–590.

Durrant, P. (2015). Lexical bundles and disciplinary variation in university students' writing: mapping the territories. *Applied Linguistics*, 38(2), 165–193.

Ebeling, S. O. and Hasselgard, H. (2015). Learner corpora and phraseology, in S. Granger, G. Gilquin and F. Meunier (eds.) *The Cambridge Handbook of Learner Corpus Research*. Cambridge: Cambridge University Press, 207–229.

Ellis, N. C., Simpson-Vlach, R., Römer, U., O'Donnell, M. B. and Wulff, S. (2015). Learner corpora and formulaic language in second language acquisition research, in S. Granger, G. Gilquin and F. Meunier (eds.) *The Cambridge Handbook of Learner Corpus Linguistics*. Cambridge: Cambridge University Press, 357–378.

Firth, J. R. (1957). *Papers in Linguistics 1934–1951*. London: Oxford University Press.

Gardner, D. (2013). *Exploring Vocabulary: Language in action*. London and New York: Routledge.

Garnier, M. and Schmitt, N. (2015). The PhaVE List: A pedagogical list of phrasal verbs and their most frequent meaning senses. *Language Teaching Research*, 19, 6, 645–666.

Granger, S. (2009). Commentary on part I: Learner corpora: A window onto the L2 phrasicon, in A. Barfield and H. Gyllstad (eds.) *Researching Collocations in Another Language: Multiple interpretations*. Basingstoke: Palgrave Macmillan, 60–65.

Gray, B. and Biber, D. (2015). Phraseology, in D. Biber and R. Reppen (eds.) *The Cambridge Handbook of English Corpus Linguistics*. Cambridge: Cambridge University Press, 125–145.

Greaves, C. and Warren, M. (2010). What can a corpus tell us about multi-word units?, in A. O'Keeffe and M. McCarthy (eds.) *The Routledge Handbook of Corpus Linguistics*. London and New York: Routledge, 212–226.

Halliday, M. A. K. (1961). Categories of the theory of grammar. *Word*, 17, 3, 241–292.

Halliday, M. A. K. (1966). Lexis as a linguistic level, in C. E. Bazell, J. C. Catford, M. A. K. Halliday and R. H. Robins (eds.) *In Memory of J. R. Firth*. London: Longman, 148–162.

Hoey, M. (2005). *Lexical Priming: A new theory of words and language*. London: Routledge.

Howarth, P. (1998). The phraseology of learners' academic writing, in A. Cowie (ed.) *Phraseology: Theory, analysis and applications*. Oxford: Oxford University Press, 161–186.

Hunston, S. (2002). *Corpora in Applied Linguistics*. Cambridge: Cambridge University Press.

Hunston, S. and Francis, G. (2000). *Pattern Grammar: A corpus-driven approach to the lexical grammar of English*. Amsterdam: John Benjamins.

Hyland, K. (2008). As can be seen: Lexical bundles and disciplinary variation. *English for Specific Purposes*, 27, 1, 4–21.

Kremmel, B., Brunfaut, T. and Alderson, J. C. (2015). Exploring the role of phraseological knowledge in foreign language reading. *Applied Linguistics*, 1–24. doi: doi.org/10.1093/applin/amv070.

Louw, B. (1993). Irony in the text or insincerity in the writer? The diagnostic potential of semantic prosodies, in M. Baker and E. Tognini-Bonelli (eds.) *Text and Technology: In honour of John Sinclair.* Amsterdam: John Benjamins, 157–176.

Martinez, R. and Schmitt, N. (2012). A phrasal expressions list. *Applied Linguistics*, 33, 3, 299–320.

McEnery, T. and Hardie, A. (2012). *Corpus Linguistics: Method, theory and practice.* Cambridge: Cambridge University Press.

Moon, R. (1997). Vocabulary connections: Multi-word items in English, in N. Schmitt and M. McCarthy (eds.) *Vocabulary: Description, acquisition and pedagogy.* Cambridge: Cambridge University Press, 40–63.

Myles, F. (2008). Investigating learner language development with electronic longitudinal corpora: Theoretical and methodological issues, in L. Ortega and H. Byrnes (eds.) *The Longitudinal Study of Advanced L2 Capacities.* New York: Routledge, 58–72.

Nation, I. S. P. (2016). Word lists, in I. S. P. Nation (ed.) *Making and Using Word Lists for Language Learning and Testing.* Amsterdam/Philadelphia: John Benjamins, 3–13.

Nattinger, J. R. and DeCarrico, J. S. (1992). *Lexical Phrases and Language Teaching.* Oxford: Oxford University Press.

Partington, A. (1998). *Patterns and Meanings: Using corpora for English language research and teaching.* Amsterdam: John Benjamins.

Partington, A. (2004). Utterly content in each other's company: Semantic prosody and semantic preference. *International Journal of Corpus Linguistics*, 9, 1, 131–156.

Partington, A., Duguid, A. and Taylor, C. (2013). *Patterns and Meanings in Discourse: Theory and practice in corpus-assisted discourse studies (CADS).* Amsterdam/Philadelphia: John Benjamins.

Pawley, A. and Syder, F. H. (1983). Two puzzles for linguistic theory: Native-like selection and native-like fluency, in J. C. Richards and R. W. Schmidt (eds.) *Language and Communication.* London: Longman, 191–225.

Römer, U. (2009). The inseparability of lexis and grammar: Corpus linguistic perspectives. *Annual Review of Cognitive Linguistics*, 7, 141–163.

Schmitt, D. (2016). *Beyond Caveat Emptor: Applying validity criteria to word lists.* Paper presented at Vocab@Tokyo Conference. 12–14 September 2016. Tokyo: Meiji Gakuin University.

Schmitt, N. (2004). (ed.) *Formulaic Sequences: Acquisition, processing and use.* Amsterdam/Philadelphia. John Benjamins.

Schmitt, N. (2010). *Researching Vocabulary: A vocabulary research manual.* Basingstoke: Palgrave Macmillan.

Schmitt, N. (2013). Formulaic language and collocation, in C. A. Chapelle (ed.) *The Encyclopedia of Applied Linguistics.* New York: Blackwell Publishing.

Shin, D. and Nation, I. S. P. (2008). Beyond single words: The most frequent collocations in spoken English. *ELT Journal*, 62, 4, 339–348.

Simpson-Vlach, R. and Ellis, N. (2010). An Academic Formulas List: New methods in phraseology research. *Applied Linguistics*, 31, 4, 487–512.

Sinclair, J. (1991). *Corpus, Concordance, Collocation: Describing English language.* Oxford: Oxford University Press.

Sinclair, J. (2004). *Trust the Text.* London: Routledge.

Siyanova-Chanturia, A. and Martinez, R. (2015). The idiom principle revisited. *Applied Linguistics*, 36, 5, 549–569.

Stefanowitsch, A. and Gries, S. Th. (2003). Collostructions: Investigating the interaction of words and constructions. *International Journal of Corpus Linguistics*, 8, 2, 209–243.

Stubbs, M. (1996). *Text and Corpus Analysis: Computer-assisted analysis of language and culture*. Oxford: Basil Blackwell.

Stubbs, M. (2002). *Words and Phrases: Corpus studies of lexical semantics*. Oxford: Blackwell.

Stubbs, M. (2013). Sequence and order: The neo-Firthian tradition of corpus semantics, in H. Hasselgard, J. Ebeling and S. O. Ebeling (eds.) *Corpus Perspectives on Patterns of Lexis*. Amsterdam/Philadelphia: John Benjamins, 13–34.

Tognini-Bonelli, E. (2010). Theoretical overview of the evolution of corpus linguistics, in A. O'Keeffe and M. McCarthy (eds.) *The Routledge Handbook of Corpus Linguistics*. London and New York: Routledge, 14–27.

Wray, A. (2002). *Formulaic Language and the Lexicon*. Cambridge: Cambridge University Press.

Chapter 6

Corpora and teaching vocabulary

6.1 Lexical syllabus and lexical approach

Corpus linguistics has exerted a considerable influence on the field of language teaching. The ways in which corpora have been employed in language pedagogy can be divided into two main categories: indirect and direct applications (Römer 2011; Flowerdew 2009). In the former, corpora are used to inform the design and development of syllabuses, tests and teaching materials, while in the latter corpus data are used for **data-driven learning** (DDL); that is, hands-on activities in which learners themselves engage in corpus analysis. This chapter aims to discuss these applications with respect to teaching vocabulary.

Before the advent of corpora in the 1980s, grammar tended to be the organizing principle of language teaching syllabuses. It was only when the first computerized databases became available that new perspectives on language teaching in which vocabulary was a prominent feature started to appear. For instance, Sinclair and Renouf (1988) came up with the idea of a lexical syllabus based on the frequency of occurrence as its underlying principle. This innovative approach stemmed from corpus analyses conducted within the COBUILD project, which culminated in the publication of the Collins COBUILD English Language Dictionary. As argued by Sinclair and Renouf (1988: 148), the teaching process should focus on "the commonest word forms in the language, the central patterns of usage and the combinations which they usually form". Of course this should not be taken to mean that grammar is unimportant; rather, the teaching process and your approach to different elements of language should be conceptualized in a different way (O'Dell 1997). Sinclair and Renouf (1988: 155) point out that "if the analysis of the word and phrases has been done correctly", a teaching approach that focuses on the most frequent items will enable students to learn not only lexis but also grammatical structures and their functions. Thus, a lexical syllabus is a use-centered approach, in which grammar is viewed via lexical patterning and the notion of lexico-grammar comes to the fore. As Willis (1990: 51) states, "what is traditionally termed grammar can be often called patterns". Consequently, the teaching process revolves around analyzing various examples of phraseological patterns and learners' attention is drawn to the fact that there is far more utility in the recombination of known elements than in the addition of less easily usable items (Sinclair and Renouf 1988: 155).

As far as translating these theoretical considerations into practical solutions is concerned, Willis and Willis (1988) were the first authors who implemented the idea of a lexical syllabus and proposed a language course based on it. The course was called the Collins COBUILD English and it was aimed at covering the first 2,500 most frequent words spread across three consecutive proficiency levels. Another staunch advocate of vocabulary-oriented teaching was Lewis (1993, 2002), who promoted the idea of a lexical approach in language instruction. Similarly to Willis (1990), Lewis rejects the traditional grammar–lexis dichotomy and perceives language as grammaticalized lexis. In practical terms, this means that teachers are encouraged to draw learners' attention to lexico-grammatical interdependencies and phraseological patterns that result from them. Similar arguments are provided by Meunier and Reppen (2015: 510), who elaborate on how corpus-informed teaching can focus on the lexico-grammatical and contextual aspects of language use rather than treat lexis and grammar as two separate layers of language. According to the authors (2015: 513), "corpus information on registers, frequency, and lexical preferences is key to a good understanding and use of grammar". From the perspective of learners, this suggests that in addition to learning individual words, they also need to develop an ability to comprehend and produce a large number of multiword formulaic units (see Chapter 5 for a detailed discussion of formulaic language).

As far as the organization of the lexical approach in the classroom is concerned, task-based learning was suggested as a methodology that ensures learners' engagement with different types of data and increases their exposure to authentic language (Willis 1990). What is more, the idea of a pedagogic corpus was another element of the teaching process which was emphasized by the proponents of this approach. A pedagogic corpus can be defined as a collection of written and spoken texts that L2 learners encounter in the course of their studies. By using such a corpus, learners are presented with different samples of language in use, which increases their overall L2 exposure (see section 6.4 for more details).

However, appealing as these ideas might seem, it must be said that the lexical syllabus was a less-than-overwhelming success at the time of its introduction (O'Dell 1997) and it did not become a widely adopted English language teaching (ELT) approach (see Szudarski 2012 for details). As an innovative syllabus organized around the most common vocabulary, it lacked the grammatical categories and labels language practitioners had been used to and consequently they were reluctant to use it. However, looking at it with hindsight, the lexical approach needs to be perceived as a groundbreaking approach, which demonstrates that findings from corpus analyses are pedagogically relevant and should inform decisions made in the language classroom. It has also paved the way for lexis-oriented teaching materials (e.g. McCarthy and O'Dell 2005; Dellar and Walkley 2016) which contribute to the promotion of vocabulary in applied linguistics as a whole.

6.2 Corpus-informed textbooks, dictionaries and teaching resources

This section is concerned with the indirect applications of corpora and discusses how they have informed the development of textbooks, reference books, dictionaries, pedagogically oriented lists of vocabulary and online teaching resources.

6.2.1 Textbooks and reference books

Teaching materials such as textbooks or self-study books are a key source of language input L2 learners are exposed to, in particular in contexts where English is taught as a foreign language. Therefore, it is of utmost importance that the language found in such materials reflects real-life communication that takes place in natural settings rather than be contrived solely for the purpose of covering a rigid teaching syllabus. As Meunier and Reppen (2015) argue, corpus-based research should inform the development of textbooks and this is true for both expert user and learner corpora.

From an empirical point of view, some corpus linguists have explored specific features of the language of textbooks and compared it with the language of authentic interactions. For instance, Gouverneur (2008) used the TeMa corpus, a pedagogically annotated corpus of textbooks taken from general English courses at different proficiency levels, to investigate the treatment of phraseology in pedagogical materials. More specifically, the author studied the frequency of phraseological patterns formed around high-frequency delexical verbs such as 'take' or 'make', which are known to pose challenges for L2 learners (see Chapter 7 for more information). The study demonstrated that at the intermediate level there were many exercises targeting verb-noun collocations with 'make' and 'take'. However, at the advanced level, textbook writers seemed to pay little attention to collocations formed with the delexical verbs. Additionally, Gouverneur found that there was a lack of consistency in the selection of chunks that were included in the teaching materials.

Likewise, Koprowski (2005) conducted a study in which he looked at three contemporary ELT textbooks aimed at intermediate learners. Using frequency and a range of text types as his evaluation criteria, the author analyzed the usefulness of the chunks that were presented in these materials. His research showed that many useful chunks were not included at all and, perhaps even more interestingly, not even a single phrase appeared in all the three textbooks. Koprowski (2005: 328) concluded that the selection of lexical phrases appeared to be "an unprincipled and careless selection process" based on "the personal discretion and intuition of the writers".

Similar observations have been made by other scholars. For instance, Burton (2012) and Gilmore (2015) argue that many ELT writers do not benefit from the richness of corpus analysis and fail to incorporate research findings into their materials. As Gilmore (2015: 517) observes, "textbook authors are not yet habitually checking their materials against relevant corpus data". This results in the fact that many features that characterize natural discourse (e.g. collocations) are not highlighted in reference books and/or textbooks well enough and the language that learners are exposed to differs considerably from the actual usage (Römer 2011). Granger (2015: 494) attributes this to two main reasons: a lack of awareness of the benefits of corpora among teachers and materials writers, and the amount of work that is necessary to translate corpus findings into accessible teaching materials.

However, despite this rather gloomy situation, we can also observe some positive changes. If you do a quick analysis of what is available on the market, you can find materials that are based on sound research findings rather than pure intuition and stilted examples. Some of the most notable examples are *the Touchstone* series by McCarthy, McCarten and Sandiford (2005) and *Natural English* by Gairns and Redman (2010), both of which have been developed on extensive corpus evidence. There is also a growing number of English for academic purposes (EAP) materials, which have profited from corpus analyses. Some noteworthy examples are Schmitt and Schmitt's (2005, 2011) textbooks which focus on academic vocabulary or Nesi's (2001) EASE (Essential Academic Skills in English) multimedia teaching materials based on the British Academic Spoken English (BASE) corpus. Finally, there exist many corpus-based reference works which focus on grammar. These include, among others, the *Longman Grammar of Spoken and Written English* (Biber et al. 1999), the *Cambridge Grammar of English* (Carter and McCarthy 2006) and *English Grammar Today* (Carter et al. 2011). When it comes to grammar, it is highly recommended that you consult Jones and Waller's (2015) recent guide on the use of corpora in this area.

> Task 6.1: Select three different contemporary ELT textbooks (ideally from different publishers) and try to determine the extent to which they are based on corpus data. Consider which factors influence the textbook selection process for your students. Is the authenticity of language one of them?

6.2.2 Dictionaries and lexicography

Corpora have also had a considerable impact on research within the area of lexicography (Walter 2010). In his discussion of the field of lexicography, Hanks (2012) refers to a corpus revolution and the way corpora have transformed the process of compiling dictionaries. Thanks to corpora, lexicographers rely on authentic examples of language use rather than their own intuitions while making decisions about the contents of dictionaries. In fact, in light of the usefulness of corpora, a lot of money is currently invested in the development of large databases, which then serve as a basis for writing dictionaries. As O'Keeffe et al. (2007: 17) state, "all major publishers now provide corpus-based dictionaries".

A good illustration of the usefulness of corpora is lexicographic work in the area of phraseology. By analyzing naturally occurring language, lexicographers can attest and describe specific meanings of words and phrases, which in turn informs their decisions about the organization of entries in dictionaries. At the same time, the abundance of information derived from a corpus can also be a challenge for lexicographers. While they seek to develop comprehensive dictionaries that reflect natural language use, such resources should remain practical and should not overwhelm the end user, in particular if they are a low-level learner. Referring to this issue, Hanks (2012: 409) suggests that the optimal solution would be "to take account of the corpus findings, but rather than doctoring example sentences for pedagogical purposes, select examples that are both authentic and pedagogically useful".

Except for mono- or bilingual dictionaries aimed at language learners, we should also mention less traditional examples of lexicographic work. Davies and Gardner (2010) published *A Frequency Dictionary of Contemporary American English*, which is based on the five different genres (spoken, fiction, newspapers, magazines and academic) constituting the Corpus of Contemporary American English (COCA). As the authors state, the dictionary is "designed to meet the needs of a wide range of language students and teachers, as well as those who are interested in the computational processing of English" (Davies and Gardner 2010: 1). From the perspective of language learners, the dictionary can be used as a source of insights into the 5,000 most common words in English that they are likely to encounter in various kinds of communicative situations. Another valuable resource is *A Valency Dictionary of English* by Herbst et al. (2004), where each entry is accompanied by information about its common complementation patterns. The dictionary is based on data from the COBUILD/Collins corpus, a large database of English with over 4.5 billion words. Finally, it is also worth highlighting Hanks's (2012) ongoing project devoted to the Pattern Dictionary of English Verbs (PDEV). The dictionary seeks to present "each meaning of every English verb with the stereotypical context or contexts in which the verb is used" (Hanks 2012: 424) and can be accessed here: http://www.pdev.org.uk/. Crucially, such a phraseology-driven dictionary can be perceived as an attempt at realizing Sinclair's (2004) idea of 'the ultimate dictionary' which would do full justice to the phrasal complexity of English by capturing all lexical items (both canonical as well as variant forms). It goes without saying that such a dictionary is a mammoth task but given the increasing number of researchers who strive to describe English phraseology, the field is moving closer to achieving this aim.

6.2.3 Pedagogically oriented lists of vocabulary

As already signaled in the previous chapter, one of the most beneficial ways in which corpora have contributed to vocabulary studies is the development of pedagogically oriented lists of the most frequent and useful vocabulary. As far as individual words are concerned, the most recent additions are Brezina and Gablasova's (2015) new General Service List and Gardner and Davies's (2014) new Academic Vocabulary List (see details in Chapters 4 and 8 respectively). The same holds true for phraseology, for a recent surge of interest in lexico-grammar and formulaic language has resulted in the development of numerous corpus-informed lists of phraseological units (see Chapter 5).

Such lists are valuable pedagogical resources that can be used by language teachers, materials developers and L2 learners and should help them deal with the magnitude of English phraseology. However, as already stressed in Chapter 4, it is important to remember that frequency is only one criterion that informs the process of identifying the most useful vocabulary and, to use Jones and Durrant's (2010: 392) argument, considerable human guidance is needed as well so that we are able to cater to the specific lexical needs of particular groups of learners. This under-scores the importance of taking into account teachers' and learners' opinions about the utility of different types of vocabulary that are derived from corpora.

An interesting way of addressing this problem has been presented in Omidian, Shahriari and Ghonsooly's (2017) recent study. With a view to exploring the pedagogic value of multiword units, the researchers asked fifty instructors and fifty students working in the English as a foreign language (EFL) context to rate a sample of various kinds of phraseological chunks in terms of their utility. In total, forty-five chunks were used and all of them came from three influential corpus-based lists of phraseology: Biber et al. (2004), Simpson-Vlach and Ellis (2010) and Martinez and Schmitt (2012). The top fifteen chunks from each list were selected and, interestingly, only one item, the phrase 'as well as', was shared by all of them. While this result is somewhat surprising, to a large extent it is caused by the different methodologies that were employed to create the original lists.

When it comes to the design of the task used by Omidian et al. (2017), all the target chunks were embedded in sample sentences from the academic section of COCA and the instructors and students rated them on a four-point scale (1 indicat-ing the lack of importance of a given phrase and 4 indicating its high importance). On the basis of these ratings as well as a series of interviews with some of the participants, the authors arrived at a set of insights into the pedagogic relevance of the phrases. Namely, some chunks were rated as valuable by both groups of informants and, interestingly, the majority of these chunks came from Martinez and Schmitt's (2012) PHRASE List.

Table 6.1 Examples of multiword units selected by Omidian et al. (2017)

Biber et al.'s (2004) list	Simpson-Vlach and Ellis (2010)	Martinez and Schmitt (2012)
Do you want to	In order to	Of course
I want you to	This is a	A few
I was going to	Part of the	At least

However, when the teachers' and students' answers were analyzed separately, the former were more inclined to select items from Biber et al.'s (2004) list (e.g. 'such as' or 'rather than') as well as phrases which they perceived as problematic from a learning point of view. In turn, the students tended to favor items from Martinez and Schmitt's (2012) list because they felt that such items could be employed in a variety of text types. Crucially, both groups had one element in common – they emphasized the high value of chunks that had a clear discourse function (e.g. discourse markers such as 'on the other hand'). These are important findings which demonstrate that the usefulness of words and phrases is a relative notion, with the ratings of what is pedagogically relevant likely to vary depending on specific teaching contexts.

> Task 6.2: Look at the phrases from Omidian et al.'s (2017) study presented in Table 6.1. Compare their frequency in the different sections of COCA, paying particular attention to the academic section of the corpus. If these are phrases that are typical of academic discourse, how would you teach them to a group of EAP students attending a course that you teach?

6.2.4 Corpus-based teaching resources

The impact of corpora on language pedagogy can also be observed when we look at a wide range of online interfaces and websites that pertain to vocabulary. One of the most useful web-based resources that needs to be mentioned is Tom Cobb's Compleat Lexical Tutor or Lextutor (http://www.lextutor.ca/), which we have already discussed in Chapter 4. The website offers numerous ways in which corpus data can be usefully exploited by both teachers and students. Similar options for exploring vocabulary are also available at http://www.wordandphrase.info/, which is a simplified version of the BYU-COCA interface. As envisioned by Davies and his colleagues, it is a user-friendly website developed for language learners and teachers, as they might be particularly apprehensive about using more technologically sophisticated corpus software aimed at professional linguists. Other examples of corpus-based teaching resources are presented in Table 6.2.

Table 6.2 Examples of corpus-based resources aimed at language teachers and learners

Name	Website	Application
Phrases in English	http://phrasesinenglish.org/	A website used for identifying phrases in the British National Corpus (BNC)

Sketch Engine for Language Learning	http://skell.sketchengine.co.uk/run.cgi/skell	A user-friendly interface which enables you to explore words by means of concordances and word sketches (i.e. lists of collocations and other kinds of phraseological partners)
Virtual Language Centre (VLC) Web Concordancer	http://vlc.polyu.edu.hk/concordance/WWWConcappE.htm	A website that can be used as both a teaching and self-study resource
VocabularySize.com	http://my.vocabularysize.com/	A website intended as a tribute to Paul Nation and his contributions to vocabulary studies); while validated tests of vocabulary are likely to be more accurate, this resource can be usefully applied by teachers and curriculum designers
Academic Word List (AWL) gap-maker; Academic Word List Highlighter; the Academic Word List in EAP	http://www.nottingham.ac.uk/alzsh3/acvocab/awlgapmaker.htm; http://www.nottingham.ac.uk/alzsh3/acvocab/awlhighlighter.htm; http://www.uefap.com/vocab/vocfram.htm	Websites aimed mainly at EAP teachers who wish to improve their students' academic vocabulary
HASK	http://pelcra.pl/hask_en/	A corpus-based collocation database aimed at linguists, language teachers and materials designers (see Pęzik 2014 for details)
LancsBox	http://corpora.lancs.ac.uk/lancsbox/index.php	A software package for linguists and language teachers interested in different aspects of vocabulary (see Brezina et al. (2015) for details on how to use this software to analyze collocational networks)
WordNet	https://wordnet.princeton.edu/	A large lexical database of English which functions as an online thesaurus
Global Scale of English Teacher Toolkit, Pearson	https://www.english.com/gse/teacher-toolkit	A free database of language learning objectives, grammar and vocabulary; it is designed as a global reference tool for the use of English at different proficiency levels (see Benigno and de Jong (2016) for details)

Task 6.3: Imagine you are preparing a reading comprehension class. Using the AWL Highlighter, identify academic words in any text of your choice. Note that the AWL Highlighter allows you to indicate how many sub-lists of the AWL you want to include, which means that you can adjust the difficulty level of the vocabulary depending on how proficient your students are.

6.3 Data-driven learning

Data-driven learning (DDL) was first proposed by Johns (1991) who defined it as the direct use of corpus data in the language teaching process. As an inductive approach, it is based on the premise that learners engage in their own linguistic analysis in which they focus on specific linguistic features. As Chambers (2010) notes, such corpus-aided learning can take different forms and range from concordances prepared by the teacher to learners' autonomous corpus consultation. Decisions as to which form should be used are likely to be influenced by the level and needs of our students.

There are several major benefits of DDL that are emphasized by its proponents. First of all, DDL promotes learners' active role in their linguistic development by encouraging them to discover regularities in language as it is used across natural contexts. As highlighted by Johns's (1997) oft-quoted metaphor, in DDL learners perform the role of detectives in the classroom and each of them can become a Sherlock Holmes. Since DDL gives learners "direct access to the data" (Johns 1991: 30), classroom work becomes an inductive, student-centered approach with each learner carrying out their own linguistic analysis. Further advantages of DDL are discussed by Gilmore (2015), who states that the direct use of corpora allows learners to immerse themselves in natural data and test their hypotheses about specific linguistic features. Thus, not only does DDL raise learners' awareness of the way language is used in real-life communicative situations but it also develops their autonomy by encouraging them to take responsibility for their own learning.

Such an understanding of the teaching process has important consequences for the role of teachers; they are no longer the only source of knowledge in the classroom but rather they facilitate the learning process and assist learners with their discovery. Crucially, teachers can also profit enormously from corpus consultation and analysis. Cobb and Boulton (2015) state that corpora can be treated as a tool which boosts teachers' confidence, especially in situations when they are unsure of their own linguistic competence. As shown by Römer (2009), many teachers who teach a language that is not their mother tongue do not trust their L2 linguistic competence and consequently seek guidance on specific language features. Also, O'Keeffe et al. (2007: 242) point out that corpora can be used as a resource for teachers "who wish to either improve their own language awareness" or need answers to some unexpected questions that might come up during classes. Corpora can also be used as repositories of sample sentences that demonstrate the use of a given word or chunk.

> Task 6.4: You prepare an English class and you want your students to study phrasal verbs that contain the prepositions 'up' and 'down'. Using the BYU-COCA interface, look for examples of such verbs in American English and select concordances that will serve as a basis for the class.

Up to this point our discussion has revolved around the positive aspects of DDL. However, there are also certain challenges that the implementation of DDL might entail (Gilquin and Granger 2010; Boulton 2009). First, DDL might be difficult to implement because of practicalities such as a lack of computers or corpus software. Even though technological advances have transformed the way foreign languages are taught these days, practicing teachers can easily imagine a situation in which access to fifteen computers during a language class might become problematic. In such cases, an alternative form of DDL is preparing paper-based concordances and giving them to students as worksheets. This form of DDL is probably more time-consuming than computer-based concordancing but it is worth considering if you or your students face the problem of limited access to technology.

Another thorny issue that should be mentioned is the potential of overwhelming students with corpus data. Irrespective of the form of presentation (on computer vs. on paper), some students might find it difficult to process large amounts of data, in particular when they represent lower levels of proficiency. As Yoon and Hirvela (2004) warn, from the perspective of students, analyzing concordances might seem time-consuming, tedious and off-putting, and DDL may not necessarily be perceived as a worthwhile classroom activity. Consequently, some authors suggest that DDL "may be suitable for certain learners only" (Gilquin and Granger 2010: 367) and teachers need to consider their students' expectations and learning styles before they decide to introduce elements of corpus analysis into language classes. For instance, Allan (2010) explored the impact of explicit vocabulary tasks involving the use of dictionaries and concordances on English as a second language (ESL) learners' acquisition of words and found that corpus-based vocabulary learning seems to be less effective at lower levels of proficiency (B1) in comparison with higher levels (B2 and C1). Bearing in mind the small scale of the study, the author recommends that "if concordances are used, it is advisable to provide plenty of initial training and keep the amount of data provided manageable" (Allan 2010: 124).

However, as Boulton's (2010) research demonstrates, if DDL is well planned and relies on carefully selected materials (e.g. paper-based corpus activities), it can be successfully implemented with learners at lower levels of proficiency. It appears that the attitude of a given teacher is of crucial importance; that is, he or she needs to know what their students are capable of and how the use of corpus data will impact on the learning experience as a whole. It goes without saying that to avoid failure in the implementation of DDL, learners ought to be informed well in advance that they will participate in a hands-on approach and they need to be prepared that this approach requires their active involvement.

A related problem that might interfere with the successful use of DDL is teachers' lack of expertise in employing corpus techniques. It is self-evident that teachers who wish to integrate some elements of corpus analysis into their classroom instruction need to be 'corpus literate' and comfortable with the mechanics of corpus analysis. After all, they will play a key role in introducing their students to the world of corpus linguistics. Elaborating on the status of corpora in teacher education, McCarthy (2008: 565) argues that "teachers should be central stakeholders in the corpus revolution" and rather than being passive consumers of corpus-informed materials produced by commercial publishers, they ought to become reflective practitioners who are genuinely interested in conducting their own corpus analysis and using its results for teaching purposes. Similar arguments are put forward by Callies (2016: 392–3), who observes that to popularize corpus linguistics "in the language teaching community at large", both teacher trainees and experienced educators need to acquire corpus literacy. According to Callies (2016: 394–5), corpus literacy can be defined as "the ability to use corpora for language analysis and instruction" and it comprises the following set of subcomponents:

- understanding basic concepts in corpus linguistics
- searching and analyzing corpus data
- interpreting corpus data
- using corpus data to produce teaching materials.

Thus, it transpires from the above arguments that if DDL and corpus-based inquiry are to become more widespread, training teachers in how to conduct corpus analysis and informing them about which corpora are available to them "is something that should be part of teacher education programs" (McCarthy 2008: 570). This can be achieved through both pre- and in-service teacher training programs and there is some empirical evidence confirming successful provision of such training (e.g. see Zareva 2017 for a useful discussion).

Leńko-Szymańska (2014) provides an example of a study in which a group of would-be teachers were introduced to the main tenets of corpus linguistics. Crucially, the study discusses both the benefits of such training as well as some challenges faced by the teachers throughout this process. Based on her findings, Leńko-Szymańska (2014: 272) asserts that we cannot benefit from the use of corpora in the classroom "until teacher trainees gain confidence in handling corpus-processing software and in interpreting the output of their analyses". As the author explains, developing corpus skills in would-be teachers "has the advantage of enabling them to assess the needs of their own students in the future, to decide on appropriate corpus-based and data-driven techniques, and to choose suitable resources which can meet these demands" (Leńko-Szymańska 2014: 272). Another encouraging example of promoting corpus literacy is Ebrahimi and Faghih's (2017) study into online teacher education programs. The authors demonstrate how to create conducive conditions that lead to the successful delivery of corpus training. In this context it is worth mentioning that for several years a team of linguists from Lancaster University have been delivering a well-received massive open online course (MOOC) in corpus linguistics (https://www.futurelearn.com/courses/corpus-linguistics). If you are interested in learning how to use corpora for a range of purposes, it is highly recommended that you sign up for this course.

As a final note in this section, it needs to be admitted that while on a theoretical level the field seems to agree that there is a lot of scope for the direct use of corpus evidence in language education, in practical terms "explicit data-driven techniques are rarely incorporated into regular teaching procedures" (Leńko-Szymańska and Boulton 2015: 3) and the uptake of corpus research by ELT practitioners is rather low (Gilmore 2015). As already observed, one area where the applications of corpus research have been less than impressive is the extent to which corpus findings have been translated into the language content that is presented in textbooks. As Gilmore maintains (2015: 515), while more and more corpus-informed materials become available on the market, "for a wide range of discourse features such as lexico-grammatical items or **speech acts** ELT textbooks often provide learners with distorted or partial representations of the target language". In a similar vein, Römer (2011: 206) states that "much work still remains to be done in bridging the gap between research and practice". According to the author, the following tasks should be completed to continue the promotion of corpus linguistics:

- focus more on the corpus literacy of teachers and practitioners
- pay more attention to learners' needs
- conduct more empirical work on corpus-based descriptions of specialized discourses.

These are without a doubt major challenges for the field and they need to be addressed through establishing closer links between corpus linguists, materials designers and teachers. However, Gilmore (2015) remains optimistic and points out that the impact of corpus research findings on classroom practices will increase in the future. A recent meta-analysis of sixty-four studies into the use of corpora in language learning also provides optimistic findings. This is how Boulton and Cobb (2017: 386) conclude their analysis:

DDL is perhaps most appropriate in foreign language contexts for under-graduates as much as graduates, for intermediate level as much as advanced, for general as much as specific/academic purposes, for local as much as large corpora, for hands-on concordancing as much as for paper-based explora-tion, for learning as much as reference, and particularly for vocabulary and lexico-grammar.

In a nutshell, it can be said that "DDL works pretty well in almost any con-text where it has been extensively tried" (Boulton and Cobb 2017: 386). Given that many corpora can be accessed free of charge and they are accompanied by resources on how to apply them to language teaching (e.g. see Timmis (2015) for a guide on the use of corpora in ELT), it is imperative that we raise teachers' awareness of the benefits of corpus-informed teaching (Nation 2001). It is hoped that with the continuing growth of corpus linguistics, more and more teachers, materials developers and language teaching practitioners will start introducing elements of this methodology into their everyday work.

6.4 Pedagogic and teaching-oriented corpora

As mentioned above, Willis (1990) promoted the idea of what he called "a pedagogic corpus", which is a teaching-oriented corpus created from all the spoken and written language encountered by learners during their language course. Such a corpus is designed to play a key role in the implementation of a lexically oriented language teaching program. For instance, a pedagogic corpus can aid teachers in their classroom work by informing their decisions concern-ing the lexical content of their classes. What is more, pedagogic corpora benefit learners by helping them to deal with the unfamiliarity of language data found in a general corpus. As explained by Hunston (2002: 187), what is special about a pedagogic corpus is that "when an item is met in one text, examples from previous (and future) texts can be used as additional evidence", which contributes to a good coverage of the most useful vocabulary.

The benefits of a pedagogic corpus are also discussed by Meunier and Gouverneur (2009: 286), who perceive it as "a large enough and representative example of the language, spoken and written, a learner has been or is likely to be exposed to via teaching material, either in the classroom or during self-study activities". However, Chambers (2015) maintains that many language practition-ers do not adhere to such a broad understanding of a pedagogic corpus. Rather, they tend to perceive it as "a small genre-specific corpus meeting a specific need identified by a single teacher-researcher or by a project team wishing to create an online resource" (Chambers 2015: 448). It is important to point out that such do-it-yourself, teaching-oriented corpora can be easily built by individual teach-ers (e.g. recording a series of lessons and storing them as a small database) and become a useful tool for improving their teaching practices and solving specific problems that pertain to their local teaching context.

It also needs to be emphasized that pedagogically oriented corpora can be adopted for the process of teachers' professional development. The Corpus of Meetings of English Language Teachers developed by Vaughan (2010) is a good example of how a small corpus (40,000 words) of teachers' interactions taking place outside the classroom can provide valuable insights into the teaching profession. Vaughan collected data from two teaching communities in Mexico and Ireland, and her research yielded valuable information about the teachers' day-to-day business and everyday practices. Similarly, Farr (2003) worked with the Post Observation Teacher Training Interactions (POTTI) corpus, which consisted of over 80,000 words collected from a teacher education program in Ireland. In her analysis of conversations between trainers and trainees, the author focused on issues such as hedged directives or tokens of engaged listenership. This allowed her to delve into the process of teacher training and the development of professional identity (O'Keeffe et al. 2007). Analyzing such data can shed some light on teachers' classroom behavior in terms of the language they use, which in turn creates an opportunity for some reflection upon their teaching (Burns 2010).

Finally, pedagogically oriented corpora can also take the form of small-scale learner corpora that consist of the language produced by L2 learners (see Chapter 7 for more information on learner language). As Chambers (2015) explains, such corpora can be used for identifying the most frequent errors learners tend to struggle with. This in turn can lead to corpus-informed form-focused instruction that targets the most problematic aspects of L2 such as collocations (see Szudarski and Carter 2016 for an example).

6.5 Exemplary study: Charles (2012) on students' attitudes toward do-it-yourself corpus-building

The aim of this section is to present details of Charles's (2012) study into the use of small-scale, do-it-yourself (DIY) corpora by fifty students of EAP at Oxford University. The students came from different L1 backgrounds and represented as many as thirty-three different academic disciplines. All of them were advanced-level graduate students who participated in a language course consisting of six two-hour sessions held over the course of six weeks. To explore the students' attitudes toward the use of DIY corpora as a way of improving their writing skills, Charles designed and administered two questionnaires at the beginning and end of the course. The results of the questionnaires revealed that most students approved of the idea of building and employing their own corpora, with about 90% of them agreeing that the corpus-based instruction was helpful in the process of writing discipline-specific texts.

As far as the practical use of the students' DIY corpora is concerned, all the participants were given numerous opportunities to analyze data from their small, purpose-built corpora. The corpora consisted of at least ten research articles each, with the size ranging from 37,000 to 99,000 words. The main aim of the study was to demonstrate to the students how to use corpus tools (e.g. frequency and collocation analyses) as a way of improving their writing skills and expressing themselves via different linguistic means (i.e. a wide variety of grammatical or lexical choices). Most of the participants focused on studying the patterns of occurrence of specific language features (e.g. pronouns) and analyzed how they fulfill different rhetorical functions typical of successful academic writing. For instance, they explored different ways of criticizing other authors' research or modifying their own claims.

To enable all the students to carry out such analyses, Charles familiarized them with AntConc (Anthony 2014), a free and user-friendly piece of corpus software (see Chapter 2). A decision to put a lot of emphasis on training the students in how to carry out corpus analysis was based on the belief that they needed to develop a certain level of expertise if they were to become autonomous corpus users once the course was over. Convincingly, the students' answers to the questionnaires showed that a high percentage (94%) intended to use corpora in the future. What is more, the students were also asked whether they consulted the corpora for revising or composing their texts and as many as 78% of them admitted that the corpora of research articles from specific disciplines were helpful in terms of formulating ideas and conveying them in conventionalized ways that are expected from proficient EAP writers. Lastly, it is also worth mentioning one student's reservations about the level of the language found in their corpus. The student observed that "the quality of English language is not always up to standard even in good articles", which points to the importance of the value of texts that serve as a basis for creating DIY corpora. In general, L2 learners' understanding of what constitutes a linguistic norm is likely to vary depending on the context of their study. However, the fact that currently more and more individuals working in academia are non-native speakers of English lends support to calls for research into the use of English as an academic lingua franca (see Chapter 7 for a detailed discussion).

Despite all the advantages of the corpus consultation described above, Charles (2012) acknowledges that the study is not devoid of certain limitations. First of all, six weeks is a relatively short period of time to accurately measure and track the impact of corpus-based instruction on L2 skills development. Second, the course was open access and did not involve any formal assessment, which meant that only 34% of the students attended all the sessions. Finally, five different classes, with about eighteen students each, participated in the study, which made it difficult for the researcher to attend to the individual needs of particular students. However, while all of these factors are likely to have influenced the validity of the findings reported by Charles, if you have ever tried to conduct research in classroom conditions, you will agree that this kind of empirical work is fraught with such challenges.

Summary

This chapter has addressed the impact of corpora on teaching vocabulary and discussed both the indirect and direct applications of corpus data. With reference to the former, we have presented the importance of corpus data for the development of teaching syllabuses, textbooks, dictionaries, pedagogical wordlists and online resources. As regards the direct use of corpus data in the language classroom, we have discussed the pros and cons of DDL. Finally, we have demonstrated the potential of purpose-built pedagogic and teaching-oriented corpora.

References

Allan, R. (2010). Concordances versus dictionaries: Evaluating approaches to word learning in ESOL, in R. Chacon-Beltran, C. Abello-Contesse and M. del Mar Torreblanca-Lopez (eds.) *Insights into Non-native Vocabulary Teaching and Learning*. Bristol: Multilingual Matters, 112–125.

Anthony, L. (2014). AntConc (Version 3.4.4) [computer software]. Tokyo: Waseda University.

Benigno, V. and de Jong, J. (2016). The "Global Scale of English Learning Objectives for young learners": A CEFR-based inventory of descriptors. In M. Nikolov (ed.) *Assessing Young Learners of English: Global and local perspectives*. New York: Springer, 43–64.

Biber, D., Conrad, S. and Cortes, V. (2004). If you look at....: Lexical bundles in university teaching and textbooks. *Applied Linguistics*, 25, 3, 371–405.

Biber, D., Johansson, S., Leech, G., Conrad, S. and Finegan, E. (1999). *Longman Grammar of Spoken and Written English*. Harlow: Pearson Education Limited.

Boulton, A. (2009). Data-driven learning: Reasonable fears and rational reassurance. *Indian Journal of Applied Linguistics*, 35, 1, 81–106.

Boulton, A. (2010). Data-driven learning: Taking the computer out of equation. *Language Learning*, 60, 3, 534–572.

Boulton, A. and Cobb, T. (2017). Corpus use in language learning: A meta-analysis. *Language Learning*, 67, 2, 348–393.

Brezina, V. and Gablasova, D. (2015). Is there a core general vocabulary? Introducing the New General Service List. *Applied Linguistics*, 36, 1, 1–22.

Brezina, V., McEnery, T. and Wattam, S. (2015). Collocations in context: A new perspective on collocation networks. *International Journal of Corpus Linguistics*, 20, 2, 139–173.

Burns, A. (2010). *Doing Action Research in English Language Teaching: A guide for practitioners*. New York: Routledge.

Burton, G. (2012.) Corpora and coursebooks: Destined to be strangers forever? *Corpora*, 7, 1, 91–108.

Callies, M. (2016). Towards corpus literacy in foreign language teacher education: Using corpora to examine the variability of reporting verbs in English, in R. Kreyer, B. Güldenring and S. Schaub (eds.) *Angewandte Linguistic in Schule und Hochschule: Neue Wege für Sprachunterricht und Ausbildung*. Frankfurt: Peter Lang, 391–415.

Carter, R. and McCarthy, M. (2006). *Cambridge Grammar of English*. Cambridge: Cambridge University Press.

Carter, R., McCarthy, M., Mark, G. and O'Keeffe, A. (2011). *English Grammar Today: An A–Z spoken and written grammar*. Cambridge: Cambridge University Press.

Chambers, A. (2010). What is data-driven learning?, in A. O'Keeffe and M. McCarthy (eds.) *The Routledge Handbook of Corpus Linguistics*. London and New York: Routledge, 345–358.

Cobb, T. (2016). *Compleat Lexical Tutor (LexTutor)* [online]. Available: www.lextutor.ca [20 June 2016].

Chambers, A. (2015). The learner corpus as a pedagogic corpus, in S. Granger, G. Gilquin and F. Meunier (eds.) *The Cambridge Handbook of Learner Corpus Linguistics.* Cambridge: Cambridge University Press, 445–464.

Charles, M. (2012). 'Proper vocabulary and juicy collocations': EAP students evaluate do-it-yourself corpus building. *English for Specific Purposes*, 31, 2, 93–102.

Cobb, T. and Boulton, A. (2015). Classroom applications of corpus analysis, in D. Biber and R. Reppen (eds.) *The Cambridge Handbook of Corpus Linguistics.* New York: Cambridge University Press, 478–497.

Davies, M. and Gardner, D. (2010). *A Frequency Dictionary of Contemporary American English: Word sketches, collocates, and thematic lists.* London: Routledge.

Dellar, H. and Walkley, A. (2016). *Teaching Lexically: Principles and practice.* Peaslake, UK: Delta Publishing.

Ebrahimi, A. and Faghih, E. (2017). Integrating corpus linguistics into online language teacher education programs. *ReCALL*, 29, 1, 120–135.

Farr, F. (2003). Engaged listenership in spoken academic discourse: The case of student-tutor meetings, *Journal of English for Academic Purposes*, 2, 1, 67–85.

Flowerdew, J. (2009). Corpora in language teaching, in M. H. Long and C. Doughty (eds.) *The Handbook of Language Teaching.* Oxford: Wiley-Blackwell, 327–350.

Gairns, R. and Redman, S. (2010). *Natural English.* Oxford: Oxford University Press.

Gardner, D. and Davies, M. (2014). A new Academic Vocabulary List. *Applied Linguistics*, 35, 3, 305–327.

Gilmore, A. (2015). Research into practice: The influence of discourse studies on language descriptions and task design in published ELT materials. *Language Teaching*, 48, 4, 506–530.

Gilquin, G. and Granger, S. (2010). How can data-driven learning be used in language teaching?, in A. O'Keeffe and M. McCarthy (eds.) *The Routledge Handbook of Corpus Linguistics.* London and New York: Routledge, 359–370.

Gouverneur, C. (2008). The phraseological patterns of high-frequency verbs in advanced English for general purposes: A corpus driven approach to EFL textbook analysis, in F. Meunier and S. Granger (eds.) *Phraseology in Foreign Language Learning and Teaching.* Amsterdam/Philadelphia: John Benjamins, 223–246.

Granger, S. (2015). The contribution of learner corpora to reference and instructional materials design, in S. Granger, G. Gilquin and F. Meunier (eds.) *The Cambridge Handbook of Learner Corpus Research.* Cambridge: Cambridge University Press, 485–510.

Hanks, P. (2012). The corpus revolution in lexicography. *International Journal of Lexicography*, 25, 4, 398–436.

Herbst, T., Heath, D., Roe, I. F. and Götz, D. (2004). *A Valency Dictionary of English: A corpus-based analysis of complementation of English verbs, nouns and adjectives.* Berlin and New York: Mouton de Gruyter.

Hunston, S. (2002). *Corpora in Applied Linguistics.* Cambridge: Cambridge University Press.

Johns, T. (1991). Should you be persuaded: Two examples of data-driven learning, in T. Johns and P. King (eds.) *Classroom Concordancing, ELR Journal 4.* Birmingham: Centre for English Language Studies, University of Birmingham, 1–16.

Johns, T. (1997). Contexts: The background, development and trialling of a concordance-based CALL program, in A. Wichmann, S. Fligelstone, T. McEnery and G. Knowles (eds.) *Teaching and Language Corpora.* London: Longman, 100–115.

Jones, C. and Waller, D. (2015). *Corpus Linguistics for Grammar: A guide for research.* London and New York: Routledge.

Jones, M. and Durrant, P. (2010). What can a corpus tell us about vocabulary teaching materials?, in A. O'Keeffe, A. and M. McCarthy (eds.) *The Routledge Handbook of Corpus Linguistics.* London and New York: Routledge, 387–400.

Koprowski, M. (2005). Investigating the usefulness of lexical phrases in contemporary coursebooks. *ELT Journal* 59, 4, 322–332.

Leńko-Szymańska, A. (2014). Is this enough? A qualitative evaluation of the effectiveness of a teacher-training course on the use of corpora in language education. *ReCALL*, 26, 2, 260–278.

Leńko-Szymańska, A. and Boulton, A. (2015). Introduction: Data-driven learning in language pedagogy, in A. Leńko-Szymańska and A. Boulton (eds.) *Multiple Affordances of Language Corpora for Data-driven Learning.* Amsterdam/Philadelphia: John Benjamins, 1–14.

Lewis, M. (1993). *The Lexical Approach: The state of ELT and a way forward.* Hove: Language Teaching Publications.

Lewis, M. (2002). *Implementing the Lexical Approach: Putting theory into practice.* Hove: Thomson.

Martinez, R. and Schmitt, N. (2012). A phrasal expressions list. *Applied Linguistics*, 33, 3, 299–320.

McCarthy, M. (2008). Accessing and interpreting corpus information in the teacher education context. *Language Teaching*, 41, 4, 563–574.

McCarthy, M. and O'Dell, F. (2005). *English Collocations in Use.* Cambridge: Cambridge University Press.

McCarthy, M., McCarten, J. and Sandiford, H. (2005). *Touchstone Student's Book 1.* Cambridge: Cambridge University Press.

Meunier, F. and Gouverneur, C. (2009). New types of corpora for new educational challenges: Collecting, annotating and exploiting a corpus of textbook material, in K. Aijmer (ed.) *Corpora and Language Teaching.* Amsterdam: John Benjamins, 179–201.

Meunier, F. and Reppen, R. (2015). Corpus versus non-corpus-informed pedagogical materials: Grammar as the focus, in D. Biber and R. Reppen (eds.) *The Cambridge Handbook of English Corpus Linguistics.* Cambridge: Cambridge University Press, 498–514.

Nation, I. S. P. (2001). Using small corpora in investigate learner needs: Two vocabulary research tools, in M. Ghadessy, A. Henry and R. L. Roseberry (eds.) *Small Corpus Studies and ELT: Theory and practice.* Amsterdam/Philadelphia: John Benjamins, 31–45.

Nesi, H. (2001). EASE: A multimedia materials development project, in K. Cameron (ed.) *CALL – The Challenge of Change.* Exeter: Elm Bank Publications, 287–292.

O'Dell, F. (1997). Incorporating vocabulary into the syllabus, in N. Schmitt and M. McCarthy (eds.) *Vocabulary: description, acquisition and pedagogy.* Cambridge: Cambridge University Press, 258–278.

O'Keeffe, A., McCarthy, M. and Carter, R. (2007). *From Corpus to Classroom.* Cambridge: Cambridge University Press.

Omidian, T., Shahriari, H. and Ghonsooly, B. (2017). Evaluating the pedagogic value of multi-word expressions based on EFL teachers' and advanced learners' value judgments. *TESOL Journal*, 8, 2, 489–511.

Pęzik, P. (2014). Graph-based analysis of collocational profiles, in V. Jesenšek and P. Grzybek (eds) *Zora 97: Phraseologie im Wörterbuch une Korpus (Phraseology in dictionaries and corpora).* Maribor, Bielsko-Biała, Budapest, Kansas, Praha: Flozofska Fakuteta, 227–243.

Römer, U. (2009). Corpus research and practice: What help do teachers need and what can we offer?, in K. Aijmer, K. (ed.) *Corpora and Language Teaching*. Amsterdam: John Benjamins, 83–98.

Römer, U. (2011). Corpus research applications in second language teaching. *Annual Review of Applied Linguistics*, 31, 205–225.

Schmitt, D. and Schmitt, N. (2005). *Focus on Vocabulary: Mastering the academic word list*. New York: Pearson Longman Education.

Schmitt, D. and Schmitt, N. (2011). *Focus on Vocabulary 2: Mastering the academic word list*. New York: Pearson Longman Education.

Simpson-Vlach, R. and Ellis, N. (2010). An Academic Formulas List: New methods in phraseology research. *Applied Linguistics*, 31, 4, 487–512.

Sinclair, J. (2004). *Trust the Text*. London: Routledge.

Sinclair, J. and Renouf, A. (1988). A lexical syllabus for language learning, in R. Carter and M. McCarthy (eds.) *Vocabulary and Language Teaching*. London: Longman, 140–160.

Szudarski, P. (2012). Lexical syllabus, in C. Chapelle (ed.) *The Encyclopedia of Applied Linguistics*. Oxford and New York: Wiley-Blackwell. http://onlinelibrary.wiley.com/doi/10.1002/9781405198431.wbeal0696/full.

Szudarski, P. and Carter, R. (2016). The role of input enhancement and input flood in the acquisition of collocations by EFL learners. *International Journal of Applied Linguistics*, 26, 2, 245–265.

Timmis, I. (2015). *Corpus Linguistics for ELT: Research and practice*. London and New York: Routledge.

Vaughan, E. (2010). How can teachers use a corpus for their own research?, in A. O'Keeffe M. McCarthy (eds.) *The Routledge Handbook of Corpus Linguistics*. London and New York: Routledge, 471–484.

Walter, E. (2010). Using a corpus to write dictionaries, in A. O'Keeffe and M. McCarthy (eds.) *The Routledge Handbook of Corpus Linguistics*. London and New York: Routledge, 426–443.

Willis, D. (1990). *The Lexical Syllabus: A new approach to language teaching*. London: Harper Collins.

Willis, D. and Willis, J. (1988). *Collins COBUILD English Course*. London: Collins COBUILD.

Yoon, H. and Hirvela, A. (2004). ESL student attitudes towards corpus use in L2 writing. *Journal of Second Language Writing*, 13, 4, 257–283.

Zareva, A. (2017). Incorporating corpus literacy skills into TESOL teacher training. *ELT Journal*, 71, 1, 69–79.

Chapter 7

Corpora and learner vocabulary

7.1 Learner language

Learner language is "the oral or written language produced by learners" (Ellis and Barkhuizen 2005: 4) and it is one of the major topics in the field of second language acquisition (SLA). Research in this area revolves around the key notion of interlanguage. Selinker (1972) was one of the first authors to suggest that learner language emerges during the course of learning and needs to be seen as a system with its own structure. As Tarone (2015) explains, learner language should be perceived as a dynamic process and it is characterized by a set of distinctive features. This means that the linguistic output produced by second language (L2) learners deserves to be studied as a notion in its own right rather than being explored through comparisons with expert performance and treated as an imperfect imitation of native-speaker norms.

According to Barlow (2005), the way the system of interlanguage evolves depends on a number of factors and these include: L1 transfer, learner strategies, paths of development, input quality and genre/register influences. There exists a large body of SLA research which explores the impact of these factors on the quality of the language used by learners. However, as Gilquin (2015: 9) states, many earlier studies were based on relatively small sets of data and it was not until the advent of learner corpora that more systematic analyses of L2 learners' linguistic performance became possible. In other words, it can be said that learner corpora as sources of insights into learner language have opened up new possibilities by providing us with a wide range of powerful research techniques.

7.2 Characteristics of learner corpora

Learner corpora can be defined as electronic collections of language data produced by L2 learners and, as underlined by Granger, Gilquin and Meunier (2015), they are a useful tool for investigating a variety of issues related to the process of language acquisition. First, learner corpora allow different kinds of automated manipulations of data, which speeds up the analysis and enables new avenues of research into the nature of interlanguage. As stated by Cobb and Horst (2015: 205), thanks to learner corpora it is possible to conduct more refined searches of learner language and produce better descriptions of their changing competence at the level of grammar, lexicon and other linguistic aspects. What is more, because learner corpora are large collections of data containing millions of words, "they are arguably more representative than smaller data samples involving a limited number of learners" (Granger et al. 2015: 1). This increases the robustness of findings and makes the study of learner production more systematic (Cobb and Horst 2015). Finally, what is particularly useful about learner corpora is error annotation; that is, detailed information about the types of errors that are frequently found in learner data. Such additional information allows us to make comparisons between the samples of language produced by L2 learners representing different L1 backgrounds. In light of these arguments, it is not surprising that learner corpus research is quickly developing as a new strand within corpus linguistics (see Granger et al. (2015) for a useful summary) and the aim of the following paragraphs is to discuss the usefulness of learner data from the perspective of vocabulary studies. Given that a comprehensive overview is beyond the scope of this book (see Pravec 2002), we will only describe the most notable examples of learner corpora.

One of the most commonly used learner corpora is the International Corpus of Learner English (ICLE). The corpus was developed by Granger and her colleagues (Granger et al. 2002) from the Centre for English Corpus Linguistics at Université catholique de Louvain in Belgium, a leading research center in the area of learner corpora, and it consists of 3.7 million words of written language (argumentative essays) produced by learners of English from sixteen countries (http://www.uclouvain.be/en-cecl-icle.html). What is more, ICLE has a spoken counterpart, the Louvain International Database of Spoken English Interlanguage (LINDSEI), which consists of 1,100,000 words (interview data) collected from learners from eleven countries (http://www.uclouvain.be/en-cecl-lindsei.html). Another corpus compiled at Louvain is the Longitudinal Database of Learner English (LONGDALE) and it is composed of learner data collected over three years (http://www.uclouvain.be/en-cecl-longdale.html). Such data are of particular value because longitudinal corpora contain data collected over long periods of time and therefore they allow more robust analyses of changes in learners' use of language as they improve their L2 proficiency. Lastly, Magali Paquot from the Centre for English Corpus Linguistics is leading a project on the development of the Varieties of English for Specific Purposes Database (VESPA) corpus (http://www.uclouvain.be/en-cecl-vespa.html). This is a specialized corpus of learner English collected from across a broad range of academic disciplines, genres and different L1 backgrounds.

Another example of a learner corpus is the International Corpus of Crosslinguistic Interlanguage developed by Tono et al. (2012). The corpus represents the writing of primary school to pre-university learners of English across different proficiency levels and L1 backgrounds (http://cblle.tufs.ac.jp/llc/icci/search.php?menulang=en). It is also worth mentioning the International Corpus Network of Asian Learners of English (Ishikawa 2015). The corpus is a collection of written and spoken data collected from learners of English in ten countries in Asia (http://language.sakura.ne.jp/icnale/online.html). Another large database is the Cambridge Learner Corpus, a multimillion-word collection of learner English collected by Cambridge University Press (CUP) as part of their ongoing work on the Cambridge English Corpus (http://www.cambridge. org/about-us/what-we-do/cambridge-english-corpus). So far, access to this corpus has been limited only to individuals working for CUP. However, recently it was announced that the learner corpus will be released as an open-source tool and a large part of the data (over 4 million words) will be made available through Sketch Engine (Barker and Grieves 2016). Given the amount and diversity of the data, the fact that individual users (e.g. language teachers) will be able to use this corpus free of charge needs to be seen as an excellent opportunity to produce better corpus-based descriptions of learner English.

Task 7.1: Check interfaces of the learner corpora described in this section and compare their functionalities. Which of these corpora suit your needs and how could you use them for research/teaching purposes?

7.3 Learner vocabulary

As indicated in the section above, learner corpus research is a vibrant area of study and researchers working in this area have explored different features of language including grammar, vocabulary, phonology and pragmatics, to name just a few. Considering the purposes of this book, the following sections focus on vocabulary and point to examples of the use of learner corpora as a way of gaining insights into L2 learners' lexical competence.

7.3.1 Contrastive interlanguage analysis

One of the most popular ways of analyzing learner data is contrastive interlanguage analysis (CIA), an approach originated by Granger (1996, 2002, 2015a). Its main aim is to uncover typical features of learner language by juxtaposing it with expert (usually native-speaker) user corpora. Examples of such expert corpora that you can access are corpora of proficient student writing such as the Michigan Corpus of Academic Spoken English (MICASE) or British Academic Written English Corpus (BAWE) (see Chapter 2 for details).

Such collections of expert language use serve as benchmarks against which learner production can be assessed. More specifically, a large part of learner corpus research has focused on exploring learners' overuse, underuse and misuse of specific language features (e.g. discourse markers or multiword units). A good illustration of this kind of analysis is Laufer and Waldman's (2011) study of English as a foreign language (EFL) learners' collocational competence. The authors compiled a corpus of written language (300,000 words produced by Israeli learners of English at different proficiency levels) and compared it with LOCNESS, a corpus of young adult native speakers. Their analysis revealed that, irrespective of the proficiency level, learners used far fewer collocations than native speakers and even at the advanced levels collocational errors continued to persist. Interestingly, similar problems with the use of L2 collocations were reported by other authors. For instance, relying on a corpus of essays written by L1 German learners of English, Nesselhauf (2005) demonstrated that L2 users' production of collocations was much less varied than that of native speakers, with many learners showing a tendency to overuse a small set of lexical teddy bears (Hasselgren 1994). Nesselhauf also analyzed different types of errors that were made by L2 learners and found that one of the key factors that accounted for a large number of miscollocations (e.g. 'make homework' instead of 'do home-work') was a negative transfer from German.

Task 7.2: Using the ICNALE online interface (http://language.sakura.ne.jp/icnale/online.html), look for examples of collocations with the verb 'make'. Try to find examples produced by different L1 groups of Asian learners of English. Can you find any collocations that differ from the production of native speakers?

Another form of CIA research that has been highly popular is making comparisons between samples of language produced by learners from different L1 back-grounds (e.g. linguistic output produced by L1 French and L1 German learners of English). This approach is particularly useful for establishing whether mis-takes that characterize L2 learners' output result from crosslinguistic differences between specific languages or whether they represent more universal invariants found across different L1 populations (Granger 2015a). As Gilquin et al. (2007: 323) note, "one important finding emerging from learner corpus-based studies in general and EAP in particular is that some of the linguistic features that character-ize learner language are shared by learners from a wide range of mother tongue backgrounds". Cobb and Horst (2015) add that such CIA comparisons are also amenable to analyzing the impact of age, proficiency level, task conditions and other factors on the use of particular words and longer lexical units by L2 learners. Interestingly, there is already some learner corpus work which has investigated the effects of these factors on the development of L2 phraseology. For instance, Leńko-Szymańska (2014) has found that for younger (teenage) EFL learners, proficiency seems to be a key element that influences the acquisition of lexical bundles, while Paquot (2013, 2014) provides evidence for the active role of L1 in L2 learners' use of such multiword units.

A convincing demonstration of CIA research that compares learners from different L1 backgrounds is Altenberg and Granger's (2001) investigation of the use of the verb 'make' by EFL learners. The authors chose this verb as representative of a group of frequent English verbs that often become delexicalized when they form collocations (e.g. 'make a contribution' or 'make progress'). To study the distribution of such collocations in L2 students' writing, Altenberg and Granger analyzed data produced by advanced Swedish and French learners of English and juxtaposed it with native-speaker performance. Their results revealed that even at the advanced level of proficiency the use of phraseological patterns around 'make' caused difficulty for the learners. What is more, since similar tendencies were observed across the two groups of learners, the authors suggested that, even though L1 transfer is a major factor influencing L2 learners' use of collocations, other factors should be explored as well. For instance, it is important to consider the impact of the context of learning and the role of proficiency effects, for they might have a bearing on the quality of learners' lexical output (see Granger 2015a for more details).

At the same time, however, it needs to be stated that despite its popularity, the CIA methodology has also been called into question. Specifically, some scholars criticize it for being confined to the dichotomous native vs. non-native view of language performance. As Hunston (2002: 211) notes, learner corpus research might take it for granted that "learners have native-speaker norms as a target". Trying to defend the premises of CIA, Granger (2015a: 13–14) states that not only learner corpus research but also many other SLA studies compare learners of different proficiency levels against native-speaker performance as an underlying norm. In a similar vein, Huat (2012: 195) explains that comparing learners and native speakers does not necessarily mean that learner language is "a deficient version of that of an idealized monolingual native speaker". Rather, interlanguage should be perceived as an independent linguistic system and consequently investigated as a separate construct.

What is more, Granger (2015a) makes it clear that the terms 'overuse' and 'underuse' should be treated as neutral notions. As maintained by Gilquin and Paquot (2008: 38), these are descriptive rather than prescriptive terms and "they merely refer to the fact that a linguistic form is found significantly more or less in the learner corpus than in the reference corpus". Consequently, if we approach native-speaker corpora from this perspective, they are treated as baselines for making comparisons rather than universal norms of ultimate attainment set for all L2 learners (irrespective of their individual needs). Further, in a recent reappraisal of the field, Granger (2015a: 17) takes note of "the strong variationist trend that characterizes current language studies" and introduces a revisited version of the CIA methodology. Namely, the author puts forward the notion of Reference Language Varieties (RLV) that encapsulate not only British and American English but also varieties that come from countries where English is spoken as a second language (e.g. India or the Philippines). Finally, the use of English as a lingua franca (see below for more details) can serve as a model and a point of reference for the analysis and assessment of learner language. It is an original proposal, which shows that relying on the traditional native vs. non-native dichotomy is not necessarily the only viable option available to us. As aptly summarized by McCarthy (2016: 110),

> the evidence from corpora levels the playing field between native users and expert non-native users of the language, with native users having no greater claim to objectivity in observation of how they use their language than the keen non-native observer.

7.3.2 English as a lingua franca (ELF) corpora

English as a lingua franca (ELF) is a new research paradigm which focuses on the global status of English and its increasing use as a preferred tool for communication among speakers from different L1 backgrounds (see Jenkins 2015 for more details). As stated by Seidlhofer (2012: 137), ELF "is not a language or variety as such but a linguistic resource" that should be studied in its own right rather than being perceived as a deviant version of the English used by native speakers. In view of this definition, ELF constitutes an important linguistic phenomenon and in recent years there has been a growing interest in this topic. Crucially for the purposes of this book, some work in this area has been based on corpus data and the following paragraphs seek to describe some examples of corpora representing the use of English in ELF contexts.

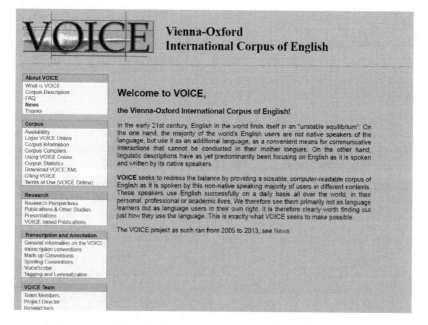

Figure 7.1 Interface of the VOICE corpus

The first ELF corpus to be discussed is the VOICE corpus (https://www.univie.ac.at/voice/), which was developed at the University of Vienna. The corpus is based on recordings of face-to-face interactions in educational, leisure and professional settings, and consequently it has been employed to explore the use of English in these contexts. Figure 7.1 displays the interface of the VOICE corpus.

Another useful example is the ELFA corpus (http://www.helsinki.fi/englanti/elfa/elfacorpus), which consists of spoken academic data recorded in university contexts including lectures, seminars, presentations and conference discussions. The corpus is freely available to anyone who is interested in the use of international English for academic purposes. Interestingly, in light of the success of this project, Anna Mauranen and her team from the University of Helsinki have also built a written corpus of academic ELF texts. The corpus is called the Corpus of Written English as a Lingua Franca in Academic Settings or WrELFA (http://www.helsinki.fi/englanti/elfa/wrelfa.html) and it comprises 1.5 million words which represent three text types: unedited research papers, PhD examiner reports and research blogs. To illustrate how ELF corpus data can be employed to analyze the use of vocabulary, we will briefly discuss Carey's (2013) study into academic phraseology.

Using data from the ELFA, a preliminary version of the WrELFA (around 300,000 words) and the MICASE (which served as a benchmark of native-speaker production) which served as a benchmark of native-speaker production, Carey (2013) investigated the use of conventional vs. approximate forms of chunks. The author focused on the frequency of multiword discourse markers (e.g. 'from my point of view' or 'so to speak') and how they were distributed across spoken and written ELF discourse. His analysis pointed to some interesting examples of unconventional or approximate forms of chunks (e.g. 'in my point of view' or 'on my point of view'), with the rate of their frequency being similar across both sets of the ELF data. However, on the whole such approximations were in the minority because many examples of the chunks identified by Carey were perfectly acceptable phraseological items and did not differ from the phraseology produced by L1 users. This suggests that at least in this sample the output produced by ELF speakers was not very different from the language of native speakers. Of course, these are only preliminary findings but given the growing interest in the use of ELF, you may consider conducting a similar kind of analysis and contribute to a better understanding of the use of vocabulary by speakers of English as a global language.

Task 7.3: Using the Asian Corpus of English (http://corpus.ied.edu.hk/ace/index.php?m=search&a=index), find examples of the use of two discourse markers: 'from my point of view' and 'so to speak'. Are these conventional or approximate forms of chunks?

7.3.3 Learner corpora and tracking L2 lexical growth

As discussed in Chapter 3, lexical knowledge is a multifaceted construct that is conceptualized in a number of ways, with vocabulary size, or the number of words known in a given language, being one of the most prevalent operationalizations. In fact, approaching the construct of vocabulary from this perspective has had important implications for research into lexical growth as most work in this area has taken the form of treatment studies exploring the effects of different interventions on L2 learners' vocabulary gains (Schmitt 2010). However, while cross-sectional studies (data collected at a given point in time) are informative, what is really needed to delve into the mechanics of mastering L2 lexis is longitudinal research < that is, longer experiments which follow learners over extended periods of time and explore how their lexical competence changes as they increase their overall language proficiency. Unfortunately, few vocabulary studies are based on longitudinal data (see Schmitt (1998) or Horst and Collins (2006) for notable exceptions) because carrying out this kind of research presents certain challenges. Namely, as Schmitt (2010) explains, longitudinal studies are more time-consuming as they require more complicated designs and more involvement from participants. Luckily, the situation can be remedied by the use of learner corpora, which can be usefully employed for tracking the lexical growth of L2 learners (e.g. Levitzky-Aviad and Laufer 2013). With the growing availability of computerized collections of learner language, more and more studies can benefit from corpus techniques and gain insights into the process of developing L2 lexicon. The following paragraphs aim to provide you with some examples of such research.

The first study to be described is Siyanova-Chanturia's (2015) investigation of the use of adjective-noun collocations by L1 Chinese learners of beginner Italian. The learners attended an intensive language program at a university in Italy. To analyze changes in their collocational competence, the author compiled a corpus of their writing (17,912 words). The corpus consisted of short compositions (150–200 words) written at three different points during the program (after seven, fourteen and twenty-one weeks of learning), which allowed the author to take a longitudinal perspective. The corpus analysis revealed that over the course of five months the learners' production improved in that the essays they wrote at the end of the language program contained more examples of higher-frequency and strongly associated (high mutual information (MI) scores) collocations. In other words, the learners' use of L2 collocations became more idiomatic when it was compared to the production of native speakers. These findings can be interpreted as evidence of the learners' phraseological development and they also suggest that L2 phraseological competence can be improved even during the early stages of the language acquisition process.

Another study based on learner corpus data is Bestgen and Granger (2014). The authors used the Michigan State University Corpus of English made up of student essays to explore the phraseological growth of L2 learners. In total, 171 essays written by fifty-seven ESL university-age learners were selected and all of the texts were rated twice (at several months' interval) by two experts. With a view to analyzing changes in the learners' phraseology, the authors employed an innovative method called the CollGram technique. This is an automated approach which uses data from a reference corpus (the COCA Corpus) to assign three scores to each bigram (a pair of contiguous words) found in the learners' essays. These three scores are a mean MI score, a mean T-score and a proportion of bigrams that are absent from the reference corpus. As Bestgen and Granger (2014: 31) emphasize, these measures "quantify the collocational strength of each text" produced by the learners, which allows them to assess the quality of the output from L2 learners. A longitudinal analysis of the first and last essays revealed improvement in the learners' writing. But this was observed only in relation to high-frequency collocations identified on the basis of T-scores (e.g. 'it is' or 'out of') because low-frequency collocations with high MI scores (e.g. 'toxic substances' or 'bulletin board'), which are a typical feature of native writing, were not statistically different. This confirms earlier research (e.g. Durrant and Schmitt 2009) suggesting that L2 users tend to overuse higher-frequency collocations with high T-scores but underuse lower-frequency items with high MI scores. However, a different picture emerged when Bestgen and Granger (2014) computed correlations between the ratings of the essays and the three scores of collocational strength. Only the MI scores correlated significantly with the quality of the essays, which suggests that strongly associated collocations whose MI scores are high are likely to have an influence on raters' judgment of learner language.

It is worth adding that in a subsequent study, Granger and Bestgen (2014) employed the same CollGram methodology to study differences between the phraseological competence of intermediate and advanced EFL learners. Using data from 223 texts taken from the ICLE corpus, the authors found a clear difference in the use of collocations between advanced and intermediate learners. The former employed more lower-frequency, strongly associated collocations than the latter and therefore the higher-proficiency learners can be said to produce more native-like output. Granger and Bestgen (2014: 248) conclude that since a mixture of high- and low-frequency collocations characterizes the phraseological competence of L2 learners, it is important to combine both measures of collocational strength so that it is "possible to highlight two aspects of phraseology, each of which appears to play a part in foreign language acquisition". In short, all of these studies point to the value of learner corpora as a powerful tool for tracking L2 lexical and phraseological growth.

7.4 Learner vocabulary, language learning and assessment

The field of language testing and assessment (LTA) deals with "measuring the language proficiency of individuals in a variety of contexts and for a range of purposes, assessing language knowledge, performance or application"

(Barker 2010: 633). In recent years language testing specialists have become increasingly interested in the use of corpora for developing valid and reliable measures of proficiency. This is particularly true for learner corpora which "present an option to inform, supplement and possibly advance the way proficiency is operationalized" (Callies, Diez-Bedmar and Zaytseva 2014: 74). In a useful account of research in this area, Callies and his colleagues distinguish between three main groups of applications of learner corpora in LTA:

- corpus-informed applications (corpus data are used as evidence that informs the content of tests and the validation of human ratings)
- corpus-based applications (corpus data are used as evidence for the identification of distinct features and/or descriptors for proficiency levels)
- corpus-driven applications (learner data are used to assess L2 proficiency, with no a priori assumptions being made and learner corpora serving as a basis for data-driven analyses).

This classification reflects the major theoretical divisions within corpus linguistics which we have already discussed in Chapter 2 (corpus-driven vs. corpus-based approaches). However, Callies and Götz (2015) rightly point out that in practice there is often a lot of overlap between different approaches and consequently drawing clear-cut distinctions in terms of how corpora inform LTA is not always necessary. What is of higher importance is that learner data can be used throughout various stages of the lifecycle of a language test (Barker 2010: 639).

Naturally there are also certain challenges associated with the use of learner corpora for testing purposes. Referring to these issues, Callies, Diez-Bedmar and Zaytseva (2014: 77) state that the usefulness of corpus-based analysis for language testing is dependent both on the quality of the information that a corpus provides and how the data are analyzed and interpreted. By way of illustration, if you have access to a learner corpus which is composed of exam scripts collected from learners at different proficiency levels, it is critical that you consider factors such as task features and test settings as they are likely to have had an impact on the language stored in the corpus. Thus it is important that if you decide to use corpus data for the purpose of writing test items, you should also take into account how the contexts in which the learner data were collected "may have influenced the language contained in the corpus and whether such language use is relevant for the analysis at hand" (Callies, Diez-Bedmar and Zaytseva 2014: 77). In what follows I describe details of the English Profile Project, which is a useful demonstration of how learner corpora can inform the development of resources useful for language learning, teaching and testing.

7.4.1 English Profile Project and Common European Framework

The English Profile Project or EPP (http://www.englishprofile.org/) is a collaborative and interdisciplinary research program based on the Cambridge Learner Corpus, a large corpus of more than 55 million words taken from Cambridge examination scripts. As McCarthy (2016: 101) explains, the project brings together a number of institutions involved in language education and aims to fulfill two goals. The first one is to describe characteristics of learner English in terms of what learners can and cannot do with the language at six proficiency levels of the Common European Framework of Reference for Languages or CEFR scale (Council of Europe 2001). The other goal of the EPP is to obtain corpus evidence that will serve as a basis for the description of learner English. The CEFR is a highly influential model of communicative competence that uses 'can-do' or functional statements as a way of describing learners' language proficiency. It consists of six main levels: two basic levels (A1 and A2), two intermediate levels (B1 and B2) and two proficient levels (C1 and C2). These six sublevels have been envisioned as a proficiency scale and they seek to reflect learners' trajectory as they make progress in a foreign/second language. The CEFR framework is descriptive in nature and it is language-independent, which means that it can be used to describe L2 competence in different languages and irrespective of where they are learned.

As far as the role of corpora within the EPP is concerned, they serve as a source of empirical evidence of learner English at different levels of proficiency (McCarthy 2016). Of note is the fact that the EPP is divided into two main parts: the English Vocabulary Profile or EVP (http://www.englishprofile.org/wordlists) and the English Grammar Profile or EGP (http://www.englishprofile.org/english-

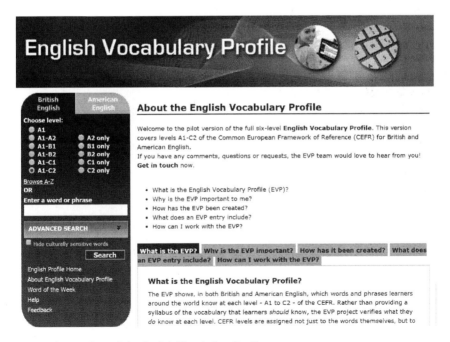

Figure 7.2 Interface of the English Vocabulary Profile

grammar-profile). Both of them are useful teaching resources that can be accessed free of charge by registering on the website of the project (see Figure 7.2 for the vocabulary interface). For instance, when it comes to practical applications, the EVP can be used to identify words and phrases that are typical of a specific proficiency level on the CEFR scale. To show you the usefulness of the tool, Figures 7.3 and 7.4 present examples of idioms that represent the language at the B2 level. Interestingly, the same search for American English yields fewer examples (only eight idioms), which shows that even at the same proficiency level (B2) learners of specific varieties of English might exhibit certain differences in their use of vocabulary.

It is worth adding that the EVP website contains a special tool called Text Inspector (http://www.englishprofile.org/wordlists/text-inspector) that enables you to upload different texts and analyze their lexical difficulty by showing their content at different levels of the CEFR.

Task 7.4: Imagine you are teaching a group of intermediate students (B1) and are planning your class. Select any text from the Internet you would like to use and analyze its lexical difficulty by means of the Text Inspector tool. Which phrases are you going to focus on? How are you going to practice them?

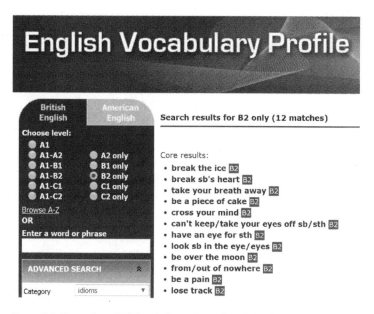

Figure 7.3 Examples of B2-level idioms from British English

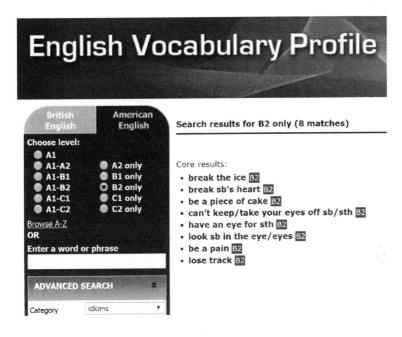

Figure 7.4 Examples of B2-level idioms from American English

As a last point in this section, I will describe a recent study by Leńko-Szymańska (2015) based on the EVP. Exploring the functionality of the EVP, the author used it as a tool for assessing samples of learner language. This exploratory study is one of the first attempts at determining whether EVP-based ratings of learner texts can be employed to assign learner output to specific CEFR proficiency levels. Drawing on data from the International Corpus of Crosslinguistic Interlanguage (ninety essays written by Austrian, Polish and Spanish learners of English), the author asked human raters to mark L2 learners' essays according to the CEFR proficiency descriptors. Statistical analyses revealed strong positive correlations between clusters of essays (grouped according to their lexical features) and the global CEFR levels assigned to them by human raters. This confirms that EVP-based descriptions of learner texts can be a good measure of learners' overall proficiency and reflect progression through different stages of interlanguage development. However, while this methodology holds a lot of potential, it also carries some risk of circularity as the EVP itself is based on human ratings. What is more, Leńko-Szymańska (2015) admits that the manual assignment of essays to specific levels is laborious and time-consuming and therefore more research into the EVP is encouraged so that it can be "converted into an automatic or semi-automatic tagging tool" and render the assessment process a more manageable task.

7.4.2 Phraseology as a token of L2 proficiency

It is important to state that L2 growth can also be assessed at the level of phraseology and the use of formulaic sequences can be treated as a marker of proficiency and fluency (Bartsch 2004). As discussed by Paquot and Granger (2012), increased L2 proficiency is often linked with a more native-like co-selection of lexical units. One way of capturing this process is tracking the phraseological development of L2 learners and consequently there is a call for more efforts to compile corpora that represent different proficiency levels (Ebeling and Hasselgard 2015: 216). Ideally these should be longitudinal corpora as a better understanding of SLA can be gained only through the analysis of longitudinal data which manifest the language produced by the same learners over longer periods of time (Myles 2008).

Chen and Baker's (2016) recent study is a good illustration of how L2 phraseological knowledge can be explored by means of corpora. Drawing on data from the Longman Learner Corpus, the scholars explored the frequency of lexical bundles in the language produced by L2 learners. The aim of the study was to determine whether lexical bundles as important elements of discourse competence can serve as criterial features which distinguish between different proficiency levels (B1, B2 and C1 of CEFR). According to Hawkins and Filipovic (2012: 11), such criterial features denote certain linguistic properties of learner language that are "characteristic and indicative of L2 proficiency at each of the CEFR levels and that distinguish high levels from lower levels". Chen and Baker's analysis provided an interesting set of results: lower-proficiency students' use of lexical bundles was more similar to the language of conversation (e.g. language that is more personal, exhibits features of informality and relies on colloquialisms), while higher-proficiency students' output resembled academic language in the sense that it was impersonal and contained more nominal components. On the basis of these results, Chen and Baker (2016: 877) argue that B2 is "the stage that starts to show signs of transition, whereby learners begin to grasp the distinction between formal and informal writing" (see Table 7.1 for examples of lexical bundles at the three levels).

Interestingly, in terms of differences between the specific levels of proficiency, B2 bundles were seen as more interactive and conversational, while C1 bundles resembled the style of formal writing, which partially results from the different

Table 7.1 Examples of lexical bundles at different CEFR levels (based on Chen and Baker 2016)

Bundles common to all three levels	Bundles at B1 level	Bundles at B2 level	Bundles at C1 level
on the other hand	if you want to	a lot of problem(s)	it is obvious that
at the same time	is very important for	a lot of time	as well as the
for a long time	I hope I can	it is also a	it is believed that

pragmatic roles that chunks play (see Chapter 9 for more details). The study thus confirms the importance of formulaicity in assessing the overall linguistic skills of L2 learners as they progress through different proficiency levels. As Chen and Baker (2016: 877) rightly point out, "there exist distinctive pragmatic and stylistic developmental features across proficiencies" and given that such information is missing from the CEFR, more fine-grained proficiency descriptors are needed to better understand and describe the ways in which phraseology serves as a marker of L2 proficiency. Evidence for this can be found in O'Donnell et al. (2013) who investigated the use of formulaic sequences (identified on the basis of four different corpus measures) in the language produced by native and non-native speakers of English at different levels of proficiency (graduate vs. undergraduate students). Their study revealed that while different operationalizations of formulaic language led to different patterns of results, L2 writers tend to use fewer examples of chunks than native speakers and higher-proficiency graduate students exhibit a more native-like behavior than lower-proficiency undergraduate students. This shows therefore that phraseological competence can be treated as a token of L2 proficiency and, as stated above, assessing students' L2 development by means of learner corpora has much to offer in relation to both the theory and practice of SLA.

7.5 Learner corpora and materials development

Another important area where learner corpora can be usefully applied is the design of language teaching materials (Meunier and Reppen 2015). In her recent account of the use of learner corpora in language pedagogy, Granger (2015b: 486) distinguishes between the direct and indirect applications. Similarly to our discussion in Chapter 6, the direct use of learner corpora refers to data-driven learning (DDL) or hands-on experimentation with corpus data (by both teachers and learners), while the indirect use involves the collection and analysis of learner corpora with a view to developing teaching materials, dictionaries and other pedagogic pedagogical resources (e.g. Liu, Wible and Tsao 2011).

Unfortunately, despite all the benefits of learner corpora that have been emphasized throughout this chapter, it needs to be stated that so far the impact of learner corpus research on the process of writing textbooks has been rather modest (Granger 2015b). For instance, both Harwood (2005) and Burton (2012) have identified a lack of fit between natural language represented in corpora and textbook language found in contemporary textbooks. As discussed in Chapter 6, it appears that in spite of the wealth of corpus findings as well as the growing number of large, open-access corpora, textbook writers still rely on intuition as the main criterion for which vocabulary is included in teaching materials and which words are prioritized in language education.

These arguments notwithstanding, it needs to be said that the situation is gradually improving and there are certain signs that more and more materials designers turn to corpora for guidance about the specific nature of learner English. An encouraging example of this is the presence of frequent usage notes or error warnings in some textbooks and dictionaries, whose aim is to raise students' awareness of the most problematic lexical items. For instance, Lu and Wei (2016) argue that including examples of misused phraseology in collocation dictionaries could improve learners' phraseological competence. In turn, elaborating on this issue, Granger (2015b) argues that errors should not be the only aspect of learner corpus research that feeds into the development of teaching materials. The author goes on to state that equally useful insights can be gained from corpus-based findings on learners' under- and overuse of specific lexical or grammatical features. This is in line with what we have already signaled in the earlier sections of this chapter. Namely, the study of learner language is broader than error analysis and consequently the field as a whole has to do more to translate its empirical findings into language pedagogy. As Chambers (2015: 463) rightly points out, there is "a considerable need for research into the integration of learner corpus data in language learning and teaching in ways which are feasible for teachers who are not researchers in applied linguistics". As Mukherjee and Rohrbach (2006) assert, the compilation of do-it-yourself learner corpora by teachers can serve as a solution which will link research in corpus linguistics and language teaching. One step toward accomplishing this goal is encouraging individual teachers to compile small-scale corpora of the work produced by their learners (see Chapter 6 for details). Encouragingly, the corpus literature contains an ever-increasing number of studies that show teachers who are willing to take up this challenge and engage actively with the use of learner data in the classroom (e.g. see section 7.6 for an exemplary study).

The last point to be made with reference to learner corpora is that corpus-informed materials can be particularly helpful in English for academic purposes (EAP) and English for specific purposes (ESP) contexts, where generic materials are less likely to meet the specific needs of learners. Convincing examples are provided by Jones and Durrant (2010) and Gilquin et al. (2007) who demonstrate how corpus-based analyses of learner data have successfully informed the development of teaching materials. In one of her corpus-based studies, Flowerdew (2001) also uses a small learner corpus, the Hong Kong University of Science and Technology Learner Corpus, alongside expert user corpora as a basis for the creation of EAP materials. The author explains how exercises involving the analysis of corpus data can be used to raise L2 learners' awareness of the importance of collocational patterns, pragmatic appropriateness and discourse features. At the same time, however, the study also indicates that the introduction of corpus-based materials into the classroom might lead to certain difficulties such as students' resistance to data-driven learning or the risk of them getting bored if too many exercises of this kind are used. This stresses the role of the teacher as a key element of the successful implementation of corpus-informed teaching.

In short, although learner corpus research is still a relatively new field whose findings are "scattered and therefore not easily accessible to materials designers" (Granger 2015b: 495), there is already some empirical evidence pointing to the usefulness and relevance of learner corpora in relation to the development of teaching materials. Considering the growing availability of such corpora and the wealth of insights they can provide, you are encouraged to make use of these resources as a way of enhancing vocabulary learning and teaching.

7.6 Exemplary study: Cotos (2014) and the use of learner corpora for teaching purposes

This section describes Cotos's (2014) study as an instance of a successful attempt at employing learner corpora for improving L2 vocabulary. As Cotos (2014: 206) herself explains, the aim of the study was to explore the potential and capacity of do-it-yourself, small learner corpora for heightening the value of DDL. In a pedagogical intervention introduced by Cotos, thirty-one ESL graduate students studying at an American university were presented with corpus-based activities, the aim of which was to improve the use of linking adverbials (e.g. 'however', 'therefore', 'in addition') and, more broadly, academic writing skills. The intervention itself lasted three weeks and during this time the students completed a series of pattern discovery exercises that targeted different kinds of linking adverbials. Each student had at their disposal a corpus of research articles from their respective discipline (around 30,000 words) and their task was to analyze the use of linking adverbials when it comes to their linguistic forms, rhetoric functions and textual distribution.

As far as the methodological design of the study is concerned, Cotos relied on a number of research tools and collected data from different sources. First, the learners' academic writing was collected at three different time points: before the intervention (pre-experiment), immediately after the intervention (immediate post-experiment) and four weeks after the intervention (delayed post-experiment). This enabled the author to make comparisons in the students' writing before and after the DDL intervention was implemented. In addition, Cotos included pre- and post-tests to check the learners' knowledge of linking adverbials. Each time, the students were given two tests which involved identifying different cohesive devices in excerpts of academic writing and completing a multiple-choice classification task. All of the tested adverbials were selected from the corpus used during the intervention. Finally, to tap into the students' perceptions of DDL, Cotos administered two open-ended questionnaires, administered before and after the implementation of the intervention.

Perhaps the most innovative aspect of the study was the fact that both native-speaker and learner data were used as a basis for DDL. The students were divided into two groups: the native-speaker corpus group (sixteen students) and the learner corpus group (fifteen students). While the former explored the use of linking adverbials only on the basis of native-speaker data (that is, original research articles), the latter were given both native-speaker and learner data (that is, their own writing stored in the corpus). It is commendable that Cotos decided to include examples from the learners' writing as a source of insights into the structure of academic writing as this shows how learner corpus data can be included in the process of language instruction. This methodological solution also allowed her to compare the effectiveness of these two different approaches and given the lack of research in this area, the study can serve as a source of inspiration for language practitioners.

The results of the study revealed that both groups of students increased their knowledge of linking adverbials, which provided evidence in favor of the effectiveness of DDL as a way of improving L2 writing skills. Interestingly, when the results of the native-speaker corpus group and the learner corpus group were compared, the latter performed better, with the learner output exhibiting a varied and more appropriate use of linking adverbials. What is more, the positive effects of DDL were also corroborated by the analysis of the questionnaires. On the whole, the students supported the inclusion of corpus data in the teaching process and, perhaps most importantly, the use of examples from their own writing was perceived as a strong motivator for further work on their writing skills. Not only did the corpus samples help the students notice inaccuracies in their output, but the analysis of their own essays also seems to have contributed to their increased involvement in the learning process as a whole. This of course does not mean that examples from the native-speaker data were not helpful, as many students from the native-speaker corpus group pointed to the writing of L1 writers as a model for their learning. However, the successful implementation of the learner corpus data needs to be highlighted because it indicates that "the use of local learner corpora combined with native-speaker corpora can strengthen DDL instruction" (Cotos 2014: 203).

Summary

In this chapter we have discussed the importance of learner corpora as a powerful tool for studying learner vocabulary. We started by describing features of such corpora and types of methodologies that can be applied to analyze learner data. Subsequently, we presented a number of ways in which learner corpora can facilitate research into L2 lexical learning as well as tracking L2 learners' lexical development over time. Finally, we have explained how learner corpora can be usefully applied to assess learner language and develop teaching materials.

References

Altenberg, B. and Granger, S. (2001). The grammatical and lexical patterning of MAKE in native and non-native student writing. *Applied Linguistics*, 22, 2, 173–195.

Barker, F. (2010). How can corpora be used in language testing?, in A. O'Keeffe, A. and M. McCarthy (eds.) *The Routledge Handbook of Corpus Linguistics*. London and New York: Routledge, 633–645.

Barker, F. and Grieves, S. (2016). Using learner data in Cambridge English – The CLC: Past, present and future. Paper presented at the 10th Anniversary English Profile Seminar Cambridge, 5 February 2016.

Barlow, M. (2005). Computer-based analyses of learner language, in R. Ellis and G. Barkhuizen (eds.) *Analysing Learner Language*. Oxford: Oxford University Press, 335–358.

Bartsch, S. (2004). *Structural and Functional Properties of Collocations in English: A corpus study of lexical and pragmatic constraints on lexical co-occurrence*. Tübingen: Narr.

Bestgen, Y. and Granger, S. (2014). Quantifying the development of phraseological competence in L2 English writing: An automated approach. *Journal of Second Language Writing*, 26, 28–41.

Burton, G. (2012.) Corpora and coursebooks: Destined to be strangers forever? *Corpora*, 7, 1, 91–108.

Callies, M., Diez-Bedmar M. B and Zaytseva, E. (2014). Using learner corpora for testing and assessing L2 proficiency, in P. Leclerq, H. Hilton and A. Edmonds (eds.) *Measuring L2 Proficiency: Perspectives from SLA*. Clevedon: Multilingual Matters, 71–90.

Callies, M. and Götz, S. (2015). Learner corpora in language testing and assessment: Prospects and challenges, in M. Callies and S. Götz (eds.) *Learner Corpora in Language Testing and Assessment*. Amsterdam/Philadelphia: John Benjamins, 1–9.

Carey, R. (2013). On the other side: Formulaic organizing chunks in spoken and written academic ELF. *Journal of English as a Lingua Franca*, 2, 2, 207–228.

Chambers, A. (2015). The learner corpus as a pedagogic corpus, in S. Granger, G. Gilquin and F. Meunier (eds.) *The Cambridge Handbook of Learner Corpus Linguistics*. Cambridge: Cambridge University Press, 445–464.

Chen, Y.-H. and Baker, P. (2016). Investigating criterial discourse features across second language development: Lexical bundles in rated learner essays, CEFR B1, B2 and C1. *Applied Linguistics*, 37, 6, 849–880.

Cobb, T. and Horst, M. (2015). Learner corpora and lexis, in S. Granger, G. Gilquin and F. Meunier (eds.) *The Cambridge Handbook of Learner Corpus Linguistics*. Cambridge: Cambridge University Press, 185–206.

Council of Europe (2001). *Common European Framework of Reference for Languages: Learning, teaching, assessment*. Cambridge: Cambridge University Press.

Cotos, E. (2014). Enhancing writing pedagogy with learner corpus data. *ReCALL*, 26, 2, 202–224.

Durrant, P. and Schmitt, N. (2009). To what extent do native and non-native writers make use of collocations? *IRAL International Journal of Applied Linguistics in Language Teaching*, 47, 2, 157–177.

Ebeling, S. O. and Hasselgard, H. (2015). Learner corpora and phraseology, in S. Granger, G. Gilquin and F. Meunier (eds.) *The Cambridge Handbook of Learner Corpus Research*. Cambridge: Cambridge University Press, 185–206.

Ellis, R. and Barkhuizen, G. (2005). *Analysing Learner Language*. Oxford: Oxford University Press.

Flowerdew, L. (2001). The exploitation of small learner corpora in EAP materials design, in M. Ghadessy, A. Henry and R. L. Roseberry (eds.) *Small Corpus Studies and ELT: Theory and practice*. John Benjamins: Amsterdam/Philadelphia, 363–379.

Gilmore, A. (2015). Research into practice: The influence of discourse studies on language descriptions and task design in published ELT materials. *Language Teaching*, 48, 4, 506–530.

Gilquin, G. (2015). From design to collection of learner corpora, in S. Granger, G. Gilquin and F. Meunier (eds.) *The Cambridge Handbook of Learner Corpus Research*. Cambridge: Cambridge University Press, 9–34.

Gilquin, G., Granger, S. and Paquot, M. (2007). Learner corpora: The missing link in EAP pedagogy. *Journal of English for Academic Purposes*, 6, 4, 319–335.

Gilquin, G. and Paquot, M. (2008). Too chatty: Learner Academic Writing and Register Variation. *English Text Construction*, 1, 1, 41–61.

Granger, S. (1996). From CA to CIA and back: An integrated approach to computerized bilingual and learner corpora, in K. Aijmer, B. Altenberg and M. Johansson (eds.) *Languages in Contrast: Text-based cross-linguistic studies*. Lund Studies in English 88. Lund: Lund University Press, 37–51.

Granger, S. (2002). A bird's eye view of learner corpus research, in S. Granger, J. Hung and S. Petch-Tyson (eds.) *Computer Learner Corpora, Second Language Acquisition and Foreign Language Learning*. Amsterdam and Philadelphia: John Benjamins, 3–33.

Granger, S. (2015a). Contrastive interlanguage analysis: A reappraisal. *International Journal of Learner Corpus Research*, 1, 1, 7–24.

Granger, S. (2015b). The contribution of learner corpora to reference and instructional materials design, in S. Granger, G. Gilquin and F. Meunier (eds.) *The Cambridge Handbook of Learner Corpus Research*. Cambridge: Cambridge University Press, 485–510.

Granger, S. and Bestgen, Y. (2014). The use of collocations by intermediate vs. advanced non-native writers: A bigram-based study. *IRAL International Review of Applied Linguistics in Language Teaching*, 52, 3, 229–252.

Granger, S., Dagneaux, E. and Meunier, F. (2002). *International Corpus of Learner English*. Université catholique de Louvain: Centre for English Corpus Linguistics.

Granger, S., Gilquin, G. and Meunier, M. (2015). Introduction: Learner corpus research – Past, present and future, in S. Granger, G. Gilquin and F. Meunier (eds.) *The Cambridge Handbook of Learner Corpus Research*. Cambridge: Cambridge University Press, 1–5.

Harwood, N. (2005). What do we want EAP teaching materials for? *Journal of English for Academic Purposes*, 4, 2, 149–161.

Hasselgren, A. (1994). Lexical teddy bears and advanced learners: A study into the ways Norwegian students cope with English vocabulary. *International Journal of Applied Linguistics*, 4, 237–260.

Hawkins, J. A. and Filipovic, L. (2012). *Criterial Features in L2 English: Specifying the reference levels of the Common European Framework*. English Profile Studies Volume 1. Cambridge: UCLES/Cambridge University Press.

Horst, M. and Collins, L. (2006). From faible to strong: How does their vocabulary grow? *Canadian Modern Language Review*, 63, 1, 83–106.

Huat, C. M. (2012). Learner corpora and second language acquisition, in K. Hyland, C. M. Huat and M. Handford (eds.) *Corpus Applications in Applied Linguistics*. London and New York: Continuum, 191–207.

Hunston, S. (2002). *Corpora in Applied Linguistics*. Cambridge: Cambridge University Press.

Ishikawa, S. (2015). Lexical development in L2 English learners' speeches and writings. *Procedia – Social and Behavioral Science*, 198, 202–210.

Jenkins, J. (2015). Repositioning English and multilingualism in English as a lingua franca. *Englishes in Practice*, 2, 3, 49–85.

Jones, M. and Durrant, P. (2010). What can a corpus tell us about vocabulary teaching materials?, in A. O'Keeffe, A. and M. McCarthy (eds.) *The Routledge Handbook of Corpus Linguistics*. London and New York: Routledge, 387–400.

Laufer, B. and Waldman, T. (2011). Verb-noun collocations in second language writing: A corpus analysis of learners' English. *Language Learning*, 51, 1, 647–672.

Leńko-Szymańska, A. (2014). The acquisition of formulaic language by EFL learners: A cross-sectional and cross-linguistic perspective. *International Journal of Corpus Linguistics*, 19, 2, 225–251.

Leńko-Szymańska, A. (2015). The English Vocabulary Profile as a benchmark for assigning levels to learner corpus data, in M. Callies and S. Götz (eds.) *Learner Corpora in Language Testing and Assessment*. Amsterdam/Philadelphia: John Benjamins, 115–140.

Levitzky-Aviad, T. and Laufer, B. (2013). Lexical properties in the writing of foreign language learners over eight years of study: Single words and collocations, in C. Bardel, C. Lindqvist and B. Laufer (eds.) *L2 Vocabulary Acquisition, Knowledge and Use: New perspectives on assessment and corpus analysis*. Amsterdam: Eurosla, 127–148.

Liu, A. L.-E., Wible, D. and Tsao, N.-L. (2011). A corpus-based approach to automatic feedback for learners' miscollocations, in A. Frankenberg-Garcia, L. Flowerdew and G. Aston (eds.) *New Trends in Corpora and Language Learning*. London: Continuum, 107–120.

Lu, H. and Wei, X. (2016). Towards an integrated collocation dictionary plus advanced EFL learners: Greater availability and equal accessibility. *International Journal of Lexicography*, 29, 2, 156–183.

McCarthy, M. (2016). Putting the CEFR to good use: Designing grammars based on learner-corpus evidence. *Language Teaching*, 49, 1, 99–115.

Meunier, F. and Reppen, R. (2015). Corpus versus non-corpus-informed pedagogical materials: Grammar as the focus, in D. Biber and R. Reppen (eds.) *The Cambridge Handbook of English Corpus Linguistics*. Cambridge: Cambridge University Press, 498–514.

Mukherjee, J. and Rohrbach, J.-M. (2006). Rethinking applied corpus linguistics from a language-pedagogical perspectives: New departures in learner corpus research, in B. Kettemann and G. Marko (eds.) *Planning, Gluing and Painting Corpora: Inside the applied corpus linguists' workshop*. Frankfurt: Peter Lang, 205–232.

Myles, F. (2008). Investigating learner language development with electronic longitudinal corpora: Theoretical and methodological issues, in L. Ortega and H. Byrnes (eds.) *The Longitudinal Study of Advanced L2 Capacities*. Hillsdale, NJ: Lawrence Erlbaum Associates, 58–72.

Nesselhauf, N. (2005). *Collocations in a Learner Corpus*. Amsterdam: Benjamins.

O'Donnell, M. B., Römer, U. and Ellis, N. (2013). The development of formulaic language in first and second language writing: Investigating effects of frequency, association, and native form. *International Journal of Corpus Linguistics*, 18, 1, 83–103.

Paquot, M. (2013). Lexical bundles and L1 transfer effects. *International Journal of Corpus Linguistics*, 18, 3, 391–417.

Paquot, M. (2014). Cross-linguistic influence and formulaic language: Recurrent word sequences in French learner writing, in L. Roberts, I. Vedder and J. H. Hulstijn (eds.), *EUROSLA Yearbook 14*. Amsterdam/Philadelphia: John Benjamins, 240–261.

Paquot, M. and Granger, S. (2012). Formulaic language in learner corpora. *Annual Review of Applied Linguistics*, 32, 130–149.

Pravec, N. A. (2002). Survey of learner corpora. *ICAME Journal*, 26, 81–114.

Schmitt, N. (1998). Tracking the incremental acquisition of second language vocabulary: A longitudinal study. *Language Learning*, 48, 2, 281–317.

Schmitt, N. (2010). *Researching Vocabulary: A research manual*. Basingstoke: Palgrave Macmillan.

Seidlhofer, B. (2012). Corpora and English as a lingua franca, in K. Hyland, M. H. Chau and M. Handford (eds.) *Corpus Applications in Applied Linguistics*. London and New York: Continuum, 135–149.

Selinker, L. (1972). Interlanguage. *IRAL International Review of Applied Linguistics in Language Teaching*, 10, 3, 209–231.

Siyanova-Chanturia, A. (2015). Collocation in beginner learner writing: A longitudinal study. *System*, 53, 148–160.

Tarone, E. (2015). Enduring questions from the interlanguage hypothesis, in Z. Han and E. Tarone (eds.) *Interlanguage: Forty years later.* Amsterdam/Philadelphia: John Benjamins, 8–26.

Tono, Y., Kawaguchi, Y. and Minegishi, M. (eds.) (2012). *Developmental and Crosslinguistic Perspectives in Learner Corpus Research.* Amsterdam/Philadelphia: John Benjamins.

Chapter 8

Specialized corpora and vocabulary

8.1 Specialized corpora

So far in this book we have approached corpora as large collections of linguistic material which enable thorough analyses of different aspects of language use. However, one criticism that is sometimes leveled at corpus linguistics is that it relies on general-purpose corpora composed of decontextualized data. As argued by Widdowson (2000), collating large amounts of computerized text does not enable linguists to say much about the original use of specific language features. What seems to be a solution to this problem is the notion of specialized (sometimes also called 'specialist') corpora, which are smaller collections of words built with a view to representing a particular type of discourse. As argued by Koester (2010: 67), such corpora "allow a much closer link between the corpus and the contexts in which the texts in the corpus were produced", which suggests that they are more suitable for the analysis of language use in specific target domains.

According to Flowerdew (2004), there are several parameters according to which the specialization of a corpus can be achieved: a specific purpose for compilation, contextualization, genre and type of discourse, subject matter/topic and variety of English. This implies that the degree of specialization of a corpus is likely to vary and to a large extent it is determined by the particular research questions you wish to pursue. The same is true when it comes to the size of specialized corpora. Cheng (2012: 166) notes that such corpora "can usually be measured in the thousands or low millions of words", but what matters more than their size is the purpose for which they are created. Similarly, Handford (2010) points out that some specialized corpora are large (e.g. the Cambridge and Nottingham Business English Corpus which contains a million words) but others are much smaller and comprise fewer than 100,000 words. A good illustration of this is Koester's (2006) corpus of American and British Office Talk (60,000 words). However, even though these corpora differ considerably in terms of their size, both are regarded as specialized databases because they document the use of language in specific contexts.

While a smaller size is an important feature of specialized corpora, it is by no means the only issue that needs to be considered. Other corpus design features such as the sampling and representativeness of data are equally important. This is perhaps less of a concern if you rely on professional corpora such as the British National Corpus (BNC) or Corpus of Contemporary American English (COCA); these general corpora are constructed in such a way that they are divided into sections that represent different registers of language use (e.g. academic or spoken language) and consequently each of these sections can be treated as a specialized corpus. However, if you wish to compile your own corpus of specialized language, you need to ensure it is representative of the specific type of discourse under study. Otherwise, findings based on this corpus might be biased and fail to reflect the actual variation that characterizes the type of language under study. For example, Coxhead (2000) created a corpus of academic language and used it to extract a list of academic words that predominate in academic discourse (see below for more details). However, Durrant (2014) points out that Coxhead's corpus was skewed toward two subject areas (i.e. law and commerce constituted 50% of the data) and as a result it is not a well-balanced representation of academic language.

8.2 Register and genre analysis

In the previous section, we have discussed the importance of specialized corpora and their role in studying specific kinds of data. In this section, we devote our attention to register and genre analysis as approaches which focus on variation resulting from specialized uses of language across different contexts.

Register can be defined as a kind of language associated with a particular situation of use (Biber and Conrad 2009). Since registers represent different types of communicative situations and contexts, they differ in terms of lexical, grammatical and discourse features, and a large part of corpus research is concerned with studying such register variation. Accordingly, the aim of register analysis is to identify "a set of linguistic features of the text that reflect the social context in which it is produced" (McCarthy 1991: 32). One of the most comprehensive register-specific descriptions of English is Biber et al.'s (1999) Longman Grammar of Spoken and Written English, which was developed on the basis of a large corpus comprising four major registers: conversation, fiction, newspaper language and academic prose. By juxtaposing these data, the authors were able to establish how the registers differed in terms of the frequency of specific linguistic features. For instance, academic prose was found to contain more nouns, adjectives and prepositions than the other three registers.

It is worth stressing that genre analysis is a similar approach and it is used to study specialized uses of vocabulary in different types of discourse. As summarized by Bowles (2012), there is a large body of genre-oriented research into the nature of academic, business and professional communication. In broad terms, genre refers to "language use in a conventionalized communicative setting in order to give expression to a specific set of communicative goals of a disciplinary or social institution" (Bhatia 2004: 23). To put it another way, genres can be defined as culturally recognized forms of language (or types of text) such as research articles or phone calls which we associate with particular situations (Cheng 2012). Importantly for the purposes of this book, specialized corpora have been instrumental in revealing the structural identity of particular genres and uncovering lexico-grammatical regularities within them (Hyland 2012: 31). Examples of genres that have been investigated by means of corpus data include, among others, business meetings (Handford 2010), call center interactions (Friginal 2008), professional letters (Upton 2002) and service encounters (McCarthy 2000).

What becomes evident from the above paragraphs is that there is some degree of similarity between the notions of register and genre. However, as Biber's (2010: 242) informative overview of corpus-based analysis of specialized language points out, most studies have adopted a register perspective. This is partly because corpora have traditionally been developed on the premise that they should represent language use across different registers. For instance, COCA consists of five sections which represent five different registers: speech, academic language, fiction, magazines and newspapers. This design creates a perfect opportunity to explore register-specific variation and, when it comes to vocabulary, you can compare its use across different types of discourse.

Task 8.1: Using the 'sections' option on the BYU-COCA interface, compare the most frequent verbs in two different registers of English: fiction vs. academic. Figure 8.1 shows how to conduct this search, with frequency as a sorting criterion. How much do the data from the two registers differ from each other? Once you have made some initial observations, carry out a similar analysis for other word classes (e.g. adjectives).

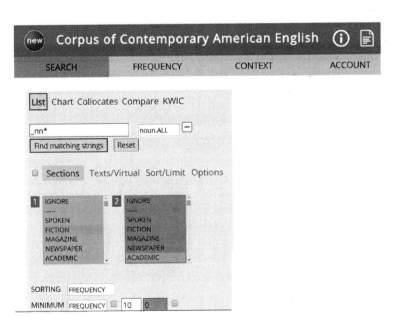

Figure 8.1 A BYU-COCA search for the most frequent nouns in two registers: fiction and academic

8.3 Languages for specific purposes and specialized vocabulary

Languages for specific purposes (LSP) refers to the area of applied linguistics devoted to the study, description and teaching of different types of language used by specific discourse communities (Cortes 2013). In light of the fact that in this book we focus on English corpus linguistics, the subsequent discussion will center on English for specific purposes (ESP). ESP is defined as "language research and instruction that focuses on the specific communicative needs and practices of particular social groups" (Hyland 2007: 391). Two main areas that are of interest to ESP researchers are English for academic purposes (EAP) (see section 8.4 for details) and English for occupational purposes (EOP) (e.g. varieties of English used in medical, legal or business contexts).

In his overview of ESP, Paltridge (2013) highlights the central role of corpora in exploring the use of language for specific purposes. The author notes that although EAP has been the dominant line of enquiry within ESP, specialized corpora have benefited the field in numerous ways, with research studies encompassing topics as different as the language of taxation websites and the type of speech used in court trials. As Nesi (2013: 421) notes, ESP is "closely associated with the use of genres within discourse communities, entailing an understanding of context and communicative purposes". In practical terms, this means that linguists working in the area of ESP are interested in exploring the features (e.g. lexical, grammatical or discoursal) that are typical of specialized language use and ESP corpora, which represent the language of specific domains, are powerful tools that assist such research. The following paragraphs explain how you can use them as a source of insights into the nature of specialized types of vocabulary.

As far as ESP or technical vocabulary is concerned, broadly speaking it can be conceptualized as "the vocabulary of a particular area of study or professional use" (Nesi 2013: 116). Coxhead (2013) lists several reasons for the central role of vocabulary in ESP research. First, establishing what constitutes the lexicon of a given field is of key importance to teachers and learners. For instance, they can use this information to accommodate language provision and design classroom materials in such a way that they suit the specific needs of particular ESP groups. As is emphasized by Nation and Webb (2013: 3), "identifying the technical vocabulary is useful because it sheds light on the low-frequency words which may be of greatest value to learners with specific academic purposes". Furthermore, knowledge of specialized vocabulary enables language users to develop a new sense of identity, because the fact that they use the same kind of language as other members of a given discourse community helps them engage with and participate more fully in the life of this community. Finally, specialized or technical vocabulary deserves our attention because little is known about the size of such vocabulary. Nation (2008: 10) argues that technical vocabulary might range from 1,000 up to 5,000 words depending on the subject area considered. Thus, studying the distribution of words in different ESP corpora can help us better understand the use of language in specialized contexts.

8.3.1 Identification of ESP vocabulary

The process of identifying ESP or technical vocabulary can take several forms such as consulting experts or technical dictionaries (Coxhead 2013). However, given the purposes of this book, we will outline the methods that employ corpus-based methodologies.

A good illustration of the use of corpora for this purpose can be found in Chung's (2003) study. To identify technical vocabulary in anatomy and applied linguistics, the researcher built a specialized corpus of two disciplines and juxtaposed it with a large general corpus. By comparing the frequency of words across the two corpora, Chung found that in the anatomy texts, 31.2% of the running words (one in every three words) were technical, whereas in the applied linguistics texts this figure amounted to around 20% (one word in every five was technical). However, many of these technical words were also found to have a high frequency outside the area of applied linguistics, which shows that academic disciplines tend to vary in terms of how much they rely on technical vocabulary. A related challenge that is entailed in analyzing ESP vocabulary is that many high-frequency words acquire specialized meanings while being used in specific contexts. This contributes to the difficulty of establishing the scope of such lexis (Coxhead 2013). It is worth adding that Coxhead (2000) is the author of a seminal study focused on the Academic Word List (AWL), which demonstrates how corpora can assist the development of lists of specialized vocabulary. A detailed description of the list and how it was created can be found in section 8.4 devoted to EAP.

Another issue that should be highlighted is that corpus-based research into specialized ESP contexts has focused not only on identifying individual words but also on phraseological chunks and longer patterns. Referring to this issue, Gilquin et al. (2007: 320) point out that corpus investigations have provided detailed descriptions of the distinctive features of academic discourse and "its highly specific phraseology". This is in line with our discussion of phraseology presented in Chapter 5 and Chapter 7, in which we have emphasized that corpora provide us with invaluable tools for exploring the distribution of multiword units across different registers and types of language use (e.g. see Nesselhauf 2005, Laufer and Waldman 2011 or Cobb and Horst 2015 for insights into learner English).

8.3.2 ESP vocabulary and language pedagogy

Corpus-based research into ESP has important implications for language instruction. Commenting on the relevance of ESP corpora to language pedagogy, Nesi (2013) highlights their central role in data-driven learning and the development of teaching materials. This is what Römer (2011) and Flowerdew (2009) refer to as the direct and indirect applications of corpus linguistics in language teaching (see Chapter 6 for a detailed discussion). As Gavioli (2005: 69) notes, "concordances provide a way to look at typical (or atypical), conventional (or non-conventional) usage of lexis and textual or genre structures", which provides us with a window into the 'idiomaticity' of specialized domains of language use.

Similar arguments in favor of the use of corpora in ESP pedagogy are put forward by Flowerdew (2015). The author encourages teachers to use findings from corpus research into the specialized uses of language to guide their ESP course and skills-based, genre-oriented teaching. In fact, there is some empirical evidence (e.g. studies by Charles (2014), Lee and Swales (2006) and Flowerdew (2016)) which shows that through the creation of smaller, purpose-built specialized corpora and the use of corpus-based activities, teachers can raise students' awareness of genres, help them improve their writing skills and gain a better understanding of how vocabulary contributes to the shape of specific kinds of texts.

Thus specialized corpora can benefit both teachers and learners who work in the field of ESP and, as more and more corpora become publicly available, the increasing use of corpora is a welcome development. Further evidence for the popularity of corpus-informed ESP materials can also be found in the growing number of teaching resources such as Tim Johns's (2016) kibitzers (http://lexically.net/TimJohns/) or Granger and Paquot's (2010) Louvain EAP dictionary (https://www.uclouvain.be/en-322619.html). The former is a particularly useful tool for EAP students as the content of this web-based dictionary is customizable in terms of specific disciplines and L1 backgrounds.

8.4 Academic vocabulary and English for academic purposes (EAP)

English for academic purposes (EAP) is arguably the most prominent example of how corpora have enhanced research into specialized language use. As highlighted by Hyland (2012: 30), "it is difficult to imagine a domain of applied linguistics where corpus studies have had a greater influence". In light of this, the following paragraphs present examples of corpus-based studies that focus on the analysis and description of academic vocabulary.

8.4.1 Academic Word List (AWL)

One of the most influential corpus-based lists of academic vocabulary is Coxhead's (2000) Academic Word List (AWL). It is a list of 570 word families derived from a written corpus of academic texts (3.5 million words) representing four broad areas: arts, commerce, law and science. As noted by Coxhead (2011: 357), on average the AWL provides a roughly 10% coverage of academic language, which means it covers around 10% of running words in any academic text. Given these benefits, the mastery of AWL words came to be known as a vital element of understanding academic English. The list is divided into ten sub-lists, with the first sub-list containing sixty most frequent items, the second sub-list containing the next sixty items and so on. All of the sub-lists can be downloaded from the following website: http://www.victoria.ac.nz/lals/resources/academicwordlist/awl-headwords.

As regards practical implications of the AWL, it has been widely used for both research and teaching purposes. The list has been particularly welcomed by language teachers and materials developers who treat it as a major resource for the promotion of academic vocabulary among EAP learners. To take a well-known resource, Schmitt and Schmitt (2005) published a textbook called *Focus on Vocabulary* which offers numerous examples of activities built around the most frequent academic words. What is more, the AWL has been incorporated into the VocabProfile program available at Lextutor (Cobb 2016), which enables researchers and language teachers to identify academic words in different kinds of texts. Figure 8.2 shows what the VocabProfile interface looks like. Note that to see examples of AWL words in any text, you have to use the classic version of the program (click on the button CLASSIC on the right-hand side of the website).

> Task 8.2: Use the classic version of the VocabProfile program (http://www. lextutor.ca/vp/comp/) to identify examples of academic words from Coxhead's AWL list in two different online articles: one about sport and the other about health. Which text contains more examples of academic vocabulary?

As a last point in this section, it should be added that despite its many virtues, the AWL has also received some criticism. First, Gardner and Davies (2014) argue that it is problematic that the list does not contain the first 2,000 most frequent word families from West's (1953) General Service List of English Words (GSL) (see Chapter 4 for details). According to the authors, Coxhead's decision to exclude the GSL words makes it difficult "to separate the high-frequency words that tend to be important in other areas of focus" (Gardner and Davies 2014: 309). Some criticism of the AWL has also been leveled by Hyland and Tse (2007). The authors argue that the list masks discipline-specific variation, which is a key feature of language in use. To put it another way, words behave differently when they are used in particular domains or disciplines and consequently a single list that purports to contain the 'core' of academic vocabulary cannot do justice to the lexical richness and sophistication of different subject areas. In light of these arguments, it is important to add that there have been attempts to produce discipline-specific lists of technical vocabulary and specialized corpora have been instrumental in conducting this research. Some recent examples of lists of technical vocabulary include Liu and Han's (2015) list of environmental vocabulary and Valipouri and Nassaji's (2013) listing of chemistry words.

8.4.2 Academic Vocabulary List (AVL)

Another corpus-based list that needs to be discussed is Gardner and Davies's (2014) Academic Vocabulary List (AVL). The list consists of 3,014 lemmas extracted from the academic section of COCA (120 million words) which comprises data

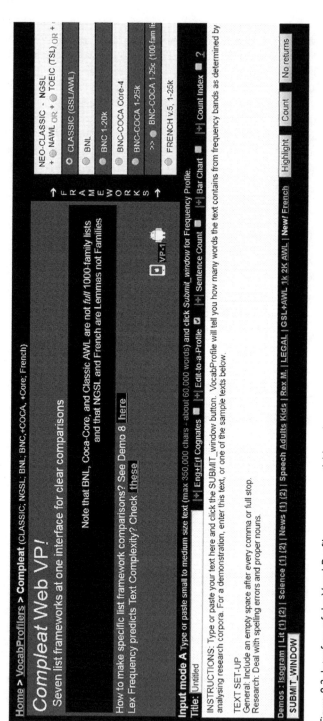

Figure 8.2 Interface of the VocabProfile program available at Lextutor

from nine different academic disciplines. The development of the list was guided by several criteria: frequency (all target lemmas had to be 50% more frequent in the academic corpus), range (they had to occur in at least seven of the nine academic disciplines), dispersion (they had to be evenly distributed across the whole corpus) and a measure of discipline-specificity, according to which "the word cannot occur more than three times the expected frequency (per million words) in any of the nine disciplines" (Gardner and Davies 2014: 316).

Thanks to this methodological rigor, the AVL is an excellent illustration of cutting-edge corpus research and it is likely to be widely adopted in both vocabulary research and pedagogy. In addition to the core 3,014 lemmas, the AVL can also be viewed in the format of word families (the top 2,000 word families are available free of charge from the following website: http://www.academicwords.info/download.asp). Gardner and Davies decided to include this format to enable direct comparisons with Coxhead's (2000) AWL which uses word families as its organizing unit.

Task 8.3: Table 8.1 displays the first twenty most frequent word families from the Academic Word List and the Academic Vocabulary List. Compare the lists and consider what they reveal about academic vocabulary.

Table 8.1 Twenty most frequent word families in the AWL and AVL

	AWL	AVL
1	analysis	study
2	approach	develop
3	area	group
4	assessment	system
5	assume	relate
6	authority	research
7	available	social
8	benefit	result
9	concept	use
10	consistent	provide
11	constitutional	however
12	context	increase
13	contract	experience
14	create	level
15	data	process
16	definition	culture
17	derived	history
18	distribution	active
19	economic	support
20	environment	individual

It is vital to add that the AVL can also be explored via a web-based interface available at http://www.wordandphrase.info/academic/frequencyList.asp. The interface uses information from the academic section of COCA and as a dynamic tool, it offers you several ways of conducting corpus research. First, you can analyze the frequency of words in a range of academic disciplines (e.g. business or medicine). Second, the interface helps you separate core academic vocabulary (the core 3,000 lemmas) from subject-specific technical vocabulary used in a given discipline. Furthermore, since the interface is equipped with color coding (yellow for core academic words and red for technical words), you can keep track of different categories of academic words. Finally, you can also input a text (e.g. an article that you want to use for teaching purposes) and explore its lexical content in terms of how many academic and technical words it contains. This functionality is similar to the VocabProfile tool described before and it is available at this link: http://www.wordandphrase.info/academic/analyzeText.asp.

> Task 8.4: Use the Analyze text tool available at http://www.wordandphrase. info/academic/frequencyList.asp to explore the distribution of academic words in the text about health you have selected for Task 8.2. Does it contain any academic words from the AVL?

8.4.3 Academic phraseology

Corpus-based research into academic vocabulary has also addressed issues related to the use of phraseological chunks, often called n-grams or lexical bundles in the literature on academic communication. As stressed in Chapter 5, a tendency of words to co-occur and form multiword units is a key feature of naturally occurring language and academic discourse is no exception in this regard (Biber and Barbieri 2007). This means that as well as exploring the occurrence of individual words across different academic texts, corpus linguists have been concerned with identifying the most frequent chunks and investigating what role they play in building the structure of academic texts.

One particular type of chunks that has attracted a lot of attention in the field of EAP are lexical bundles (or n-grams). They can be defined as "two or more words that repeatedly occur consecutively in a corpus" (Cheng 2012: 72). In a similar way, Paquot and Granger (2012) perceive lexical bundles as contiguous sequences of three-, four- or five-word clusters, which are identified by means of a purely statistical, frequency-driven approach. This means that lexical bundles include both grammatically complete (e.g. 'that's a good idea', 'on the other hand') as well as incomplete (e.g. 'in the case of the', 'it should be noted that') units. Seminal work in this area has been conducted by Biber and his colleagues (e.g. Biber et al. 1999, 2004), who have demonstrated that lexical bundles are an important feature of academic texts and they serve a range of important functions such as expressing stance (e.g. 'I think it was') or organizing discourse (e.g. 'if you look at'). What follows is a discussion of some corpus-based studies which have led to the compilation of lists of academic phraseology.

The first list of academic lexical bundles we will present is Simpson-Vlach and Ellis's (2010) Academic Formulas List (AFL). Using data from several corpora (the Michigan Corpus of Academic Spoken English (MICASE), the BNC and Hyland's (2004) corpus of research articles), the authors identified the most important chunks found in academic speech and writing. There are three versions of the list: a core version with 207 chunks that are common to both modes of communication, a version with the 200 most frequent spoken chunks and a version with the 200 most frequent written chunks. Importantly, in addition to frequency and mutual information which are two criteria that compare the occurrence of chunks in academic vs. non-academic texts, another factor that Simpson-Vlach and Ellis took into account was expert judgment. More specifically, the authors asked EAP instructors to rate all the chunks in terms of their utility, which allowed them to devise a special measure called formula teaching worth (FTW). Table 8.2 presents the first twenty items from the AFL ranked according to their FTW scores.

Table 8.2 Examples of academic chunks from the AFL list sorted by FTW score

		Speech		Writing		FTW
		Raw freq	Freq per million	Raw freq	Freq per million	
1	in terms of	726	337	597	282	3.53
2	at the same time	198	92	208	98	2.56
3	from the point of view	23	11	30	14	2.44
4	in order to	330	153	540	255	2.35
5	as well as	147	68	539	255	2.08
6	part of the	432	201	457	216	1.96
7	the fact that	383	178	430	203	1.96
8	in other words	315	146	188	89	1.90
9	the point of view of	22	10	31	15	1.89
10	there is a	307	143	472	223	1.72
11	as a result of	57	26	158	75	1.58
12	this is a	657	305	160	76	1.57
13	on the basis of	50	23	174	82	1.50
14	a number of	190	88	455	215	1.50
15	there is no	107	50	391	185	1.45
16	point of view	177	82	128	60	1.41
17	the number of	171	79	521	246	1.38
18	the extent to which	21	10	111	52	1.36
19	as a result	131	61	264	125	1.35
20	in the case of	68	32	286	135	1.32

Including expert judgment is an important methodological improvement because it shows that even though the frequency of occurrence plays a key role in identifying the most salient chunks, other factors should also be considered in the process of developing pedagogically oriented lists of academic language.

Task 8.5: Compare the frequencies of the top five lexical bundles from the AFL in the academic vs. non-academic sections of COCA. Use Rayson's online corpus calculator (http://ucrel.lancs.ac.uk/llwizard.html) to check whether the frequency values differ in terms of statistical significance.

A similar method of selecting academic chunks has been adopted by Ackermann and Chen (2013) in their study devoted to the production of the Academic Collocation List (ACL). The authors based their analysis on the written component of the Pearson International Corpus of Academic English (25 million words) and, by combing a quantitative, frequency-based analysis with a qualitative expert review, they arrived at over 2,400 collocations which made up their ACL. What Ackermann and Chen emphasize about their list is that the expert judgment was used not only for the selection of the collocations but also for the refinement of the list, which makes it particularly valuable to both EAP students and teachers. The list can be accessed via the following link: http://pearsonpte.com/research/academic-collocation-list/.

The last example to be discussed is Liu's (2012) list of 228 academic chunks. The list is based on the academic data derived from the BNC and COCA, which enabled the author to investigate the frequency of the target chunks in both British and American English. In addition, Liu organized them according to their discourse functions, using three main categories: referential/ideational expressions, stance expressions and discourse organizers. Information about the discourse functions of chunks is particularly useful for teachers and materials developers as they can use it to create tailor-made materials that will cater to the specific academic needs of EAP students. Table 8.3 presents examples of chunks together with their discourse functions.

Task 8.6: Select five chunks from Liu's (2012) list and explore their occurrence in the academic section of COCA. Try to find examples of concordances which demonstrate the specific discourse functions of the chunks.

Table 8.3 Examples of pragmatic functions of academic chunks (adapted from Liu 2012)

Referential/ideational

Framing/intangible framing attributes	Tangible framing attributes	Identification/identity specification	Qualifying	Quantity specification	Referential place/text/direction	Referential time/sequence	Reporting/description/interpretation	Multifunctional
according to (det + N); (be) based on (det + N)	in the form of (det/N); (as/in) the size of (det + N)	there be no NP; there be det + N	at all; as a whole	a/the (large/small) number of; (as) (a) part of (det + N)	in + the name of a country/ state/ region; In this article/ chapter	(at/by) the end of (det + N); (at) the time of (det + N)	NP suggest that; NP show that	the use of (det + N); (be) associated with (det + N)

Discourse/textual organizers

Linking	Topic introduction
such as (det + N); for example	as to wh-clause/ NP; let us/me + infinitive

Stance/interpersonal/impersonal expressions

Epistemic stance	Attitudinal/modality stance
I/we argue that; I/we believe that	be able to VP; tend to VP

8.5 Other examples of specialized corpora

The last section of this chapter discusses translation, literary and age- and gender-differentiated corpora as further examples of specialized corpora. Our aim is to illustrate that such corpora afford a number of opportunities for research into the distribution and use of vocabulary across a wide range of contexts.

8.5.1 Specialized corpora and translation studies

Corpora consisting of translations are the first example of specialized corpora to be discussed. As mentioned in Chapter 1, there are two main types of corpora that are used in translation studies: parallel corpora, which consist of texts written in a source language and their translations into a target language, and comparable corpora, which consist of texts written in different languages but designed according to the same criteria. As Kübler and Aston (2010) state, although parallel texts (source plus target texts) have long been used as a tool in the work of translators, it is the advent of large computerized collections of such texts that has led to the emergence of corpus-based translation studies as a new research area (see Mikhailov and Cooper (2016) for a book-length account of the use of corpora in translation and comparative studies).

As Kenning (2010) explains, both parallel and comparable corpora are employed in the area of translation studies and the purposes for which they are used are three-fold. First, translators treat them as a resource which helps them resolve different problems that might be encountered while translating texts from one language into another. Second, many scholars preoccupied with translation and its products rely on such corpora as a basis for their research. To take a prominent example, Baker (1995) pioneered corpus-based work on the character of translated texts and the role of translation universals as features inherent in the translation process. Finally, specialized corpora of translated texts have also become a key tool for developing translation skills and training future generations of translators.

To illustrate the way corpus techniques can be employed to study the vocabulary of translated texts, I will briefly outline a study conducted by Biel (2012). The study aimed at investigating the collocational and phraseological patterning of both British and Polish legal texts. Relying on two comparable corpora (318,087 words in the UK corpus and 52,068 words in the Polish corpus), Biel identified a number of key terms, that is, words that occurred with a high frequency in both databases. 'Company', 'director' and 'share' were examples of such words. Biel also focused on the collocational patterning of legal texts in both languages and found that it was governed by similar conceptual metaphors (e.g. 'company is a person'). However, there were also some differences in the distribution of collocations, which the author attributed to language-specific phraseological constraints. Such constraints result from cross-linguistic differences in the structure of legal texts in Polish and English and they are likely to cause difficulty during the translation process.

8.5.2 Literary corpora and corpus stylistics

Recent years have also seen a rise in the use of corpora for analyzing literary texts. This area of corpus studies has come to be known as corpus stylistics and, as Mahlberg (2016: 139) explains, it "employs methods from corpus linguistics to study literary texts". In a similar fashion, McIntyre and Walker (2010) highlight the value of corpus linguistics in stylistic analyses of texts, in particular its capacity to provide more systematic evidence and add more objectivity to the subjective nature of literary criticism (Mahlberg 2013; Stubbs 2005). Considering that stylistics focuses on individual texts, we should not expect stylisticians and literary critics to engage in large-scale quantitative projects. Rather, corpus-based stylistic studies are likely to make use of different types of corpus methods (e.g. frequency or keyword analysis) to interpret the style of a given text or author. In light of these arguments, therefore, it is fair to say that corpus stylistics as an area of study encompasses a range of corpus approaches that assist in the literary analysis of the language of poetry, drama and films (McIntyre and Walker 2010).

With a view to demonstrating the details of a corpus-based stylistic analysis, we will refer to a recent study published by Mahlberg et al. (2013). Using data from a corpus of novels written by Charles Dickens, the authors explored the notion of suspended quotations, a specific kind of textual unit that contributes to the individual style of Dickens. According to Mahlberg et al. (2013), suspended quotations (or suspensions) can be defined as interruptions of the speech of a fictional character by the narrator. The following sentence is one of the examples retrieved from the corpus of Dickens's novels:

"I am very glad indeed," **said Mrs. Jellyby in an agreeable voice,** "to have the pleasure of receiving you. I have a great respect . . .

Figure 8.3 An example of a suspended quotation found in a corpus of Charles Dickens's novels (taken from Mahlberg et al. 2013)

Approaching the data from a number of angles, Mahlberg et al. found that suspended quotations play a special role in the language of Charles Dickens. Specifically, they contain information about the body language of characters from his novels and they also help to convey the specific meaning of reporting verbs such as 'exclaimed' and 'continued'. Interestingly, the study also revealed that the occurrence of suspensions can be studied across different novels and consequently contribute to a better understanding of the specific style of Dickens's prose. It is worth adding that the corpus of Dickens's novels can be accessed free of charge via a web-based tool called CLiC (http://clic.bham.ac.uk/). Figure 8.4 displays a screenshot from this interface.

As Mahlberg (2016) explains, CLiC is equipped with a number of tools that are relevant to stylistic analysis. Examples of search options include: the whole text, quotes (text within quotation marks), non-quotes (text outside of quotation marks),

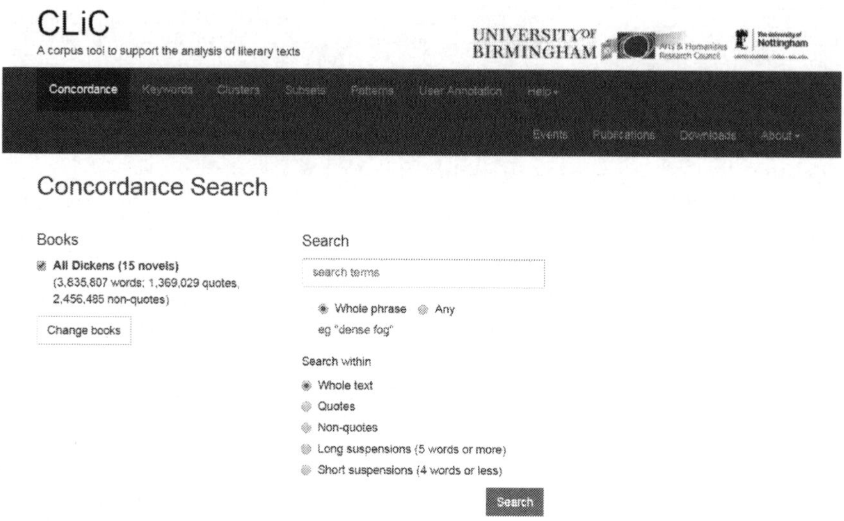

CLiC
A corpus tool to support the analysis of literary texts

UNIVERSITY OF
BIRMINGHAM

Concordance   Keywords   Clusters   Subsets   Patterns   User Annotation   Help▾

Events   Publications   Downloads   About▾

Concordance Search

Books

☑ **All Dickens (15 novels)**
(3,835,807 words; 1,369,029 quotes,
2,456,485 non-quotes)

Change books

Search

search terms

◉ Whole phrase   ○ Any
eg "dense fog"

Search within
◉ Whole text
○ Quotes
○ Non-quotes
○ Long suspensions (5 words or more)
○ Short suspensions (4 words or less)

Search

Figure 8.4 Interface of the CLiC corpus

short suspensions (four words or fewer) and long suspensions (five words or more). What is more, the CLiC tool enables several other kinds of corpus analysis such as keyword or n-gram analysis and they can be employed to explore different aspects of the style of Dickens or other authors (click on the 'Change books' option to see other books that can be searched). By way of illustration, Mahlberg et al. (2013) demonstrate how the n-gram analysis of Dickens's novels yields insights into the phraseology used by specific characters. More specifically, the authors elaborate on how different phraseological patterns fulfill important textual functions such as indicating different manners of speaking or showing the narrator's interpretation of particular situations described in the novels. Considering all the functionalities of the CLiC interface, it needs to be flagged up as an example of cutting-edge corpus research that holds a lot of potential for stylistic analyses of texts and their lexical structure.

> Task 8.7: Explore search tools of the CLiC interface (http://clic.bham.ac.uk/).
> How would you use them in your own corpus stylistic analysis?

8.5.3 Age- and gender-differentiated corpora

Age- and gender-differentiated corpora are another type of specialized corpora. These are corpora which allow the researcher to explore the impact of sociolinguistic variables such as gender, age and social class on the use of vocabulary. As stated by Friginal and Hardy (2014) in a recent overview, corpus-based sociolinguistics is a new line of research that is quickly expanding and focuses on issues such as lexical variation in the use of language across different social contexts (e.g. workplace discourse), dialectology and diachronic change.

To present an example of research in this area, we will briefly discuss Barbieri's (2008) study into age-based variation in the use of vocabulary. The study was based on a sample of the American Conversation corpus (around 400,000 words) and it explored the effects of age on the distribution of different lexical features which included, among others, slang, stance markers, fillers (called inserts in the study), pronouns, adverbs and discourse markers. To delve into the effects of age on these features, the researcher used keyword analysis (see Chapter 2 for details) and compared two different groups, younger speakers aged fifteen to twenty-five vs. older speakers aged thirty-five to sixty. In terms of the methodology, Barbieri relied on a way of demonstrating which words from the target corpus were characteristically unusual (i.e. occur with a high frequency) in comparison with their frequency in a reference corpus. The author's analysis produced a number of interesting findings. Namely, younger speakers were found to "make outstandingly frequent use of a range of slang and swear words, inserts, attitudinal or personal affect adjectives, intensifiers, discourse markers, first and second person singular reference, and particular quotative verbs" (Barbieri 2008: 77). A detailed discussion and interpretation of these results is beyond the scope of this book but even these general observations prove that specialized, sociolinguistically differentiated corpora have much to offer in relation to the study of variation in the use of words and other elements of discourse.

Other examples of sociolinguistically oriented corpus work include Murphy's (2012) analysis of male and female talk in Irish English or Macaulay's (2002) study of the impact of age, gender and social class on the use of discourse markers. These studies constitute evidence that sociolinguistic research can greatly benefit from the increasing availability of age- and gender-differentiated corpora. By gaining insights into the complex relationship between social and cultural phenomena, we can better understand how social differentiation impacts on the use of specific linguistic forms.

As a last point, it needs to be admitted that while all of the areas of specialized language described in this section hold a lot of potential for employing corpus methods and techniques, there are also certain challenges that the use of corpora might entail. For instance, Murphy (2012) warns against exploring sociolinguistic variables in isolation as naturally occurring language is a complex process where many variables interact with one another and consequently a more interdisciplinary approach is required to produce accurate and reliable descriptions of language in use. Also, Mahlberg (2013) comments on the difficulty of translating theoretical considerations that underpin corpus stylistics into more practical solutions. The author calls for more work into new functionalities of corpora and more effective methodologies so that both corpus linguists and stylisticians can start reaping benefits from the integration of the fields. These are important tasks that lie ahead if we wish to see further developments in the field of corpus-based research as it transgresses traditional borders within applied linguistics.

8.6 Exemplary study: Martinez, Beck and Panza's (2009) study into academic vocabulary in agriculture research articles

In this section we will discuss Martinez et al.'s (2009) study as an example of how specialized corpora can be used to identify field-specific vocabulary. The study integrates corpus and genre approaches as it explores one specific genre – research articles in agricultural sciences. As the authors explain, the aim of their research was to investigate the frequency of academic words from Coxhead's (2000) AWL in a corpus of research articles written in the field of agriculture. In addition, given that words take on different shades of meaning depending on which contexts and disciplines they are used in (Hyland and Tse 2007), Martinez et al. also studied the specialized behavior of academic vocabulary as it was used in one specific genre of one specific field.

As far as methodology is concerned, the study was based on a specialized corpus of research articles called AgroCorpus. It consisted of over 800,000 words retrieved from 218 articles published by academics working in English-speaking universities. The corpus was compiled taking into account criteria such as representativeness, use of whole texts and availability of electronic versions. Since research articles have a fixed structure composed of subsections (e.g. Abstract, Introduction, Methodology, Discussion, Results), some of them were excluded from the word count. That is, numbers, abstracts, acknowledgements, references, captions and appendices were not included. Thanks to this corpus design, the authors were able to explore the frequency of academic words not only in terms of total numbers but also across different sections of research articles. This is a very interesting methodological solution that allowed Martinez et al. to gain more fine-grained insights into the genre under study and both quantitative and qualitative approaches were used to analyze the data. Using WordSmith tools, the authors identified the most frequent academic words in their corpus and built word families around them. This was done to ensure direct comparisons with Coxhead's analysis, where word families were the unit of counting.

The results of the study revealed that the AgroCorpus contained only ninety-two word families from the AWL, which points to the discipline-specificity of the agricultural vocabulary and contrasts with Coxhead's (2000) corpus, which represented more general academic vocabulary collected from several different disciplines. What is more, many highly frequent academic words in the AgroCorpus belonged to West's (1953) GSL list. It turns out that some of the most frequent words in English might be used as specialized words in academic texts, which puts into question Coxhead's decision to exclude the GSL as a source of academic vocabulary. Further insights into the nature of agricultural vocabulary were also gained from the analysis of lexical coverage. In Martinez et al.'s study the AWL vocabulary accounted for 9.06% of the AgroCorpus, while in Coxhead's study this figure was higher, reaching 10%. In addition, when the ninety-two word families from the AgroCorpus were juxtaposed with the most frequent word families from Coxhead's corpus, only twenty-six items coincided. These were fairly general academic words (e.g. 'significant', 'analysis', 'data', 'area' and 'variation') that are likely to be frequently used in different academic texts, regardless of discipline. This strengthens the argument that the type of data stored in a corpus has a profound impact on the results of our analysis.

Interestingly, Martinez et al. also explored the frequency of academic words across the different subsections of research articles in their corpus. The highest number of AWL families was found in the Introduction subsection, and the lowest in the Results subsection. This finding points to the role of academic vocabulary in building the structure of scientific texts. It is understandable that introductions of research articles appear to contain the highest number of academic words, for this is the section where literature reviews are presented and academic terms are explained. Examples of the most frequent words from the Introductions of research articles in the corpus include 'area', 'stress', 'region' and 'accumulation'. Finally, the qualitative analysis of data from the AgroCorpus revealed that some words "were used with technical rather than academic meaning" (Martinez et al. 2009: 191). A good illustration of this is the word 'culture', which carries a more specialized meaning when it appears in scientific texts (e.g. 'cell culture' or 'liquid culture'). The same applies to collocational patterns that accompany words. In academic or technical texts, they might take on different meanings and become more field-specific (e.g. technical collocations such as 'management strategies' or 'adaptation strategy').

In terms of practical implications, Martinez et al.'s study offers strong evidence that discipline-specific lexical variation is an important factor that you need to take into account when you try to identify academic vocabulary. The study also shows that in ESP contexts it is critical to consider the specific lexical needs of learners as you prioritize the types of vocabulary that they should know (Granger 2015; Granger et al. 2015).

Summary

The aim of this chapter has been to underline the importance of specialized corpora in the study of vocabulary. First, we have discussed the characteristic features of such corpora. Next, we have explained how they can be employed to study specific uses of vocabulary and the lexical variation they entail. Finally, to demonstrate the usefulness of specialized corpora, we have presented examples of their applications in a range of areas including ESP, EAP, translation studies, literary linguistics, stylistics and sociolinguistics.

References

Ackermann, K. and Chen, Y. (2013). Developing the Academic Collocation List (ACL): A corpus-driven and expert-judged approach. *Journal of English for Academic Purpose*, 12, 4, 235–247.

Baker, M. (1995). Corpora in translation studies: An overview and suggestions for future research. *Target*, 7, 2, 223–243.

Barbieri, F. (2008). Patterns of age-based linguistic variation in American English. *Journal of Sociolinguistics*, 12, 1, 58–88.

Bhatia, V. K. (2004). *Worlds of Written Discourse.* London: Continuum.

Biber, D. (2010). What can a corpus tell us about registers and genres?, in A. O'Keeffe and M. McCarthy (eds.) *The Routledge Handbook of Corpus Linguistics.* London and New York: Routledge, 241–254.

Biber, D. and Barbieri, F. (2007). Lexical bundles in university spoken and written registers. *English for Specific Purposes*, 26, 263–286.

Biber, D. and Conrad, S. (2009). *Register, Genre, and Style.* Cambridge: Cambridge University Press.

Biber, D., Conrad, S. and Cortes, V. (2004). If you look at …: Lexical bundles in university teaching and textbooks. *Applied Linguistics*, 25, 3, 371–405.

Biber, D., Johansson, S., Leech, G., Conrad, S. and Finegan, E. (1999). *Longman Grammar of Spoken and Written English.* Harlow: Longman.

Biel, Ł. (2012). Areas of similarity and difference in legal phraseology: Collocations of key terms in UK and Polish Company law, in A. Pamies, J. M. Pazos Bretaña and L. Luque Nadal (eds.) *Phraseology and Discourse: Cross-linguistic and corpus-based approaches.* Baltmannsweileer: Schneider Verlag, 225–233.

Bowles, H. (2012). Analyzing languages for specific purposes discourse. *Modern Language Journal*, Focus issue, 96, 43–58.

Charles, M. (2014). Getting the corpus habit: EAP students' long-term use of personal corpora. *English for Specific Purposes*, 35, 30–40.

Cheng, W. (2012). *Exploring Corpus Linguistics: Language in action.* London and New York: Routledge.

Chung, T. M. (2003). A corpus comparison approach for terminology extraction. *Terminology*, 9, 2, 221–245.

Cobb, T. (2016). *Compleat Lexical Tutor (LexTutor)* [online]. Available: www.lextutor. ca [20 June 2016].

Cobb, T. and Horst, M. (2015). Learner corpora and lexis, in S. Granger, G. Gilquin and F. Meunier (eds.) *The Cambridge Handbook of Learner Corpus Linguistics.* Cambridge: Cambridge University Press, 185–206.

Cortes, V. (2013). Corpora in language for specific purposes research, in C. A. Chapelle (ed.) *The Encyclopedia of Applied Linguistics.* New York: Blackwell Publishing.

Coxhead, A. (2000). A new Academic Word List. *TESOL Quarterly*, 34, 2, 213–238.

Coxhead, A. (2011). The Academic Word List 10 years on: Research and teaching implications. *TESOL Quarterly*, 45, 2, 355–362.

Coxhead, A. (2013). Vocabulary and ESP, in B. Paltridge and S. Starfield (eds.) *The Handbook of English for Specific Purposes.* Boston, MA: Wiley-Blackwell, 115–132.

Durrant, P. (2014). Discipline and level specificity in university students' written vocabulary. *Applied Linguistics*, 35, 3, 328–356.

Flowerdew, J. (2009). Corpora in language teaching, in M. Long and C. Doughty (eds.) *The Handbook of Language Teaching*, London: Wiley-Blackwell, 327–350.

Flowerdew, L. (2004). The argument for using specialized corpora to understand academic and professional language, in U. Connor and T. Upton (eds.) *Discourse in the Professions: Perspectives from corpus linguistics*. Amsterdam: John Benjamins, 11–33.

Flowerdew, L. (2015). Corpus-based research and pedagogy in EAP: From lexis to genre. *Language Teaching*, 48, 1, 99–116.

Flowerdew, L. (2016). A genre-inspired and lexico-grammatical approach for helping postgraduate students craft research grant proposal. *English for Specific Purposes*, 42, 1–12.

Friginal, E. (2008). Linguistic variation in the discourse of outsourced call centers. *Discourse Studies*, 10, 715–736.

Friginal, E. and Hardy, J. A. (2014). *Corpus-based Sociolinguistics: A guide for students*. New York and London: Routledge.

Gardner, D. and Davies, M. (2014). A new Academic Vocabulary List. *Applied Linguistics*, 35, 3, 305–327.

Gavioli, L. (2005). *Exploring Corpora for ESP Learning*. Amsterdam/Philadelphia: John Benjamins.

Gilquin, G., Granger, S. and Paquot, M. (2007). Learner corpora: The missing link in EAP pedagogy. *Journal of English for Academic Purposes*, 6, 319–335.

Granger, S. (2015). Contrastive Interlanguage analysis: A reappraisal. *International Journal of Learner Corpus Research*, 1, 1, 7–24.

Granger, S., Gilquin, G. and Meunier, M. (2015). Introduction: Learner corpus research – Past, present and future, in S. Granger, G. Gilquin and F. Meunier (eds.) *The Cambridge Handbook of Learner Corpus Research*. Cambridge: Cambridge University Press, 1–5.

Granger, S. and Paquot, M. (2010). Customising a general EAP dictionary to meet learner needs, in S. Granger and M. Paquot (eds.) *eLexicography in the 21st Century: New challenges, new applications*. Louvain-la-Neuve: Presses universitaires de Louvain, 87–96.

Handford, M. (2010). What can a corpus tell us about specialist genres?, in A. O'Keeffe and M. McCarthy (eds.) *The Routledge Handbook of Corpus Linguistics*. London and New York: Routledge, 255–269.

Hyland, K. (2004). *Disciplinary Discourses: Social interactions in academic writing*. Ann Arbor, MI: University of Michigan Press.

Hyland, K. (2007). English for specific purposes: Some influences and impacts, in J. Cummins and C. Davison (eds.) *International Handbook of English Language Teaching*. New York: Springer, 391–402.

Hyland, K. (2012). Corpora in academic discourse, in K. Hyland, C. M. Huat and M. Handford (eds.) *Corpus Applications in Applied Linguistics*. London and New York: Continuum, 30–46.

Hyland, K. and Tse, P. (2007). Is there an "academic vocabulary"?, *TESOL Quarterly*, 41, 2, 235–253.

Johns, T. (2016). Kibbitzers [online]. Available: http://lexically.net/TimJohns/ [28 September 2016].

Koester, A. (2006). *Investigating Workplace Discourse*. London: Routledge.

Kenning, M.-M. (2010). What are parallel and comparable corpora and how can we use them?, in A. O'Keeffe and M. McCarthy (eds.) *The Routledge Handbook of Corpus Linguistics*. London and New York: Routledge, 486–500.

Koester, A. (2010). Building small specialized corpora, in A. O'Keeffe and M. McCarthy (eds.), *The Routledge Handbook of Corpus Linguistics.* London and New York: Routledge, 66–79.

Kübler, N. and Aston, G. (2010). Using corpora in translation, in A. O'Keeffe and M. McCarthy (eds.) *The Routledge Handbook of Corpus Linguistics.* London and New York: Routledge, 501–515.

Laufer, B. and Waldman, T. (2011). Verb-noun collocations in second language writing: A corpus analysis of learners' English. *Language Learning*, 61, 2, 647–672.

Lee, D. and Swales, J. (2006). A corpus-based EAP course for NNS doctoral students: Moving from available specialized corpora to self-compiled corpora. *English for Specific Purposes*, 25, 1, 56–75.

Liu, D. (2012). The most frequently-used multi-word constructions in academic written English: A multi-corpus study. *English for Specific Purposes*, 31, 25–35.

Liu, J. and Han, L. (2015). A corpus-based environmental academic word list building and its validity test. *English for Specific Purposes*, 39, 1–11.

Macaulay, R. (2002). You know, it depends. *Journal of Pragmatics*, 34, 6, 749–767.

Mahlberg, M. (2013). Corpus analysis of literary texts, in C. A. Chapelle (ed.) *The Encyclopedia of Applied Linguistics.* Oxford: Blackwell Publishing.

Mahlberg, M. (2016). Corpus stylistics, in V. Sotirova (ed.) *The Bloomsbury Companion to Stylistics.* London: Bloomsbury Academic, 139–156.

Mahlberg, M., Smith, C. and Preston, S. (2013). Phrases in literary contexts: Patterns and distributions of suspensions in Dickens's novels. *International Journal of Corpus Linguistics*, 18, 1, 35–56.

Martinez, I. A., Beck, S. C. and Panza, C. B. (2009). Academic vocabulary in agriculture research articles: A corpus-based study. *English for Specific Purposes*, 28, 3, 183–198.

McCarthy, M. (1991). *Discourse Analysis for Language Teachers.* Cambridge: Cambridge University Press.

McCarthy, M. (2000). Mutually captive audiences: Small talk and the genre of the close-contact service encounters, in J. Coupland (ed.) *Small Talk.* Harlow: Pearson Education, 84–109.

McIntyre, D. and Walker, B. (2010). How can corpora be used to explore the language of poetry and drama?, in A. O'Keeffe and M. McCarthy (eds.) *The Routledge Handbook of Corpus Linguistics.* London and New York: Routledge, 516–530.

Mikhailov, M. and Cooper, R. (2016). *Corpus Linguistics for Translation and Contrastive Studies.* London and New York: Routledge.

Murphy, B. (2012). Exploring response tokens in Irish English – A multidisciplinary approach: Integrating variational pragmatics, sociolinguistics and corpus linguistics. *International Journal of Corpus Linguistics*, 17, 3, 325–348.

Nation, I. S. P. (2008). *Teaching Vocabulary: Strategies and techniques.* Boston, MA: Heinle Cengage.

Nation, I. S. P. and Webb, S. (2013). *Researching and Analyzing Vocabulary.* Boston, MA: Heinle Cengage.

Nesi, H. (2013). ESP and corpus studies, in B. Paltridge and S. Starfield (eds.) *The Handbook of English for Specific Purposes.* Boston, MA: Wiley-Blackwell, 407 London and New York 426.

Nesselhauf, N. (2005). *Collocations in a Learner Corpus.* Amsterdam: Benjamins.

Paltridge, B. (2013). Genre and English for specific purposes, in B. Paltridge and S. Starfield (eds.) *The Handbook of English for Specific Purposes.* Boston, MA: Wiley-Blackwell, 347–366.

Paquot, M. and Granger, S. (2012). Formulaic language in learner corpora. *Annual Review of Applied Linguistics*, 32, 130–149.

Rayson, P. (2015). Log-likelihood calculator [online]. Available: http://ucrel.lanc.ac.uk/llwizard.html [25 November 2015].

Römer, U. (2011). Corpus research applications in second language teaching. *Annual Review of Applied Linguistics*, 31, 205–225.

Schmitt, D. and Schmitt, N. (2005). *Focus on Vocabulary: Mastering the academic word list.* New York: Pearson Longman Education.

Simpson-Vlach, R. and Ellis, N. (2010). An Academic Formulas List: New methods in phraseology research. *Applied Linguistics*, 31, 4, 487–512.

Stubbs, M. (2005). Conrad in the computer: Examples of quantitative stylistic methods. *Language and Literature*, 14, 1, 5–24.

Upton, T. (2002). Understanding direct mail letters as a genre. *International Journal of Corpus Linguistics*, 7, 3, 65–85.

Valipouri, L. and Nassaji, H. (2013). A corpus-based study of academic vocabulary in chemistry research articles. *Journal of English for Academic Purposes*, 12, 248–263.

West, M. (1953). *A General Service List of English Words.* London: Longman.

Widdowson, H. (2000). On the limitations of linguistics applied. *Applied Linguistics*, 21, 1, 3–25.

Chapter 9

Discourse, pragmatics and vocabulary

9.1 What is discourse and discourse analysis?

Discourse is a notoriously difficult term to define but in general "it refers to units of language above the level of the sentence" (McEnery and Hardie 2012: 132). In a detailed definition, Thornbury (2010) enumerates three main senses of the term: discourse as connected text, discourse as language in use and discourse as social practices. Similarly, Gee (1999) distinguishes between discourse (with a little d) and Discourse (with a capital D). While the former is concerned with language in use in specific contexts, the latter involves not only linguistic practices but also systems of knowledge, beliefs and other elements of social life. This distinction is also reflected in Groom, Charles and John's (2015) discussion of discourse-oriented approaches. The authors posit that there are two basic types of discourse analysis: the first one concentrates on the structure of different kinds of interactions and the other is the study of conventionalized meanings, values and ideologies held by specific social groups.

What transpires from the above definitions is that discourse analysis is an umbrella term and it encompasses a set of mainly qualitative methods and practices aimed at exploring specific examples of language in use and studying how meaning emerges in the process of interaction (Biber, Connor and Upton 2007). Corpus linguistics, in turn, tends to be perceived as a quantitative methodology, which relies on frequency data and statistical procedures and seeks to reveal typical patterns of natural language use. It becomes evident then that there are inherent differences between these two approaches to the study of language. Nevertheless, both discourse analysis and corpus linguistics are interested in naturally occurring linguistic data (Flowerdew 2012) and consequently they can be usefully integrated and complement each as is manifested by findings from corpus-assisted discourse studies (e.g. Partington 2004; Partington, Duguid and Taylor 2013). Operating on this premise, in the following sections you will learn how research at the interface of discourse analysis and corpus linguistics can provide new insights into vocabulary as a key element of authentic discourse.

9.2 Interface between discourse analysis and corpus linguistics

According to Thornbury (2010: 276), the optimal way of integrating corpus and discourse approaches is to combine computation and interpretation "in mutually informing cycles of investigation". As discourse analysis is a fundamentally interpretative activity based on qualitative analyses (Groom et al. 2015), supporting its findings with robust corpus statistics can add validity to claims about specialized types of language use (Baker and McEnery 2015). On the other hand, Handford (2010) rightly states that even though corpora have much to say about language in terms of statistical data, they can lack detailed contextual information, which is usually gleaned from interpretative analyses of the use of language in specific contexts. In short, it can be argued that a synergy of both methodologies offers new possibilities for exploring a wide range of linguistic issues.

In a comprehensive overview of corpus approaches to discourse analysis, Conrad (2002) distinguishes four main areas of work within this area: i) specific features of language in use, ii) realizations of specific functions of language, iii) varieties of language and iv) occurrences of linguistic features throughout a text. A similar classification is provided by Flowerdew (2012), who includes yet more categories: i) textual approaches that focus on language choices, meanings and patterns, ii) critical approaches that explore discourse as ideology (e.g. critical discourse analysis) and iii) contextual approaches that foreground sociolinguistic and situational factors. This suggests that there is a lot of potential for corpus-based inquiry of language use at the level of discourse, and given that the number of corpora representing specialized types of discourse is quickly increasing, further integration of corpus and discourse approaches is desirable.

However, we should also bear in mind that combining discourse analysis and corpus linguistics might pose certain methodological challenges. Baker and McEnery (2015) point to issues such as: a bias that a researcher brings into their analysis, reporting unrevealing findings (e.g. a rise in the frequencies of specific words as a result of some political or economic events) and violating ethical standards in the process of data collection. These are potential pitfalls that you need to be aware of, regardless of which aspects of the corpus–discourse interface you decide to pursue.

9.3 Lexical features of discourse

Vocabulary participates in shaping the internal structure of texts and fulfills a number of functions related to the use of language at the level of discourse. The following paragraphs aim to demonstrate this by discussing examples of lexical features that contribute to textual cohesion and explaining how discourse analysis can highlight the importance of lexis in the construction and organization of discourse. We seek to show how automatic corpus searches supplemented by qualitative analyses of language in use with respect to both context (a situation in which a given piece of discourse is produced) and co-text (fragments of text surrounding a given item) can enable you to delve deeper into the role of lexical elements in building discourse.

The notion of lexical cohesion is of central importance to the study of discourse (see Mahlberg 2006 for details). In simple terms, it can be defined as the ways "in which the components of the surface texts are mutually connected within a sequence" (Carter 1998: 103). In other words, cohesion "expresses the continuity that exists between one part of the text and another" (Halliday and Hasan 1976: 299), whereby it contributes to the internal unity of discourse. One of the main textual mechanisms that has been explored in the context of building cohesion is reiteration. According to McCarthy (1991), reiteration involves either the direct repetition of a word or the use of a related item that carries the same meaning (e.g. a synonym, near-synonym or superordinate). To illustrate the mechanism of reiteration, the author uses the word 'furniture' and explains that it can be replaced by superordinates such as 'item', 'object' or 'thing'. All of these words express a similar meaning but in terms of hierarchical relations, they represent a more general level than 'furniture'. Other instances of general words that help to build the structure of discourse include 'people', 'idea' or 'fact' and, as attested by their high frequency in corpora, they are among the most commonly used words in English.

Task 9.1: Using data from the academic section of the Corpus of Contemporary American English (COCA), find examples of concordances in which the word 'fact' contributes to lexical cohesion.

It is of note that reiteration is not a chance event. As stated by McCarthy (1991: 66), "writers and speakers make conscious choices whether to repeat, or find a synonym, or a superordinate" in order to add new dimensions and nuances to the meaning they wish to convey. This shows that the use of varied lexical forms across longer stretches of discourse constitutes an important aspect of the meaning-creation process. Crucially, by exploring such forms you can uncover new facts about the texture of naturally occurring language.

A related discourse phenomenon that you can study by means of corpora is relexicalization. It can be defined as a specific form of paraphrasing in which speakers take up one another's vocabulary as they participate in conversations (McCarthy 1991). Some useful examples of relexicalization are provided by Buttery and McCarthy's (2012) study of lexis in spoken English. Using data from the Cambridge and Nottingham Corpus of Discourse in English (CANCODE), the authors employed techniques from discourse and conversation analysis to analyze variation in the occurrence of vocabulary across turn boundaries, that is, sequences of turns where speakers take over from one another. This methodology enabled them to shed light on the importance of lexical chains or a series of synonyms and near-synonyms used "over longer stretches of discourse" (Buttery and McCarthy 2012: 297). Figure 9.1 presents a fragment of an informal conversation in a shop which exemplifies relexicalization as a chain of positive adjectives used across two speakers' turns (all the relexicalized forms have been bolded).

As Buttery and McCarthy (2012) emphasize, such lexical phenomena can be observed both within and across speakers' turns, which points to the central role of vocabulary in both developing specific topics and creating interactional convergence between interlocutors. Thus, given that corpora provide numerous examples of authentic conversations that take place in different contexts, you can use such data to conduct research into speakers' repetition of modified lexical forms and analyze how this repetition helps them engage in the interactions in which they participate.

> Task 9.2: Figure 9.2 presents a short fragment of a conversation from the spoken section of COCA that represents the use of the word 'smashing'. The conversation took place during a TV show presented by Sean Hannity on *Fox News*. Can you identify any examples of lexical repetition and relexicalization?

Another notion of interest to discourse analysts is **intertextuality**, a property which distinguishes a text "from a random sequence of unconnected sentences" (McCarthy 1991: 65). It is a key aspect of research into discourse organization in

---

[In a shoe-shop: <$1> is the customer, <$2> is the assistant]
<$2> Probably needs adjusting but I'll check that.
<$1> Oh right. That's **lovely**.
<$2> | Okay.
<$1> | Yeah | that's **nice**.
<$2> | They're **nice** aren't they.
<$1> Yeah they are **nice**.
<$2> **Very very nice**.
<$1> Thank you.
<$2> They feel **right**?
<$1> Yeah.
<$2> Does it?
<$1> That feels **pretty good** actually.
<$2> Yes **smashing fit**.
<$1> Yeah. (CANCODE © Cambridge University Press)

Figure 9.1 A fragment of a conversation taken from Buttery and McCarthy's (2012) analysis of relexicalization

ROVE: I think that now means that – again, I'm finding it difficult to find the right place here, but that would put McCain over 800, 826. And he would need – this number wrong here at the bottom. He now needs less than 270 votes in order to get the nomination.
WALLACE: So he's really on his way?
ROVE: He's on his way.
WALLACE: Let's talk about the Democratic side. I mean, we're talking about a smashing Obama victory in Virginia, a very healthy victory in Maryland. The fact that we're able to call it so quickly. Is Hillary Clinton in trouble?
ROVE: Absolutely. But, again, remember the proportionality of the Democratic contest rules means that tonight she came in roughly, according to the FOX News count, up 23 delegates. If he continues this tonight, basically two to one victories, he will come out – he'll pick up roughly 50 delegates.

Figure 9.2 A fragment of a conversation taken from the spoken section of COCA

that it explores how "a discourse makes reference to prior and future discourses" (Cheng 2012: 160). As Cheng (2012: 159) asserts, "each discourse is part of a chain of discourses which intertwine" and vocabulary is a vital element in creating such interdependencies within texts. Evidence for the discourse-organizing function of lexis can be found in McCarthy's (1991) analysis of words such as 'problem' or 'solution'. These are words that are used to signal discourse segments (i.e. a sentence, a paragraph or even a longer piece of language) and consequently they help readers (or listeners) navigate through the structure of specific texts.

Flowerdew and Forest (2009, 2015) provide useful examples of how vocabulary contributes to intertextuality. In their corpus-based genre analysis of PhD literature reviews, the authors focus on the signaling function of words such as 'research', 'advantage', 'situation' and 'solution'. These abstract nouns are nonspecific in meaning when they are considered in isolation. However, they can exhibit much more specific meanings when they are analyzed in relation to the use of lexis in particular parts of texts. By way of illustration, Flowerdew and Forest investigated the lexico-grammatical patterning around the word 'research' and reported that collocations such as 'little research' or 'further research' are key building elements of literature reviews, where they are used to refer to gaps in research. To be more precise, these words fulfill important textual functions such as signaling moves (or rhetorical steps) that make up the structure of PhD theses.

Task 9.3: There are seventy-nine occurrences of the phrase 'further research' in the academic section of the British National Corpus (BNC). Do any of them confirm the findings of Flowerdew and Forest?

Another extensive area of research within corpus-based discourse analysis is concerned with the use and functions of discourse markers. A discourse marker (or operator) is "a word or phrase – for instance, a conjunction, adverbial, comment clause, interjection – that is uttered with the primary function of bringing the listener's attention to a particular kind of linkage of the upcoming utterance with the immediate discourse context" (Redeker 1991: 1168). Naturally, this definition centers on spoken language but such an understanding of discourse markers is equally applicable to the written mode of communication. As Rühlemann (2010: 296) notes, corpus-based research that focuses on the role of discourse markers is an extremely productive area, with studies ranging from explorations of the textual and interpersonal functions of discourse particles (e.g. Aijmer's (2002) analysis of the London-Lund Corpus of spoken English) to analyses of historical data (e.g. Lutzky's (2012) investigation of early modern English). Furthermore, there is also a substantial body of work based on learner corpora which juxtaposes the use of discourse markers by native and non-native speakers. For instance, Müller (2005) compared the use of discourse markers by American students and L1 German learners of English, while Liu (2013) studied the importance of register awareness in L2 speakers' use of multiword discourse markers.

When it comes to practical aspects of conducting this kind of corpus-based research, it must be stated that discourse markers cannot be easily identified by means of automatic searches. As a consequence, one of the most convenient methods is to look for examples of some pre-selected lexical forms (Thornbury 2010). In simple terms this means that you create an inventory of the items you are interested in (e.g. see Carter and McCarthy (2006) for an extensive list of different forms and functions of discourse markers) and subsequently explore patterns of their occurrence in a specific corpus. The most commonly studied instances include: 'fine', 'good', 'like', 'now', 'okay', 'right', 'so', 'actually', 'well', 'I mean', 'you know', 'so to speak', 'in other words' and many more. It is worth highlighting that this list contains examples of both one- and multiword discourse markers. As Buttery and McCarthy (2012: 290) underline, lexical chunks "have developed pragmatic specialisms in discourse with regard to organization and management and the signaling of stance, and operate outside of clause- and sentence boundaries, as free-standing discourse items". Thus, a large part of corpus-based analysis of discourse focuses on phraseology and the ways in which phraseological units realize different pragmatic functions (see below).

Task 9.4: Compare the frequency of the following discourse markers in the spoken and written subsections of COCA.

you know, I mean, actually, right, in other words, so to speak

To sum up, exploring how different forms of vocabulary are configured over longer stretches of discourse contributes to a better understanding of their role in the creation and maintenance of discourse flow. It turns out that through the use of specific words and lexical patterns, speakers and writers are able to segment and organize different pieces of information so that they constitute a coherent unit of discourse. By combining corpus and discourse-analytic approaches, you can gain insights into the importance of such vocabulary choices, the kinds of intertextual relationships they form within texts and the ways in which they fulfill different textual functions.

9.4 Corpora and pragmatics

Pragmatics is the study of language use in context or, to be more precise, the study of how meaning is created and interpreted in context (Cheng 2012). As stated by Adolphs (2006: 122), pragmatic analysis is concerned with "the relationship between language form, language function and language users" and considering that corpora provide access to numerous examples of authentic language, they can become a powerful tool to explore the use of words and different forms of lexical patterning in relation to how they function pragmatically. With this particular focus in mind, the following sections aim to demonstrate the mechanics of corpus pragmatics. More specifically, I seek to explain how some of the corpus techniques described throughout this book can be combined with qualitative discourse-analytic interpretative reading of concordances to raise your awareness of the pragmatic relevance of vocabulary.

However, before we present some examples of this kind of research, it needs to be stated that the use of corpora for pragmatic analysis can be fraught with practical problems. Considering that "corpora record text, not meaning" (Rühlemann 2010: 289), raw corpus material does not lend itself easily to pragmatic investigations, unless we have access to pragmatically annotated corpora such as the Speech Act Annotated Corpus for Dialogue Systems (Leech and Weisser 2003). As Rühlemann and Aijmer (2015: 10) observe, "for most pragmatic phenomena there is no one-to-one relationship between form and function". This suggests that the same pragmatic function can be realized by a number of surface forms and therefore identifying all of them in a reliable and replicable way might pose certain methodological challenges.

Thus, to gain insights into the multi-faceted links between specific lexical choices, different nuances of meaning they convey and pragmatic functions they fulfill, automatic corpus searches need to be integrated with qualitative analyses of concordance lines. As Buttery and McCarthy (2012: 288) argue, even though quantitative findings such as frequency values are informative, they are not sufficient "to account for the contribution of lexis to discourse". As a result, pragmatic analyses of corpus data tend to focus on specific examples of concordances as a source of information about "how lexical items are used in real contexts" (McCarthy 1991: 64). This then points to the fact that corpus pragmatics is an intersection between corpus linguistics and pragmatics as it "integrates the foundational methodologies" of the two fields (Rühlemann and Aijmer 2015: 15). Whether or not the field will expand, the authors note, is largely dependent on practical issues such as the introduction of automatic pragmatic annotation and the development of larger pragmatic corpora.

9.4.1 Pragmatic functions of vocabulary

One strand of corpus-based pragmatic research that you might consider undertaking is the exploration of the pragmatic effects of vocabulary use. Corpora provide a window into naturally occurring stretches of language and by analyzing the use of specific words, chunks and lexical patterns in different contexts, it is possible to delve into how they fulfill important pragmatic functions. As emphasized by Adolphs (2006: 125), "functional analyses of individual lexical items or phrases can provide an empirical angle on some of the core issues in pragmatics", such as the ways in which vocabulary eases communication and fosters interaction between interlocutors.

A convincing example of such research is O'Keeffe et al.'s (2007: 159) examination of relational language, which they define as "language which serves to create and maintain good relations between the speaker and hearer". Using conversational data from CANCODE, the authors demonstrate how automatic corpus searches supported by the qualitative interpretation of concordances provide illuminating insights into the importance of vocabulary in building everyday interactions. More specifically, O'Keeffe et al. (2007) investigate the role of lexical units in fulfilling a variety of pragmatic functions such as marking the speaker's attitude toward the proposition that is conveyed ('right', 'well', 'I mean', 'you know'), hedging or mitigating the directness of what is said ('a bit', 'I guess', 'I don't know if'), expressing vagueness and approximation ('a bit', 'a couple of', 'or something like that'), showing listenership ('I see', 'that's interesting') and many more. The authors provide numerous examples of the realization of these functions across different types of interactional exchanges. A strong case in point is the analysis of how some high-frequency lexical items function as response tokens, that is, discourse items which speakers use to acknowledge what is being said and signal to their interlocutors that they are being listened to. Instances of such items include backchanneling cues ('mm' or 'umhum'), reactives ('oh'), variations of 'yes' and 'no' (e.g. 'yeah') and one-word responses such as 'right', 'cool', 'exactly' or 'absolutely'.

Another example of how corpora can be of great help to individuals interested in the pragmatic role of vocabulary is Cheng and O'Keeffe's (2015) study into vague language. Vagueness (e.g. items such as 'about', 'approximately', 'or so') is a common feature of natural communication and it is used to express imprecision, uncertainty and over-generalization (Channell 1994; Carter and McCarthy 2006). As Carter (1998: 93) notes, determining the extent to which vagueness is used "depends on contextual factors", with informal spoken contexts producing "the highest degrees of vagueness". Importantly for the purposes of this book, vagueness can be manifested in a number of ways and lexis is one of the key carriers of vague information.

In a seminal publication devoted to this topic, Channell (1994) distinguishes between three main categories: vague additives (e.g. 'about') and tags (e.g. 'and things like that'), vague words (e.g. 'thingy') and quantifiers (e.g. 'piles of'), and vagueness resulting from implicature (or an implied meaning). Relying on corpus data, Cheng and O'Keeffe (2015) focused on the first two categories and explored the use of vague words in combination with numbers and quantifiers. Specifically, the authors looked at thirteen vague words such as 'about', 'around' and 'approximately' and compared their use in two subsections of the Hong Kong Corpus of Spoken English (consisting of both native and non-native data) and the Limerick Corpus of Irish English. Thanks to this design, it was possible to make two kinds of comparisons: intracultural (native vs. non-native English in Hong Kong) and intercultural (Hong Kong English vs. Irish English). Statistical tests revealed no significant differences between the corpora in terms of the frequency of vague language, which could be taken as evidence showing "a degree of universality in form choice". However, the authors went on to explore their data more deeply and through the qualitative reading of concordances they revealed cultural implicitness and contextually specific uses of the vague words under study. Figure 9.3 is an illustration of a short fragment of data taken from the Irish corpus. It is a conversation between a mother and a son which demonstrates how the use of vague language is challenged by the high level of directness that characterizes family discourse.

This analysis illustrates how corpus pragmatics lies at the interface of discourse-analytic and corpus approaches, with both methodologies complementing

---

(A, the son; B, the mother)
A: I'll be back later.
B: Okay.
A: Good luck.
B: What time is later Jason?
A: About half an hour.
B: Half an hour?
A: I don't know. I'd say an hour probably.
B: Are you definitely going to be back then?
A: Why?
B: Cause I'll lock the door if you aren't.
A: Lock the door away.
B: Okay.
A: I'll open it myself.
B: Okay bye.
<sound of car driving off>

Figure 9.3 A fragment of a conversation taken from Cheng and O'Keeffe's (2015) analysis of vagueness

each other and providing a wide variety of options for exploring naturally occurring language. It is important that you consider using some of these options as you embark on your own analysis of the pragmatic dimensions of vocabulary use.

> Task 9.5: Select three examples of the lexical items described in this section and study them in the spoken section of COCA. Consider their pragmatic functions and explore how they contribute to maintaining good relationships between the interlocutors participating in the piece of discourse that you analyze.

9.4.2 Speech acts

Another important aspect of pragmatic research pertaining to vocabulary centers on the notion of speech acts. In general terms, it can be said that speech acts are utterances that serve a performative function in communication (Adolphs 2006). For instance, we perform speech acts when we apologize, suggest something and agree or disagree with someone and, crucially, examples of how speakers perform such acts in their interactions can be studied via corpus data. A good exemplification of such research is Adolphs's (2008) pragmatic analysis of different ways of making suggestions in spoken English.

Ideally, if corpora were pragmatically annotated, such analyses could be carried out automatically. However, as pointed out by Cheng (2012), there are very few corpora that are tagged in terms of pragmatic markers. The only exceptions that the author mentions are the Corpus of Verbal Response Modes, the Speech Act Annotated Corpus for Dialogue Systems and a subsection of the Michigan Corpus of Academic Spoken English (MICASE). This means that the process of identifying examples of speech acts is usually carried out by combining automatic searches with qualitative analyses of concordance lines. What follows, therefore, is a short description of procedures that you can use to conduct a corpus-based study of speech acts.

> Task 9.6: Using data from the spoken part of COCA, analyze how the speech act of apologizing can be realized by means of different lexical units.

In the first part of this task, check the frequency of the lemma 'apologize' and identify examples of its different forms that function as a pragmatic marker of apology. Decide which of these forms should be included in your analysis. It is likely that there is a range of words that participate in the realization of the act of apologizing and, as a result, consider repeating the same search for the word 'sorry' (because it is likely to play a key role in this process). Once you know which forms of these words are the most frequent ones, explore their frequency and the types of collocations (and potentially other kinds of chunks) they form. As stated in the previous section, many pragmatic functions are realized by means of multiword units. In the qualitative phase of the analysis, select a sample of concordances for the forms that you have identified in the first phase and investigate how they are used across larger stretches of discourse. Such a careful analysis should enable you to produce an evidence-based profile for the speech act of apologizing.

9.4.3 Pragmatic functions of semantic prosody

As already discussed in Chapter 5, the notion of semantic prosody refers to attitudinal or connotative meanings conveyed by patterns of co-occurring words or extended units of meaning (see Hunston 2007 or Partington et al. 2013 for more details). In this section of the chapter we return to this concept but consider it from the perspective of its pragmatic (or discourse) significance because, as Sinclair (1991) states, semantic prosody is a unit of meaning that needs to be interpreted pragmatically. More specifically, we seek to discuss how corpus-based analysis of naturally occurring language provides us with an opportunity to explore the role of phraseological units in terms of the different pragmatic functions they may serve.

In her account of semantic prosody, Cheng (2012: 114) states that it can be defined as "the overall functional meaning of a lexical item". Such an understanding of the concept stems from Sinclair's (2004) approach to phraseology, in which semantic prosody occupies a central position as the underlying principle of the process of lexical co-selection. As emphasized by the author himself, semantic prosody "has a leading role to play in the integration of an item with its surroundings" (Sinclair 2004: 34), for it expresses the function of the whole lexical unit.

If we follow this claim and accept that semantic prosody determines the choice of words and their lexical patterning (i.e. their collocational and colligational company), then corpus-based explorations of sequences of co-occurring words can be used as a means of tapping into communicative intentions and needs of speakers and writers. In other words, if we assume that language users rely on semantic prosody as a way of expressing specific functional meanings, the concept itself can be employed as "a useful resource for studying pragmatic phenomena" (Rühlemann 2010: 292). According to Cheng (2012), examples of these phenomena include irony, sarcasm, persuasion and different emotional states. For instance, given that semantic prosody is linked to the point of view of a speaker or writer, you can explore how it helps to express concepts such as surprise or frustration.

To illustrate how a corpus-based analysis of the pragmatic meaning of semantic prosody can be carried out, we will use some examples provided by Sinclair (2004). Using data from the Bank of English (consisting of over 200 million words at that time), the author explored the semantic prosody of the item 'true feelings'.

On the basis of the semantic preference and frequent collocations of the phrase (e.g. 'conceal', 'hide', 'mask', 'disguise', 'deny', 'not be keenly aware of'), Sinclair concluded that its discourse function was to express reluctance or inability to talk about emotional matters. Another example that is worth mentioning is the verb 'budge'. Sinclair found that 'budge' had a strong tendency to co-occur with negative words (e.g. 'refuse' or negative forms of modal verbs). The author attributed it to the specific kind of semantic prosody that speakers use to express "frustration (or a similar emotion) at the refusal or inability of some obstacle to move" (Sinclair 2004: 145). In a similar fashion, Stubbs (2013) argues that semantic prosody concerns the speaker's evaluation and their communicative purpose in using specific configurations or combinations of words. The researcher observes that while collocation and colligation are related to form or how something is expressed, semantic prosody has to do with the speaker's motivation for the way they use language and what pragmatic force it has.

> Task 9.7: Figure 9.4 presents a selection of concordance lines for the phrase 'true feelings' taken from the BNC. Explore the semantic prosody of the phrase in terms of how it fulfills the discourse function of expressing reluctance or inability.

What is more, to highlight the crucial role of semantic prosody in discourse, Stubbs (2013) suggests splitting the concept into two separate aspects: illocutionary force (e.g. fulfilling a specific speech act) and discourse management (e.g. signaling specific text segments as parts of longer stretches of discourse). In fact, the author goes even further and calls for treating the discourse-managing function of semantic prosody as the fifth level of Sinclair's (2004) model of phraseology, in which collocation, colligation, semantic preference and semantic prosody participate in the process of lexical co-selection (see Chapter 5 for details). As Stubbs (2013: 25) aptly notes, "the model combines form, content, speech act force and discourse function, and therefore contributes to a theory, not just of language, but of communication". Thus, by examining the ways in which words co-occur and form different phraseological units, we can tap into more fine-grained shades of meaning and their pragmatic force in different acts of communication.

9.5 Exemplary study: corpora and discourse analysis by Baker (2013)

This section offers a step-by-step description of Baker's (2013) study that employs a number of corpus techniques to explore the discourse of tourism. The study is based on a small corpus of twelve holiday leaflets (17,865 words)

No of concordance	KWIC
1	problems, especially the er, he hasn't actually dealt with the **true feelings** that he had towards his father, and who instead chose to vent his rage
2	and Hari realized that he had used the laugh many times to conceal his **true feelings**.' I won't promise anything,' she said following him,'
3	I've dared set my will against his. And if they guess my **true feelings** — They'll say nothing. Not in public, at least, if you make
4	distracted. A refusal in such circumstances may well not reflect my employer's **true feelings** on the matter, but once having sustained such a dismissal, I could not
5	his safety was almost too much to bear. She tried to mask her **true feelings** from her mother and sister, but her throat ached with tension and she felt
6	Joan's seeming ill-humour was a ploy to conceal even from herself her **true feelings** — the quickening of her pulses at mention of the beloved, told a different
7	be ashamed of snobbishness — or perhaps I only taught him to keep his **true feelings** from me. But he remained — though I'm sure he honestly fought against
8	one of nature's radicals, someone to whom he could reveal his new **true feelings**. As for his own talk — that, once begun, had, as
9	Hope smiled to himself: the smile broadened, and to disguise his **true feelings** he turned the smile on Mr Crump; who was greatly encouraged as he had
10	before the Armistice was signed, she realised that she had been denying her **true feelings** for years. She had loved Connor from the day she set eyes on him
11	you do whatever you wish.' Stephen's controlled voice disguised his **true feelings**, but Christina sensed his jealousy and changed the subject.' Why don't
12	you're probably a very good husband, but you like to hide your **true feelings**." Oh, don't be so serious, Basil,' smiled
13	a statement of fact. Dexter was surprised that the TV presenter revealed her **true feelings** towards Nicola so quickly: most people in his experience,
14	'd ever seen, but which she always felt quite at odds with her **true feelings**. In fact, there were lots of things she'd like to change about
15	turned, looking at the girl, smiling at her reassuringly, keeping his **true feelings** from showing. Games. It was all one big game to DeVore.

Figure 9.4 Sample concordance lines for the phrase 'true feelings' taken from the BNC

and the author demonstrates how a simple frequency-based wordlist can be a good starting point for further analyses that "illuminate a variety of interesting phenomena" (Baker 2013: 11).

Using WordSmith tools, Baker started his analysis by producing a list of the most frequent words from his holiday corpus and compared them with data from the BNC (see Table 9.1). This comparison resulted in a number of insightful observations. For instance, although the holiday corpus was built of written data, it contained many tokens of the personal pronoun 'you', which is typically regarded as a feature of spoken language (see Chapter 4 for a discussion of differences between spoken and written vocabulary). As Baker (2013: 18) explains, the high frequency of 'you' in the holiday leaflets "suggests a personal style of writing, where the writer is directly addressing the reader".

Another observation that can be made about the holiday corpus concerns the frequency of function words. The high rate of occurrence of such words is hardly surprising because, as we already mentioned in Chapter 4, function words tend to have a high frequency, irrespective of the type of texts analyzed. However, while such grammatical words are important, it is a list of the most frequent lexical words that is likely to yield some useful insights into the specific nature of the discourse of tourism. That is why Baker (2013) emphasizes the importance of distinguishing between function (grammatical) and lexical words. Following this distinction, the author shows how words such as 'beach', 'pool' and 'studios', the most frequent lexical items from the holiday corpus, represent the type of language that is used when people describe their holidays. Interestingly, both the words 'bar' and 'bars' (plural form) occurred with a high frequency in the corpus, which sparked Baker to produce a frequency list based on lemmas. The fact that the lemma 'bar' occurred at the top of this new list is a valuable finding because it confirms that the unit of counting that drives our analysis is of paramount importance to our results (see Chapter 3).

Table 9.1 Examples of the most frequent words in the holiday corpus and BNC expressed in percentages (adapted from Baker 2013)

	Word	% frequency in the holiday corpus	% frequency in the BNC
1	The	5.55	6.20
2	And	3.62	2.68
3	To	2.64	2.66
4	A	2.44	2.21
5	Of	1.96	3.12
6	You	1.95	0.68
7	For	1.38	0.90
8	In	1.37	1.97
9	On	1.15	0.74
10	All	1.04	0.28

Going beyond the frequency values, the next stage of Baker's study focused on the analysis of clusters (n-grams) formed around words such as 'bar', 'club' and other frequent items from the corpus. While the high frequency of clusters such as 'bars and clubs' or 'loads of bars' could suggest that consuming alcohol is the most frequent concept expressed in the holiday corpus, Baker (2013: 22) warns against "jumping to conclusions too early" and continues his analysis. Namely, he explores the occurrence of verbs as another source of information about the discourse of tourism. His findings reveal that although the corpus does not contain too many verbal forms that explicitly refer to getting drunk, it is possible to identify some verbs that describe tourists' recovery from alcohol consumption (e.g. 'chilling' or 'relaxing'). From a discourse standpoint, such vocabulary can be treated as a more subtle way of suggesting that drinking is an integral part of the holiday experience.

Another aspect of Baker's analysis makes use of dispersion plots as a window into the position of specific words within holiday brochures. In simple terms, dispersion refers to the distribution of vocabulary in terms of "how evenly the occurrences of a word are spread across different texts" (Nation 2016: 6). This analysis enables Baker to delineate how the holiday brochures follow a similar structure when it comes to reflecting some ideological beliefs hidden behind the production of such texts. For instance, putting words related to work at the beginning of brochures creates the image of holidays as a form of escape for holidaymakers, which can be interpreted as a way of forgetting about work-related problems. Baker (2013: 26) also refers to how the use of language contributes to the issues of identity construction and identification as important elements that are present in the discourse of advertising.

It is also vital to note that Baker engages in a sociolinguistic (demographic) analysis of some informal words such as 'loads', 'mates' and 'cool'. The author juxtaposes the frequencies of these words in the holiday corpus vs. the BNC, which is treated as a reference corpus. Without going into too much detail, the results point to the influence of age and gender on the type of language found in the holiday corpus. Baker's (2013: 30) analysis suggests that the leaflets were written primarily for young adults, "emulating the typical language" that is normally used by these speakers. However, at the same time, the author cautions against overemphasizing the demographic frequency, as not all members of a specific age or social group will always use the same types of linguistic forms to discuss a given topic.

As a last point, it needs to be stated that Baker's study also involved some elements of a multimodal analysis of the visual content of brochures. This is a convincing exemplification of integrating different approaches within corpus-based discourse analysis, in which frequency data are only a starting point. Baker did not stop at the raw frequency statistics but delved more deeply into the corpus with a view to gaining a better understanding of language in use and eventually producing a more accurate description of the type of discourse of tourism. As Baker (2013: 33) stresses, "context plays an important role in the analysis of particular words" and therefore discourse-oriented corpus analyses need to go beyond the simple level of frequencies. On the other hand, it is worth pointing out that not all research projects that rely on corpus data will involve all the stages of the corpus analysis employed in Baker's study. To a large extent, the choice of appropriate methodologies will depend on your research interests and the research question(s) you want to pursue.

To sum up, this section has focused on the use of discourse-oriented corpus analysis as an effective way of studying the role of vocabulary in building the logical structure of discourse. We have demonstrated that combining corpus and discourse approaches affords a number of opportunities to explore the use of specific words and lexical units and how they fulfill important discourse roles and contribute to the creation and maintenance of discourse flow.

Summary

This chapter has focused on the use of corpora for exploring vocabulary at the level of discourse. First, we presented the benefits of combining corpus and discourse approaches for the purpose of analyzing the use of words and phrases. Next, we discussed the importance of discourse-oriented corpus research for studying the role of lexical features in constructing and organizing discourse. Finally, we demonstrated how corpus techniques can assist in the analysis of pragmatic functions of vocabulary use.

References

Adolphs, S. (2006). *Introducing Electronic Text Analysis: A practical guide for language and literary studies*. London and New York: Routledge.

Adolphs, S. (2008). *Corpus and Context: Investigating pragmatic functions in spoken discourse*. Amsterdam: John Benjamins.

Aijmer, K. (2002). *English Discourse Particles: Evidence from a corpus*. Amsterdam: John Benjamins.

Baker, P. (2013). Corpora and discourse analysis, in K. Hyland (ed.) *Discourse Studies Reader: Essential excerpts*. London: Bloomsbury Academic, 11–34.

Baker, P. and McEnery, T. (2015). Introduction, in T. McEnery and P. Baker (eds.) *Corpora and Discourse Studies: Integrating discourse and corpora*. Basingstoke: Palgrave Macmillan, 1–19.

Biber, D., Connor, U. and Upton, T. (2007). *Discourse on the Move: Using corpus analysis to describe discourse structure*. Amsterdam: John Benjamins.

Buttery, P. and McCarthy, M. (2012). Lexis in spoken discourse, in J. P. Gee and M. Handford (eds.) *Routledge Handbook of Discourse Analysis*. London and New York: Routledge, 285–300.

Carter, R. (1998). *Vocabulary: Applied Linguistic Perspectives*. London and New York: Routledge.

Carter, R. and McCarthy, M. (2006). *Cambridge Grammar of English: A comprehensive guide to spoken and written grammar and usage*. Cambridge: Cambridge University Press.

Channell, J. (1994). *Vague Language*. Oxford: Oxford University Press.

Cheng, W. (2012). *Exploring Corpus Linguistics: Language in action.* London and New York: Routledge.

Cheng, W. and O'Keeffe, A. (2015). Vagueness, in K. Aijmer and C. Rühlemann (eds.) *Corpus Pragmatics: A handbook.* Cambridge: Cambridge University Press, 360–378.

Conrad, S. (2002). Corpus linguistic approaches for discourse analysis. *Annual Review of Applied Linguistics,* 22, 75–95.

Flowerdew, J. and Forest, R. W. (2009). Schematic structure and lexico-grammatical realization in corpus-based genre analysis: The case of research in the PhD literature review, in M. Charles, D. Pecorari and S. Hunston (eds.) *Academic Writing: At the interface of corpus and discourse.* London: Equinox, 15–36.

Flowerdew, J. and Forest, R. W. (2015). *Signalling Nouns in English: A corpus-based discourse approach.* Cambridge: Cambridge University Press.

Flowerdew, L. (2012). Corpus-based discourse analysis, in J. P. Gee and M. Handford (eds.) *The Routledge Handbook of Discourse Analysis.* London and New York: Routledge, 174–187.

Gee, J. P. (1999). *An Introduction to Discourse Analysis: Theory and method.* London: Routledge.

Groom, N., Charles, M. and John, S. (2015). Corpora, grammar, and discourse analysis: Recent trends, current challenges, in N. Groom, M. Charles and S. John (eds.) *Corpora, Grammar and Discourse: In honour of Susan Hunston.* Amsterdam/Philadelphia: John Benjamins, 1–20.

Halliday, M. A. K. and Hasan, R. (1976). *Cohesion in English.* London: Longman.

Handford, M. (2010). What can a corpus tell us about specialist genres?, in A. O'Keeffe and M. McCarthy (eds.) *The Routledge Handbook of Corpus Linguistics.* London and New York: Routledge, 255–269.

Hunston, S. (2007). Semantic prosody revisited. *International Journal of Corpus Linguistics,* 12, 2, 249–268.

Leech, G. and Weisser, M. (2003). Pragmatics in dialogue, in R. Mitkov (ed.) *The Oxford Handbook of Computational Linguistics.* Oxford: Oxford University Press, 135–156.

Liu, A. L. (2013). Register awareness and English language learning: The case of multi-word discourse markers. Unpublished PhD thesis, University of Nottingham.

Lutzky, U. (2012). *Discourse Markers in Early Modern English.* Amsterdam/Philadelphia: John Benjamins.

Mahlberg, M. (2006). Lexical cohesion: Corpus linguistic theory and its application in English language teaching. *International Journal of Corpus Linguistics,* 11, 3, 363–383.

McCarthy, M. (1991). *Discourse Analysis for Language Teachers.* Cambridge: Cambridge University Press.

McEnery, T. and Hardie, A. (2012) *Corpus Linguistics: Method, theory and practice.* Cambridge: Cambridge University Press.

Müller, S. (2005). *Discourse Markers in Native and Non-native English Discourse.* Amsterdam/Philadelphia: John Benjamins.

Nation, I. S. P. (2016). Word lists, in I. S. P. Nation (ed.) *Making and Using Word Lists for Language Learning and Testing.* Amsterdam/Philadelphia: John Benjamins, 3–13.

O'Keeffe, A., McCarthy, M. and Carter, R. (2007). *From Corpus to Classroom.* Cambridge: Cambridge University Press.

Partington, A. (2004). Corpora and discourse: A most congruous beast, in A. Partington, J. Morley and L. Haarman (eds.) *Corpora and Discourse.* Bern: Peter Lang, 11–20.

Partington, A., Duguid, A. and Taylor, C. (2013). *Patterns and Meanings in Discourse Theory and Practice in Corpus-assisted Discourse Studies (CADS).* Amsterdam/Philadelphia: John Benjamins.

Redeker, G. (1991). Linguistic markers of discourse structure. *Linguistics,* 29, 6, 1139–1172.

Rühlemann, C. (2010). What can a corpus tell us about pragmatics?, in A. O'Keeffe and M. McCarthy (eds.) *The Routledge Handbook of Corpus Linguistics.* London and New York: Routledge, 288–301.

Rühlemann, C. and Aijmer, K. (2015). Introduction: Corpus pragmatics – Laying the foundations, in K. Aijmer and C. Rühlemann (eds.) *Corpus Pragmatics: A handbook.* Cambridge: Cambridge University Press, 1–26.

Sinclair, J. (1991). *Corpus, Concordance, Collocation.* Oxford: Oxford University Press.

Sinclair, J. (2004). *Trust the Text: Language, corpus and discourse.* London and New York: Routledge.

Stubbs, M. (2013). Sequence and order: The neo-Firthian tradition of corpus semantics, in H. Hasselgard, J. Ebeling and S. E. Ebeling (eds.) *Corpus Perspectives on Patterns of Lexis.* Amsterdam/Philadelphia: John Benjamins, 13–34.

Thornbury, S. (2010). What can a corpus tell us about discourse?, in A. O'Keeffe and M. McCarthy (eds.) *The Routledge Handbook of Corpus Linguistics.* London and New York: Routledge, 270–287.

Chapter 10

Summary and research projects

10.1 Future research in corpus linguistics

In the preceding chapters I have presented a large number of examples of corpus-based studies and explained how to employ corpus techniques to address a wide range of issues related to the use and functions of vocabulary as a key component of language. Judging by the diversity and complexity of the topics that have been covered, it is fair to say that corpus linguistics is a vibrant area of linguistic study and it is likely to continue developing in the coming years.

One of the most important directions for future research is further integration of corpus tools and methodologies. In their overview of the field, McEnery and Hardie (2012: 233) state that methodological pluralism is "critical to the future of corpus linguistics". The authors highlight the importance of triangulation, which can be defined as obtaining different types of data from multiple sources as a way of verifying the validity of the claims made. To illustrate this point, McEnery and Hardie (2012) refer to research into collocations (e.g. theories such as Hoey's (2005) lexical priming or Sinclair's (1991) idiom principle) and call for integrating corpus-based work with psycholinguistic and neurolinguistic approaches. Linking evidence from these areas is "one of the most exciting vistas for future research" and it should lead to the development of a Unified Empirical Linguistics (McEnery and Hardie 2012: 236). Likewise, Granger et al. (2015) make a similar plea with reference to learner corpus research. The researchers emphasize "the need to pull together the different research strands" so that the field as a whole expands its interdisciplinary scope and brings together findings from corpus linguistics, second language acquisition, language teaching and natural language processing.

Methodological triangulation and further integration of research traditions within corpus linguistics are also discussed by Egbert (2016). Taking stock of the field, the author elaborates on several issues that are likely to be the object of future corpus research. These include:

- the development of larger corpora
- improvements in the design of spoken corpora so that they do not lag behind technological advancement

- the compilation of hyper-monitor corpora where new data can be added daily (e.g. the NOW corpus available at http://corpus.byu.edu/now/)
- the growing popularity of virtual corpora that can be customized according to the needs of individual users
- the refinement of methods that are used for summarizing corpus data (e.g. Brezina et al.'s (2015) GraphColl as a new way of exploring collocations)
- the use of crowdsourcing as a method of collecting corpus data (e.g. Biber, Egbert and Davies's (2015) study based on the GloWbE Corpus available at http://corpus.byu.edu/glowbe).

It is worth adding that Baker and Egbert (2016) have recently published an edited volume that deals with the robustness of findings and the role of methodological triangulation in corpus linguistics. The volume summarizes an innovative project in which ten prominent corpus linguists used data from the same corpus (400,000 words) to address the same research question. Specifically, the question concerned the use of language in an online Q&A forum and how it differed across four varieties of world English (India, Philippines, United Kingdom and United States). Crucially, the ten scholars were not told which methodologies they should choose to answer this question as the aim of the project was to triangulate and assess multiple approaches that are employed in corpus-based language studies. Interestingly, only a small part of the findings overlapped between the different approaches. While it might seem like a worrying result, Baker and Egbert (2016) highlight the richness and value of insights that were gained and argue that combining different corpus methods and techniques can be complementary and lead to a more thorough understanding of issues under study.

As far as future work in vocabulary studies is concerned, Carter (2012: 15–16) points to the following topics that are particularly worthy of investigation:

- the regularity and recurrence of lexical patterns specific to spoken and written lexis
- the importance of everyday words and phrases as they are used in conversational interaction
- the application of corpus findings in vocabulary teaching and learning
- the exploration of lexical patterns in literary texts by means of corpus stylistic analysis
- the development of electronic dictionaries with entries that provide information not only on the meaning of words but also the interactive, gestural and intercultural aspects of vocabulary use
- the analysis and description of the use of vocabulary in multimodal contexts.

The last two points refer to multimodal corpus approaches. These are approaches that emphasize the multi-channeled nature of communication, in which both verbal and nonverbal elements are inextricably linked to each other and play an equally important role (Adolphs and Carter 2013; Bateman 2013). As a new area of research, multimodal corpus linguistics is concerned with the development of the new type of multimodal corpora, which, in addition to textual records, also contain other streams of data (e.g. visual video-recorded material or information on speakers' spatial positioning obtained via GPS systems). Thus, by adopting a broader perspective on the use of language and including various kinds of data, multimodal corpus approaches aim to highlight the highly interactive and dynamic nature of human communication and explore relationships between talk and bodily actions. However, as evidenced by the first findings based on multimodal corpora (e.g. see Knight, Evans, Carter and Adolphs 2009 or Adolphs, Knight and Carter 2011), there are many technical challenges that are entailed in the collection and analysis of such data (e.g. logistical difficulties associated with obtaining video data). It transpires then that one of the more pressing needs for corpus linguistics at the moment is to devise new ways of embracing non-textual material and find "appropriate mechanisms for measuring the extent to which these other data streams determine the nature of the language that is used" (Adolphs and Carter 2013: 180).

To recapitulate, corpus linguistics is a well-established methodology that is likely to continue to evolve as a powerful approach for analyzing language 'at large'. In light of the fact that "corpus linguists are increasingly sophisticated in compiling, extracting, and evaluating their data in complex and innovative ways" (Wulff et al. 2010: 6), it is safe to say that prospects for the future look bright and "the place of corpus analysis in linguistics is assured" (McEnery and Hardie 2012: 237).

10.2 Research projects

Throughout the book, I have emphasized the usefulness of corpora for exploring a variety of issues that pertain to vocabulary knowledge and use. These have included, among others, frequency-based analyses of texts, differences between spoken and written vocabulary, the role of collocations and other types of phraseological units or register- and genre-specific descriptions of vocabulary use. To encourage you to embark on your own corpus analysis, what follows is a selection of ideas for corpus-based projects that you can undertake to explore different aspects of vocabulary.

10.2.1 Project 1: The use of phrasal vs. single-word verbs in American English

Research question: What is the proportion of phrasal vs. single-word verbs in spoken and written American English?

Background: Phrasal (or multiword) verbs are an important feature of spoken English and as a result their frequencies in spoken texts are often said to be higher than in written texts. However, a large number of phrasal verbs can be substituted by one-word equivalents that convey a similar meaning. For instance, 'put out a fire' can be replaced by 'extinguish a fire'. Importantly, such one-word verbs represent higher levels of formality and therefore they might be expected to predominate in written texts. A question that then arises is: what is the proportion of phrasal vs. single-word verbs in different modes of language?

Methodology: A useful example of a corpus-based analysis in this area is Siyanova and Schmitt's (2007) study of the frequency of phrasal verbs in spoken and written English. Using both spoken (the Cambridge and Nottingham Corpus of Discourse in English (CANCODE)) and written data (the British National Corpus (BNC)), the authors compared the frequency of twenty-six phrasal verbs and their single-word equivalents. The main conclusion of the study was that one-word verbs were more frequent than multiword verbs both in the spoken (seventeen out of twenty-six verb pairs which amounted to 65% of the cases) and written language (eighteen out of twenty-six verb pairs which amounted to 69% of the cases). See Table 10.1 for the proportions of percentages for all the pairs.

Table 10.1 Frequency (in percentages) of multiword verbs vs. one-word verbs reported by Siyanova and Schmitt (2007)

multiword verb (MWV) ; one-word verb (OWV)	CANCODE MWV	CANCODE OWV	BNC MWV	BNC OWV
turn down ; decrease	56	44	35	65
go on ; continue	86	14	40	60
go up ; rise	93	7	31	69
put off ; postpone	100	0	58	42
work out ; train	72	28	67	33
mess around ; misbehave	77	23	71	29
come up ; arise	95	5	60	40
show off ; boast	88	12	56	44
tell off ; reproach	0	100	0	100
put up with ; stand	12	88	9	91
run into ; meet	3	97	5	95
come round ; come	3	97	1	99
tidy up ; organize	17	83	17	83
pull over ; stop	3	97	0	100
set up ; start	12	88	46	54
get back ; return	45	55	25	75
figure out ; understand	2	98	6	94
walk off ; leave	0	100	0	100
come up with ; suggest	35	65	20	80
hold on ; wait	8	92	19	81
bring up ; mention	11	89	14	86
come along ; join	32	68	10	90
come across as ; seem	11	89	0	100
catch up with ; join	3	97	5	95
call off ; cancel	0	100	11	89
brush up on ; revise	5	95	3	97

In your project, follow a similar methodology and use the same twenty-six pairs of phrasal and single-word verbs. However, as your research question concerns the distribution of phrasal verbs and their one-word equivalents in different registers of American English, you are encouraged to draw on data from the Corpus of Contemporary American English (COCA) and explore its different subsections. More specifically, use the Sections option to study the frequency of a given verb across the spoken and written sections of the corpus. Note that to carry out this search, you need to click on 'Sections' and in Box 1 select 'Fiction', 'Magazine', 'Newspaper' and 'Academic" (hold the shift button as you select these sections), and in Box 2 select 'Spoken'. Figure 10.1 presents a sample search for the verb 'turn down'.

For the sake of simplicity, you will use infinitive forms of the phrasal verbs (e.g. 'turn down') as the main unit of your analysis. A search for lemmas (TURN down) is slightly more difficult to conduct because it produces separate frequency values for each inflected form of the verb ('turn', 'turned', 'turning', 'turns'). All of these values would have to be summed up if you wanted to obtain the total frequency of a given verb.

Once you type a given verb in the search box and click on 'Find matching strings', a new tab opens up and provides you with the following information: the number of tokens in the spoken section (tokens 1), the number of tokens in the written section (tokens 2), the normalized frequency (per million words)

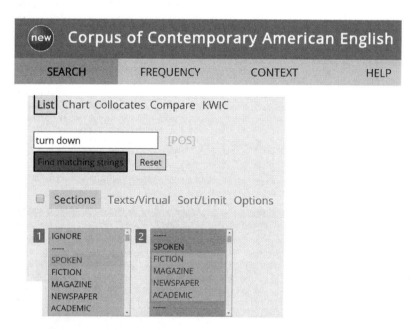

Figure 10.1 A search for the frequency of 'turn down' in the spoken and written sections of COCA

in the spoken section, the normalized frequency in the written section and a ratio indicating the relative percentage of all occurrences in the two corpus sections. Perform a similar search for all the phrasal verbs and their one-word equivalents. If you experience difficulties during any stage of your analysis, click on the 'HELP' button, which is located on the right-hand side of the interface. Table 10.2 displays frequency data for all the twenty-six pairs of verbs in the spoken and written sections of COCA.

It is worth noting that in addition to the frequency of the verbs (values per million words), the table also reports the relative percentages of multiword vs. one-word forms (the more frequent forms are bolded). These percentages were calculated following Siyanova and Schmitt's original procedures: adding the total occurrences of a given verb in both forms and calculating relative proportions.

Table 10.2 Frequency of multiword verbs vs. one-word verbs in spoken and written COCA

Multiword – one-word verb	Frequency per million words in spoken COCA	Percentage (figures are rounded)	Frequency per million words in written COCA	Percentage (figures are rounded)
turn down ; decrease	1.8 ; 5.7	24% ; **76%**	2.1 ; 19.3	10% ; **90%**
go on ; continue	78.6 ; 194	29% ; **71%**	34.9 ; 121.5	22% ; **78%**
go up ; rise	28.8 ; 41.2	41% ; **59%**	10 ; 80	11% ; **89%**
put off ; postpone	3.3 ; 2.6	**56%** ; 44%	3.6 ; 2.7	**57%** ; 43%
work out ; train	21 ; 15.9	**57%** ; 43%	13.4 ; 17.1	44% ; **56%**
mess around ; misbehave	0.9 ; 0.5	**67%** ; 33%	0.5 ; 0.4	**53%** ; 47%
come up ; arise	7.4 ; 3.3	**96%** ; 4%	29.5 ; 13.5	**69%** ; 31%
show off ; boast	2.5 ; 1.2	**67%** ; 33%	3.8 ; 4.4	46% ; **54%**
tell off ; reproach	0.02 ; 0.4	5% ; **95%**	0.03 ; 1.4	2% ; **98%**
put up with ; stand	4.7 ; 160.2	3% ; **97%**	3.5 ; 124.5	3% ; **97%**
run into ; meet	8.2 ; 148.8	5% ; **95%**	6.6 ; 136.8	5% ; **95%**
come round ; come	0.1 ; 1062.8	1% ; **99%**	0.2 ; 559.5	1% ; **99%**
tidy up ; organize	0.1 ; 8.7	2% ; **98%**	0.4 ; 14.9	2% ; **98%**
pull over ; stop	1.1 ; 235.2	1% ; **99%**	1.3 ; 174.6	1% ; **99%**
set up ; start	46.5 ; 324.5	13% ; **87%**	46.9 ; 214.4	18% ; **82%**
get back ; return	48.1 ; 89.3	35% ; **65%**	21.5 ; 150.4	13% ; **87%**
figure out ; understand	53.3 ; 319.9	14% ; **86%**	26.3 ; 178.5	13% ; **87%**
walk off ; leave	1.3 ; 198.8	1% ; **99%**	1.1 ; 177.3	1% ; **99%**
come up with ; suggest	41.2 ; 47.2	47% ; **53%**	16.8 ; 78	18% ; **82%**
hold on ; wait	29.6 ; 192	13% ; **87%**	12.1 ; 99.2	11% ; **89%**
bring up ; mention	10.7 ; 42.6	18% ; **82%**	3.4 ; 45.5	7% ; **93%**
come along ; join	5.7 ; 85.3	11% ; **89%**	4.5 ; 54.9	8% ; **92%**
come across as ; seem	1.0 ; 147.8	1% ; **99%**	0.7 ; 146.9	1% ; **99%**
catch up with ; join	3.0 ; 85.3	3% ; **97%**	2.6 ; 54.9	5% ; **95%**
call off ; cancel	0.7 ; 6.0	11% ; **89%**	0.4 ; 5.8	7% ; **93%**
brush up on ; revise	0.1 ; 1.3	8% ; **92%**	0.3 ; 3.6	7% ; **93%**

As far as the frequency of the verbs in the spoken COCA is concerned, in twenty-one out of the twenty-six pairs (81%), the one-word verbs occurred more frequently than the multiword verbs. A similar pattern was found in the written section of the corpus; namely, in twenty-three out of the twenty-six pairs (88%), the one-word equivalents were more frequent than the multiword verbs. These results confirm Siyanova and Schmitt's finding that one-word verbs had a higher frequency of occurrence in both modes of communication. In fact, the COCA data provide even stronger evidence for this claim: the higher frequency of one-word forms was found in 81% of the pairs for the spoken language and in 88% of the pairs in the written language, while in the original study (based on the BNC) these values were 65% and 69% respectively. Thus, it can be concluded that at least for the twenty-six pairs of verbs that were selected, the one-word verbs appear to be used more frequently than their multiword equivalents and this is true for both spoken and written American English.

However, there are certain limitations that need to be acknowledged. First, the polysemy of phrasal verbs was not considered in this project. As reported by Garnier and Schmitt (2015), phrasal verbs in English can carry several meanings and some of these meaning-senses are likely to be more frequent than others. In our project we did not take this issue into account because our searches were form-based. A more detailed analysis of meaning would be possible if we had access to a semantically parsed corpus, with different tags distinguishing between the specific meanings of verbs (e.g. 'work out' meaning 'train' vs. 'work out' meaning 'figure out'). A related problem is the degree of semantic equivalence between the one-word and multiword versions of verbs. In the project, we used Siyanova and Schmitt's target items, but it could be argued that there are certain differences across the twenty-six pairs in terms of how closely the one-word forms correspond to the meaning of the multiword forms.

Finally, unlike the original design, this project did not include any data from learner corpora as an additional source of information about the use of phrasal verbs by L1 and L2 users. Siyanova and Schmitt used the International Corpus of Learner English and reported that in informal spoken contexts L2 users were less likely to use multiword verbs than native speakers (as revealed by frequency patterns from the CANCODE and the BNC). It would also be interesting to replicate this finding using data from other databases. For instance, the project could be supplemented with data from the Corpus of American Soap Operas (http://corpus.byu.edu/soap/), a corpus composed of 100 million words collected from ten soap operas (scripted dialogs). Analyzing the frequency of phrasal verbs in the colloquial speech of contemporary American media would be a useful addition to the project.

10.2.2 Project 2: Morphological complexity of words

Research question: What are the most productive verb-forming suffixes in English?

Background: Morphology is the study of word structure. It focuses on **morphemes**, the smallest units of meaning that can be identified within words. For instance, the word 'unbreakable' consists of three separate morphemes: 'un', 'break' and 'able', whereas the word 'dogs' consists of two morphemes: 'dog' and 's'. At another level of analysis, 'un' and 'able' are labeled as derivational morphemes which are used to derive new words (by converting one part of speech to another). For example, if we add 'able' to the verb 'break', it becomes an adjective, 'breakable'. In turn, 's' or 'ed' are examples of inflectional morphemes; these morphemes do not change words in the sense of converting them into different parts of speech but rather they indicate specific grammatical categories such as plural, gerund or past forms (e.g. the morpheme 's' in the word 'dogs' marks its plural form).

What is more, morphemes can also be categorized according to their position within words: prefixes occur at the beginning of words (e.g. re– in 'rewrite' or un– in 'unimportant'), while suffixes appear at the end of words (–able in 'workable' or –fy in 'modify'). Being able to analyze the structure of words and identify specific examples of morphemes is a crucial aspect of lexical competence, and therefore the aim of this project is to demonstrate how conducting corpus analyses can contribute to a better understanding of morphological processes.

Methodology: To present how corpora can become a useful tool for exploring the morphological structure of words, you are encouraged to carry out a project in which you will examine the productivity of derivational morphemes in English. Specifically, you will rely on the BYU-COCA interface to study the frequency of suffixes which are used to create verbs. According to Carter et al. (2011), the most important examples of such suffixes in English include –en, –ate, –fy and –ize/–ise. It is worth highlighting that in addition to deepening your understanding of English morphology, this analysis will also offer some practical implications related to language instruction. For instance, data about the morphological productivity of particular suffixes can inform decisions as to which forms should be prioritized in language instruction and be taught to L2 learners.

Since your aim is to explore the frequency of the main verb-forming suffixes in English, you will carry out five separate searches using the following queries: *ate.[vvi*], *en.[vvi*], *fy.[vvi*], *ize.[vvi*] and *ise.[vvi*]. The symbol of an asterisk is a wildcard which stands for any missing letter, while vvi is a tag for infinitive forms of verbs. In other words, all the analyses will be based on the infinitive forms of the verbs. What is more, you will use the Chart option of the interface, which will allow you to compare the frequency of the suffixes across the five different subsections of COCA. See Figure 10.2 for a sample search for verbs ending with the –ate suffix. Finally, given that English is spoken in many countries, your research can also focus on potential differences in morphology between British and American English. You can establish this by comparing the frequency of the five suffixes in the BNC and COCA. Table 10.3 presents all the frequency data you need to complete this project.

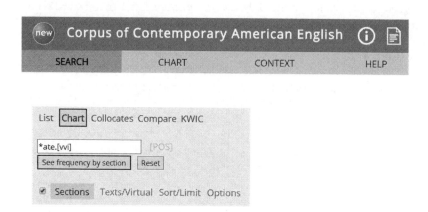

Figure 10.2 A search for the infinitive forms of verbs ending with suffix –ate

If you look at the total number of occurrences of these suffixes in COCA, it can be seen that the most productive suffix is –ate, followed by –en and –ize. The least productive item is –ise (130.48 occurrences pmw), which is rather unsurprising given the fact that COCA is a corpus of American English and –ise is a suffix that is associated with British English. It is interesting to compare these results with the data from the BNC (the last column of Table 10.3). The suffix –ate still has the highest number of occurrences but the second most frequent item is –ise, which confirms that it is a typical feature of British English. This is a valuable finding which points to the usefulness of corpus-based analyses in terms of providing insights into similarities and differences between British and American English (and potentially other varieties of the language as well). It needs to be stated that the older version of the BYU interface (http://corpus.byu.edu/coca/old/) has a special tool called 'side by side', which allows users to view data from both the BNC and COCA on one screen (see Figure 10.3). You might consider using it for some of the searches in this project.

Since COCA contains data from five different registers (spoken, fiction, magazine, newspapers and academic), you can also explore the relationship between register variation resulting from the use of English in different contexts and the distribution of the verb-forming suffixes. As Table 10.3 displays, –ate (1,386.92 pmw), –fy (283.94 pmw) and –ize (368.01 pmw) have the highest frequency in the academic section of the corpus. In contrast, the suffix –en exhibits a different pattern and has the highest frequency in the spoken section (396.76 pmw). Finally, –ise seems to have a similar level of occurrence across the different sections of the corpus, with only the language of fiction exhibiting a lower frequency.

In terms of further research options, the morphological productivity of suffixes could also be studied by looking at some other corpora available at the BYU interface. For instance, given that the Corpus of Historical American English

Table 10.3 Frequency of verb-forming suffixes in COCA and BNC (a = raw frequency; b = frequency per million words)

	Spoken COCA	Fiction COCA	Magazine COCA	Newspaper COCA	Academic COCA	Total COCA	Total BNC
-ate	64,120a	36,536	89,368	73,982	143,438	407,444	69,903
	586.15b	348.29	811.62	698.18	1,386.60		
-en	43,402	30,039	26,739	27,780	15,842	143,802	20,871
	396.76	286.36	242.84	262.16	153.18		
-fy	11,652	5,586	13,400	13,144	29,366	73,148	14,893
	106.52	53.25	121.70	124.04	283.94		
-ise	14,946	10,397	15,581	15,248	13,546	69,718	31,313
	136.63	99.11	141.50	143.90	130.98		
-ize	22,074	14,869	25,370	20,609	38,060	120,982	9,200
	201.79	141.74	230.40	194.49	368.01		

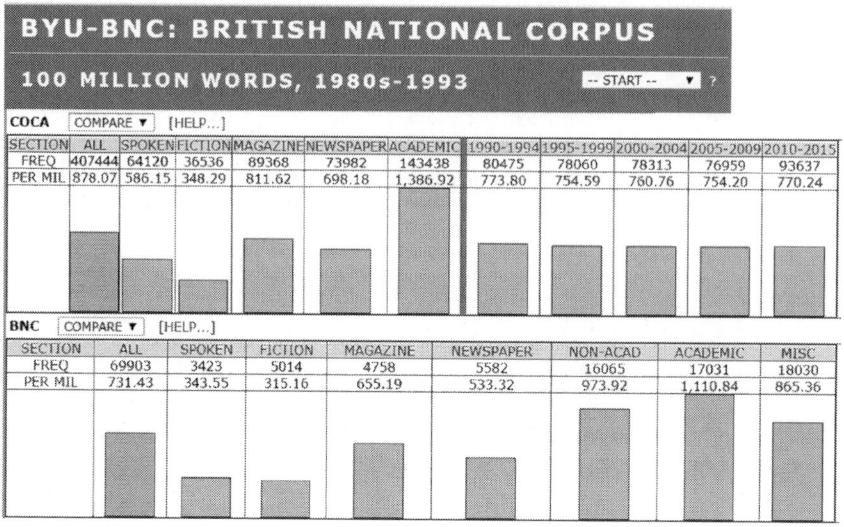
BYU-BNC: BRITISH NATIONAL CORPUS
100 MILLION WORDS, 1980s-1993
-- START --
COCA
COMPARE
[HELP...]
SECTION ALL SPOKEN FICTION MAGAZINE NEWSPAPER ACADEMIC 1990-1994 1995-1999 2000-2004 2005-2009 2010-2015
FREQ 407444 64120 36536 89368 73982 143438 80475 78060 78313 76959 93637
PER MIL 878.07 586.15 348.29 811.62 698.18 1,386.92 773.80 754.59 760.76 754.20 770.24
BNC
COMPARE
[HELP...]
SECTION ALL SPOKEN FICTION MAGAZINE NEWSPAPER NON-ACAD ACADEMIC MISC
FREQ 69903 3423 5014 4758 5582 16065 17031 18030
PER MIL 731.43 343.55 315.16 655.19 533.32 973.92 1,110.84 865.36

Figure 10.3 A side-by-side comparison of the frequency of –ate in the BNC vs. COCA

(COHA: http://corpus.byu.edu/coha/) contains data representing the use of English across different periods of time, you could investigate how the frequency of specific morphemes changes over time. Another possibility is to explore the distribution of different suffixes in the Global Web-based English (GloWbe) Corpus (http://corpus.byu.edu/glowbe/). The corpus is composed of data from twenty English-speaking countries and therefore it can be employed to make comparisons between specific varieties of English. Lastly, if you wish to conduct an even more ambitious project, you could use any of the BYU corpora to investigate the morphological productivity of many other kinds of morphemes such as verb-forming prefixes ad–, de–, im–/in– and per–.

10.2.3 Project 3: The creation of a corpus-based list of technical vocabulary

Research question: How can we use a discipline-specific corpus to create a list of technical vocabulary from the field of linguistics?

Background: As discussed in Chapter 4, technical vocabulary refers to specialized words which characterize the language of certain subject areas. According to Nation (2013), there are different ways of identifying such vocabulary and one of them is asking experts to produce a list of items that are essential for successful communication in their field. However, as this approach uses speakers' intuitions, it is likely to be subjective to a large extent because even experts (or especially experts) exhibit some bias in the process of determining the specificity of words.

Another way of identifying technical vocabulary is by creating a wordlist on the basis of a specialized corpus representing a given subject area or domain. As Chung and Nation (2004: 113) observe, technical vocabulary "occurs much more frequently in a specialized text than in general usage". This suggests then that comparing the frequency of words in a general corpus and a specialized corpus can be treated as an effective way of delineating the borders of technical language.

Methodology: To answer the research question in this project, you will make use of the Wikipedia Corpus (http://corpus.byu.edu/wiki/). It consists of 1.9 billion words (4.4 million articles) collected from the English version of Wikipedia (see Figure 10.4 for a screenshot of the Wikipedia Corpus interface).

It must be stressed that the corpus is constructed in an innovative way because it enables you to compile your own virtual corpora that you can personalize and adapt according to your specific research and teaching needs. This is particularly useful for English for academic purposes (EAP)- and English for specific purposes (ESP)-oriented work that focuses on exploring the language of different academic disciplines (e.g. establishing differences between the vocabulary of medicine and the vocabulary of economics). Such comparisons are valuable not only for the sake of linguistic description; they are also pedagogically relevant in the sense that they can be used by EAP instructors who teach different types of discipline-specific vocabulary.

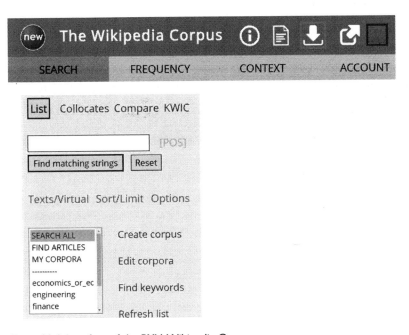

Figure 10.4 Interface of the BYU-Wikipedia Corpus

However, despite all these benefits, we should bear in mind that the Wikipedia Corpus is composed of a specific kind of linguistic data. As an online encyclopedia, Wikipedia is written and edited by a virtual community of users, who represent different nationalities, cultural backgrounds and levels of linguistic proficiency. This means that as a corpus user you have no control over the type and quality of texts that you base your analysis on. Thus, it is critical that during your project, you take into account the fact that the Wiki Corpus contains a specific type of digital language produced in the highly dynamic context of online communication.

During the first stage of this project, you need to create a virtual corpus that will represent the vocabulary used in the field of linguistics. For the purposes of this project, you will call it the Language corpus and create it via the 'Texts/Virtual' option, which you can find on the left-hand side of the interface. Click on it and use the 'create corpus' button to select websites that will comprise the Language corpus. Once a new window opens up, type in 'language or linguistics' in the Title word box and indicate that you want to include 1,000 websites (you can include more websites if you wish to compile a bigger corpus). When you hit 'submit', the interface will list examples of Wikipedia entries that contain the word 'language' or 'linguistics'. Use all of them to build your virtual corpus; this procedure will increase the size of the corpus but it gives you a rather limited level of control of the texts themselves. In the last step, type the name of the corpus into the 'Save as' box and click on 'Submit'. The Language corpus (over 1.7 million words) is now ready to use and it should appear under the tag 'My virtual corpora'. Note that this procedure can be repeated to create many other kinds of virtual corpora depending on which topics or disciplines you are keen on (see Figure 10.5 for examples of virtual corpora for different disciplines).

new	The Wikipedia Corpus	ⓘ	🗎	⬇	↗		👤	?
	SEARCH	VIRTUAL CORPORA		CONTEXT		HELP		

MY VIRTUAL CORPORA

HELP			LIST NAME ↕	# ARTICLES ↕	# WORDS ↕	FIND KEYWORDS ● SPECIFIC ○ FREQ	CREATED ↕
1	🗑	🔒	ECONOMICS_OR_EC	1000	1,007,960	NOUN VERB ADJ ADV N+N ADJ+N	239 d
2	🗑	🔒	ENGINEERING	1000	2,903,373	NOUN VERB ADJ ADV N+N ADJ+N	239 d
3	🗑	🔒	FINANCE	1000	4,149,628	NOUN VERB ADJ ADV N+N ADJ+N	239 d
4	🗑	🔒	GEOGRAPHY_OR_GE	661	776,658	NOUN VERB ADJ ADV N+N ADJ+N	239 d
5	🗑	🔒	LANGUAGE	1000	1,754,859	NOUN VERB ADJ ADV N+N ADJ+N	306 d
6	🗑	🔒	MEDICINE	1000	1,017,065	NOUN VERB ADJ ADV N+N ADJ+N	239 d

Figure 10.5 Examples of virtual corpora from different disciplines

As stated above, the aim of your project is to investigate the character of technical vocabulary used in the field of linguistics. To achieve this goal, we will make use of keyword analysis and identify words that occur with a higher frequency in a target corpus when compared to a reference corpus (see Chapter 2 for details of keyness analysis). Conveniently, the Wikipedia interface is constructed in such a way that lists of keywords are generated automatically. As can be seen in Figure 10.5, you can view separate lists of keywords for different parts of speech: nouns, verbs, adjectives and adverbs. What is more, the interface also allows you to explore lists of the most frequent collocations from your virtual corpus. There are two types of collocations that the interface generates in an automatic way: noun-noun or adjective-noun collocations. As highlighted in Chapter 5, studying ways in which words tend to co-occur and collocate is a powerful method for uncovering more nuanced aspects of meaning. Importantly, thanks to the + or − buttons, you can also change the level of specificity for your search. In other words, you can make your list of keywords more or less specific by manipulating the minimum frequency and range (the number of texts in which a given word occurs) as your criteria for exploring the Language corpus.

As discussed in Chapter 4, technical vocabulary is a separate category that is distinct from the first 2–3,000 most frequent word families regarded as the core of English lexis. However, technical vocabulary also encompasses high-frequency general-use words that take on more specialized meanings when they are used in a particular field (Schmitt 2010). Therefore, once you have created a list of the most frequent technical words from your virtual corpus (see Table 10.4 for the first 200 words), it is worth exploring whether it contains any examples of high-frequency words that carry some specialized meanings relevant to the field of linguistics.

Table 10.4 Examples of the first 200 most frequent technical words in the field of linguistics (based on data from the Wikipedia Corpus)

Rank	Word
1	LANGUAGE
2	WORD
3	DIALECT
4	VOWEL
5	VERB
6	FORM
7	SPEAKER
8	SYSTEM
9	CENTURY
10	NUMBER
11	PEOPLE
12	NOUN
13	CONSONANT

(continued)

Table 10.4 (continued)

Rank	Word
14	USE
15	CASE
16	NAME
17	PART
18	TIME
19	SYLLABLE
20	PERSON
21	TYPE
22	SCRIPT
23	OBJECT
24	EXAMPLE
25	GROUP
26	AREA
27	CLASS
28	SUFFIX
29	LETTER
30	SOUND
31	TONE
32	FEATURE
33	MEANING
34	SENTENCE
35	PRONOUN
36	SCHOOL
37	REGION
38	TERM
39	VARIETY
40	ALPHABET
41	SUBJECT
42	TEXT
43	GRAMMAR
44	WAY
45	YEAR
46	COUNTRY
47	FUNCTION
48	FAMILY
49	COMMUNITY
50	PROGRAM
51	SPEECH
52	CHILD
53	STATE
54	PHRASE
55	CODE
56	STRUCTURE
57	PERIOD
58	VOCABULARY

59	POPULATION
60	CHANGE
61	INFLUENCE
62	BOOK
63	ORDER
64	DEVELOPMENT
65	DIFFERENCE
66	ORTHOGRAPHY
67	RULE
68	PROCESS
69	PRONUNCIATION
70	ROOT
71	SIGN
72	PROGRAMMING
73	METHOD
74	PHONEME
75	ELEMENT
76	PLURAL
77	LITERATURE
78	WRITING
79	LINGUIST
80	DATA
81	WORLD
82	SET
83	STATUS
84	POSITION
85	MAN
86	RESULT
87	END
88	VALUE
89	SYNTAX
90	ORIGIN
91	VERSION
92	PREFIX
93	WORK
94	ADJECTIVE
95	OTHERS
96	LEVEL
97	ACCENT
98	SOURCE
99	STUDY
100	GOVERNMENT
101	ARTICLE
102	SINGULAR
103	STOP
104	LIST

(continued)

Table 10.4 (continued)

Rank	Word
105	DISTINCTION
106	EXPRESSION
107	THEORY
108	MEMBER
109	PLACE
110	STANDARD
111	GENDER
112	ARGUMENT
113	CHARACTER
114	STUDENT
115	STRESS
116	DICTIONARY
117	CONTEXT
118	PATTERN
119	LINGUISTICS
120	EDUCATION
121	MILLION
122	TRANSLATION
123	CLUSTER
124	MORPHEME
125	CULTURE
126	SPELLING
127	COMMUNICATION
128	INSTRUCTION
129	CLAUSE
130	INFORMATION
131	CITY
132	ASPECT
133	QUESTION
134	STEM
135	PARTICLE
136	VARIANT
137	FACT
138	TABLE
139	MARKER
140	HISTORY
141	LOANWORDS
142	ANALYSIS
143	HAND
144	DOCUMENT
145	POINT
146	APPLICATION
147	IMPLEMENTATION
148	ENDING
149	MODEL
150	INSCRIPTION
151	FIELD

Finally, your list of discipline-specific vocabulary of linguistics can be further refined by comparing it with Gardner and Davies's (2014) list of academic vocabulary (the list is available at www.wordandphrase.info). Such a comparison will allow you to determine the level of specificity of your list; that is, you will be able to establish how much it differs from a core academic list. What is more, your list from the field of linguistics could also be compared with similar lists representing other academic disciplines (e.g. see Table 10.5 for examples of technical words from medicine and economics). Such comparisons might be particularly valuable for teachers and materials developers working in the area of ESP, where the lexical content of language courses is often dictated by the particular needs of students from a variety of subject areas.

Table 10.5 Examples of the first 100 most frequent technical words in medicine and economics (based on data from the Wikipedia Corpus)

Rank	Medicine Corpus	Economics Corpus
1	MEDICINE	ECONOMICS
2	HOSPITAL	ECONOMY
3	SCHOOL	MARKET
4	YEAR	COUNTRY
5	STUDENT	GOVERNMENT
6	CARE	POLICY
7	HEALTH	YEAR
8	PATIENT	PRICE
9	PROGRAM	DEVELOPMENT
10	RESEARCH	TRADE
11	PHYSICIAN	SYSTEM
12	DISEASE	PRODUCTION
13	SERVICE	GROWTH
14	DEGREE	BUSINESS
15	TREATMENT	THEORY
16	TRAINING	PROGRAM
17	CENTER	STATE
18	PRACTICE	RATE
19	SYSTEM	SERVICE
20	COLLEGE	MEMBER
21	EDUCATION	ECONOMIST
22	TIME	TIME
23	STUDY	CAPITAL
24	MEMBER	LABOR
25	FACILITY	RESEARCH
26	DOCTOR	VALUE
27	USE	INCOME
28	COURSE	TAX
29	UNIVERSITY	MODEL
30	AREA	GOOD

31	SCIENCE	WORLD
32	BUILDING	COST
33	PART	INVESTMENT
34	COUNTRY	SCHOOL
35	BODY	INDUSTRY
36	CAMPUS	LEVEL
37	STATE	STUDY
38	FIELD	PEOPLE
39	NUMBER	ORGANIZATION
40	FACULTY	WORK
41	SPECIALTY	STUDENT
42	ORGANIZATION	AREA
43	EMERGENCY	RESOURCE
44	SURGERY	CHANGE
45	DEPARTMENT	ACTIVITY
46	INSTITUTION	CENTURY
47	GRADUATE	PERIOD
48	COMMUNITY	SECTOR
49	CANCER	WORKER
50	MILLION	PRODUCT
51	CONDITION	RIGHT
52	DRUG	MONEY
53	INFORMATION	NUMBER
54	GROUP	LAW
55	CASE	SOCIETY
56	TEACHING	ANALYSIS
57	WOMAN	INSTITUTION
58	BLOOD	ISSUE
59	DEVELOPMENT	PART
60	WORLD	EDUCATION
61	THERAPY	INTEREST
62	LEVEL	FIRM
63	PEOPLE	PROCESS
64	TEST	COMPANY
65	CLASS	TERM
66	FAMILY	DEMAND
67	PROCESS	EFFECT
68	UNIT	PROBLEM
69	STAFF	WAGE
70	NAME	POWER
71	WORK	SUPPLY
72	EFFECT	UNIVERSITY
73	RESULT	USE
74	HEART	MILLION
75	GOVERNMENT	GROUP
76	TERM	EXCHANGE

(continued)

Table 10.5 (continued)

Rank	Medicine Corpus	Economics Corpus
77	RESIDENCY	INFORMATION
78	EXAMINATION	FORM
79	CHILD	REGION
80	PROCEDURE	REFORM
81	CITY	JOURNAL
82	DIAGNOSIS	OUTPUT
83	METHOD	PROPERTY
84	LABORATORY	CONSUMER
85	CENTURY	RESULT
86	ACTIVITY	PROJECT
87	AMBULANCE	WAY
88	HISTORY	BILLION
89	CANNABIS	BANK
90	QUALITY	LAND
91	CELL	FIELD
92	ROLE	NATION
93	JOURNAL	FACTOR
94	TYPE	PERCENT
95	CURRICULUM	INCREASE
96	CLINIC	DEGREE
97	FORM	BOOK
98	DISORDER	INDIVIDUAL
99	BED	POPULATION
100	RISK	DECISION

10.2.4 Project 4: Lexical characteristics of political discourse

Research question: What are the most frequent words in the language of Tony Blair and Margaret Thatcher? Are there any chunks that keep recurring in their speeches?

Background: Political discourse is a large area of study that attracts the interest of many scholars and, as Ädel (2010) states, it "has a long-standing tradition as an object of study across many disciplines, including rhetoric, linguistics and political science". This means that depending on your specific research question, the language of politics can be studied from a number of perspectives including both quantitative and qualitative approaches. Corpus-based analysis of political discourse is one example and, as explained by Ädel (2010), there are several ways in which corpora can contribute to this area of study. These are, among others, analyzing the frequencies of linguistic features as markers of a particular style, making comparisons between different corpora, analyzing how a given topic is talked about and identifying keywords in the language of politicians. In this research project, you will be concerned with the vocabulary of Margaret Thatcher and Tony Blair, and you will analyze the lexical profile of speeches made by these two British politicians.

Methodology: To answer the research questions about the language of Tony Blair and Margaret Thatcher, you will use the Hansard Corpus (http://www.hansard-corpus.org/), which consists of 1.6 billion words collected from speeches made in the British Parliament between 1803 and 2005. Since your aim is to describe the use of vocabulary by these two specific politicians, the first step of your analysis will be to create a virtual corpus of the language that they produced. For illustrative purposes, we will do it with reference to Tony Blair but you should follow the same procedures to create a virtual corpus of the language of Margaret Thatcher.

Once you have logged into the corpus interface, find the word 'speaker' located on the left-hand side of the interface and click on the first option, 'create list' (see Figure 10.6). You will then see a search box with four columns: 'house', 'speaker', 'years' and 'party', all of which specify which data should be used to build your corpus. In the 'speaker' section, click on PM, which stands for prime ministers, and select Tony Blair. Next, in the section called 'years', type in 1997 and 2007 to indicate that you wish to include only those speeches that were made when Tony Blair served as the UK's Prime Minister. Finally, click 'find speeches', select a name for your corpus (type it in the 'save as' box) and hit 'submit'. Thanks to this simple procedure, you have created a corpus that consists of over 6,400 speeches or 930,000 words and since it is saved by the interface, you can access it whenever you need to.

It is of note that the Hansard Corpus interface allows you to create several virtual corpora depending on your interests and the types of research questions you wish to pursue. What is more, the interface is constructed in such a way that you can decide which texts you want to analyze (e.g. you can only look at the speeches of Churchill produced during the Second World War). As Figure 10.6 demonstrates, you can use several examples of virtual corpora and make comparisons between the language produced by different politicians.

Considering that the research question in this project concerns similarities and differences in the vocabulary used by Margaret Thatcher and Tony Blair, you will compare the most frequent words in the virtual corpora of their political speeches. Quite conveniently, the interface provides all the frequency information in the form of separate categories; that is, all the information is organized with reference to different word classes: nouns, verbs, adjectives and adverbs. This means that you can compare the language of the two politicians by looking at the most frequent vocabulary from their speeches. Tables 10.6 and 10.7 present the most frequent nouns and verbs found in the virtual corpora.

There are different ways in which the data can be analyzed. For instance, you can look for words that have a high frequency on both lists. Examples of such words are 'year', 'people', 'time', 'school', 'money' or 'tax' and the high rate of occurrence of these items is rather unsurprising given the topics that are normally discussed by politicians. Another kind of analysis that can be carried out involves the identification of words that are found only in the language of one politician and not the other. By way of illustration, among the first thirty most frequent nouns retrieved from the two corpora, the words 'job' and 'education' feature in the language of Thatcher

Figure 10.6 Interface of the Hansard Corpus

Table 10.6 Examples of the most frequent nouns in the language of M. Thatcher and T. Blair

	Margaret Thatcher (875,815 words)			Tony Blair (933,083 words)		
	Word	Frequency	No. of texts	Word	Frequency	No. of texts
1	YEAR	2146	1037	PEOPLE	3648	2148
2	PEOPLE	1814	1130	COUNTRY	2553	1545
3	TIME	1502	1007	YEAR	2244	1374
4	PER	1186	491	PARTY	1634	1102
5	COUNTRY	1177	807	SERVICE	1573	829
6	MATTER	1102	860	WAY	1564	1176
7	RATE	1059	531	TIME	1517	1099
8	CENT	1053	464	ISSUE	1362	952
9	SCHOOL	1021	505	MONEY	1251	807

	Word	Frequency	No. of texts	Word	Frequency	No. of texts
10	NUMBER	1020	742	HEALTH	1237	609
11	WAY	998	767	POLICY	1196	720
12	QUESTION	945	777	INVESTMENT	1059	661
13	POLICY	935	541	POSITION	1028	722
14	INCREASE	903	498	PART	981	766
15	AUTHORITY	872	527	POINT	942	795
16	MEETING	837	442	THING	860	734
17	INDUSTRY	824	491	INTEREST	860	589
18	POINT	819	602	ACTION	855	525
19	MILLION	812	435	MILLION	852	605
20	PROBLEM	742	485	PER	834	496
21	REPLY	703	696	RESULT	817	703
22	CASE	700	414	PROBLEM	816	654
23	JOB	697	474	MEASURE	811	553
24	PRICE	691	356	REASON	774	681
25	TAX	686	256	CENT	746	470
26	EXPENDITURE	683	386	TAX	741	420
27	EDUCATION	665	385	SCHOOL	733	403
28	MONEY	654	410	PROCESS	705	433
29	INFLATION	632	313	QUESTION	699	581
30	FIGURE	612	400	SYSTEM	687	459

Table 10.7 Examples of the most frequent verbs in the language of M. Thatcher and T. Blair

	Margaret Thatcher (875,815 words)			Tony Blair (933,083 words)		
	Word	Frequency	No. of texts	Word	Frequency	No. of texts
1	BE	33829	6754	BE	42145	6011
2	HAVE	13742	4702	HAVE	14178	4845
3	WILL	8657	3675	WILL	9869	4120
4	DO	3906	2281	DO	5835	3104
5	SHALL	3372	2097	SAY	3900	2342
6	CAN	2875	1625	CAN	3747	2251
7	MAKE	2561	1545	MAKE	3668	2359
8	TAKE	2265	1543	SHALL	3081	2044
9	GIVE	2228	1661	TAKE	2287	1566
10	SAY	2172	1325	GET	1894	1424
11	ASK	1889	1706	GIVE	1614	1234
12	GO	1525	986	GO	1509	1133
13	KNOW	1406	966	KNOW	1433	1102
14	GET	1203	779	WANT	1345	1021
15	MUST	1156	840	PUT	1319	1026
16	THINK	1056	798	AGREE	1249	845

(continued)

Table 10.7 (continued)

	Margaret Thatcher (875,815 words)			Tony Blair (933,083 words)		
	Word	Frequency	No. of texts	Word	Frequency	No. of texts
17	AGREE	950	767	BELIEVE	1209	950
18	BELIEVE	948	731	THINK	1143	921
19	PUT	852	630	MUST	1076	767
20	SEE	828	623	NEED	937	707
21	HOPE	819	715	COME	891	734
22	COME	804	610	WORK	832	649
23	PAY	758	434	ENSURE	819	677
24	MAY	741	505	SEE	778	649
25	INCREASE	704	502	DEAL	704	529
26	FIND	685	576	TRY	693	580
27	CONSIDER	673	530	SET	693	534
28	TRY	608	488	HAPPEN	673	550
29	WISH	604	510	SUPPORT	657	531
30	REFER	556	442	HELP	633	499

but are absent from the list of Blair's most frequent vocabulary. Likewise, the Blair list contains some nouns that are not found among Thatcher's most frequent items (e.g. 'health' or 'investment'). Crucially, the same kind of analysis can be carried out on the set of the most frequent verbs presented in Table 10.7. What do the data reveal? Are Margaret Thatcher and Tony Blair similar or different in terms of their use of verbs?

Such analyses can yield insights into the main foci of the speeches made by Margaret Thatcher and Tony Blair. More broadly, such comparisons can be treated as pointers into the Prime Ministers' political agenda and details of their policies. However, these are only tentative observations that would need to be backed up by some statistical calculations before any definite conclusions could be drawn (e.g. see Mollin (2009) for a large-scale corpus-based study of the language of Tony Blair).

What is more, considering that phraseological patterning is a useful window into the meaning that is conveyed (see Chapter 5 for details), you can also explore the most common collocations that are found in the speeches made by Margaret Thatcher and Tony Blair. Quite conveniently, examples of collocational partners are identified automatically by the interface and you can view two types of combinations: noun-noun and adjective-noun collocations (in case you wish to explore different kinds of word combinations). Table 10.8 displays examples of the most frequent noun-noun collocations in both corpora.

Similarly to the searches of individual words, you can try to identify these collocations that are shared by both lists (e.g. 'per cent', 'private sector', 'public spending', 'local authority'). Alternatively, you can look for unique phrases that are indicative of the idiolect of each of the politicians. For instance, some of the most frequent

Table 10.8 Examples of the most frequent noun-noun collocations in the language of M. Thatcher and T. Blair

	Margaret Thatcher (875,815 words)			Tony Blair (933,083 words)		
	Word	Frequency	No. of texts	Word	Frequency	No. of texts
1	PER CENT	1052	465	HEALTH SERVICE	845	461
2	LOCAL AUTHORITY	345	197	PER CENT	747	471
3	PUBLIC EXPENDITURE	277	173	PUBLIC SERVICE	207	156
4	EDUCATION AUTHORITY	209	174	INTEREST RATE	201	145
5	INTEREST RATE	198	128	OTHER COUNTRY	174	155
6	TRADE UNION	184	113	MINIMUM WAGE	146	108
7	LOCAL EDUCATION	183	150	PEACE PROCESS	138	100
8	PUBLIC SECTOR	158	114	CLASS SIZE	106	68
9	PRIVATE SECTOR	147	101	MEMBER STATE	101	58
10	PER CENT:	134	91	POLICE OFFICER	95	72
11	OTHER COUNTRY	116	96	PER CENT:	87	71
12	PRIMARY SCHOOL	102	78	PRIVATE SECTOR	85	60
13	SECONDARY SCHOOL	77	62	PUBLIC SPENDING	78	64
14	SCHOOL MEAL	72	56	GENERAL ELECTION	77	72
15	INCOME TAX	63	46	MAJORITY VOTING	77	50
16	OTHER PEOPLE	59	55	HUMAN RIGHT	75	61
17	LEAVING AGE	58	38	HEALTH CARE	75	56
18	RETIREMENT PENSION	57	48	LOCAL AUTHORITY	74	62
19	TASK FORCE	56	37	PUBLIC FINANCE	72	66
20	MONEY SUPPLY	54	28	CHILD BENEFIT	72	64
21	SCHOOL LEAVING	53	34	CRIMINAL JUSTICE	71	54
22	PUBLIC SPENDING	51	42	POST OFFICE	69	29
23	BORROWING REQUIREMENT	51	34	RIGHT THING	63	60
24	COUNCIL HOUSE	50	40	PRIMARY SCHOOL	59	51
25	BUILDING PROGRAMME	48	41	JUSTICE SYSTEM	57	44
26	PUBLIC SERVICE	47	27	POLICE NUMBER	57	40

(continued)

Table 10.8 (continued)

	Margaret Thatcher (875,815 words)			Tony Blair (933,083 words)		
	Word	Frequency	No. of texts	Word	Frequency	No. of texts
27	INCOME POLICY	47	27	TAX BURDEN	55	39
28	CAPITAL EXPENDITURE	46	29	DEBT RELIEF	55	31
29	EXCHANGE RATE	45	32	ASYLUM SEEKER	54	32
30	UNEMPLOYMENT BENEFIT	43	36	SPENDING REVIEW	53	49

collocations found in the Blair corpus include 'health service', 'health care', 'peace process', 'human right' and 'justice system'. In turn, Margaret Thatcher's speeches contained phrases such as 'trade union', 'public sector', 'leaving age' and 'money supply'. Even these several examples point to some semantic preferences that appear to emerge from the analyzed data, with Tony Blair focusing on the issues of health and justice while Margret Thatcher on the economy and public money. Of course, to substantiate these findings, a more thorough quantitative approach should follow. Also, you could conduct a more discourse-oriented study of a sample of concordance lines that would take into account the historical context in which the speeches were made. This would be in line with Ädel's (2010) argument that in corpus studies of political discourse, both qualitative and quantitative methods are needed to complement each other. However, even a simple series of searches such as the ones described above show that virtual corpora are powerful resources that open up a plethora of options for the study of language use.

Finally, in a more ambitious project, you could explore a range of other questions that are related to the use of vocabulary in political contexts. For instance, what language does Tony Blair use to describe specific topics such as 'Europe', 'economy' or 'war'? How has his vocabulary use changed over time? Are there any keywords in the language of Blair when it is compared to a reference corpus? You could also create a similar lexical profile of a prominent politician from another country and compare it with the findings about Tony Blair or Margaret Thatcher. For this purpose, you would need to compile your own corpus of political discourse by collecting data from the Internet (e.g. speeches made by Barack Obama can be found at http://obamaspeeches. com/). However, if you decide to use the Internet, you need to bear in mind that data not in the public domain may be protected by copyrights and you may need to seek permission to include them in your corpus. Lastly, it might be worth considering using the Digital Corpus of the European Parliament (https://ec.europa.eu/jrc/en/language-technologies/dcep), which is a large collection of the language produced by the European Parliament.

10.3 Final word

Corpus Linguistics for Vocabulary has been written as a practical introduction to corpus linguistics, with the aim of highlighting the usefulness of corpora for studying vocabulary and its use. As emphasized throughout all the chapters, vocabulary studies is a highly active field with a variety of issues that can be explored by means of corpus tools. Therefore, I would like to finish this book by encouraging you to explore the vast and multifaceted utility that corpus linguistics has to offer and undertake your own investigations in this fascinating area. In light of the increasing availability and functionality of corpora, it can be predicted that the number of individual students and teachers embarking on corpus-based projects will grow, and I certainly hope that *Corpus Linguistics for Vocabulary* will make a contribution in this regard as well.

References

Ädel, A. (2010). How to use corpus linguistics in the study of political discourse?, in A. O'Keeffe and M. McCarthy (eds.) *The Routledge Handbook of Corpus Linguistics*. London and New York: Routledge, 591–604.

Adolphs, S. and Carter, R. (2013). *Spoken Corpus Analysis: From monomodal to multimodal*. London and New York: Routledge.

Adolphs, S., Knight, D. and Carter, R. (2011). Capturing context for heterogeneous corpus analysis: Some first steps. *International Journal of Corpus Linguistics*, 16, 3, 305–324.

Baker, P. and Egbert, J. (eds.) (2016). *Triangulating Methodological Approaches in Corpus-linguistic Research*. New York and London: Routledge.

Bateman, J. A. (2013). Multimodal corpus-based approaches, in C. A. Chapelle (ed.) *The Encyclopedia of Applied Linguistics*. Oxford: Wiley, 1–9.

Biber, D., Egbert, J. and Davies, M. (2015). Exploring the composition of the searchable web: A corpus-based taxonomy of web registers. *Corpora*, 10, 1, 11–45.

Brezina, V., McEnery, T. and Wattam, S. (2015). Collocations in context: A new perspective on collocation networks. *International Journal of Corpus Linguistics*, 20, 2, 139–173.

Carter, R. (2012). *Vocabulary: Applied linguistic perspectives*. London and New York: Routledge.

Carter, R., McCarthy, M., Mark, G. and O'Keeffe, A. (2011). *English Grammar Today: With CD-Rom – An A–Z of spoken and written grammar*. Cambridge: Cambridge University Press.

Chung, T. M. and Nation, P. (2004). Identifying technical vocabulary. *System*, 32, 2, 251–263.

Egbert, J. (2016). *The Future of Corpus Linguistics*. A lecture given at Lancaster University. Available at http://www.lancaster.ac.uk/users/moocs/corpus/public/anniversary/future.htm.

Gardner, D. and Davies, M. (2014). A new Academic Vocabulary List. *Applied Linguistics*, 35, 3, 305–327.

Garnier, M. and Schmitt, N. (2015). The PhaVE List: A pedagogical list of phrasal verbs and their most frequent meaning senses. *Language Teaching Research*, 19, 6, 645–666.

Granger, S., Gilquin, G. and Meunier, M. (2015). Introduction: Learner corpus research – Past, present and future, in S. Granger, G. Gilquin and F. Meunier (eds.) *The Cambridge Handbook of Learner Corpus Research.* Cambridge: Cambridge University Press, 1–5.

Hoey, M. (2005). *Lexical Priming: A new theory of words and language.* London: Routledge.

Knight, D., Evans, D., Carter, R. and Adolphs, S. (2009). HeadTalk, HandTalk and the corpus: Towards a framework for multi-modal, multi-media corpus development. *Corpora*, 4, 1, 1–32.

McEnery, T. and Hardie, A. (2012). *Corpus Linguistics.* Cambridge: Cambridge University Press.

Mollin, S. (2009). "I entirely understand" is a Blairism: The methodology of identifying idiolectal collocations. *International Journal of Corpus Linguistics*, 14, 3, 367–392.

Nation, I. S. P. (2013). *Learning Vocabulary in Another Language.* Cambridge: Cambridge University Press.

Schmitt, N. (2010). *Researching Vocabulary: A research manual.* Basingstoke: Palgrave Macmillan.

Sinclair, J. (1991). *Corpus, Concordance, Collocation: Describing English language.* Oxford: Oxford University Press.

Siyanova, A. and Schmitt, N. (2007). Native and nonnative use of multi-word vs. one-word verbs. *International Review of Applied Linguistics in Language Teaching*, 45, 119–139.

Wulff, S., Gries, S. T. and Davies, M. (2010). Introduction, in S. T. Gries, S. Wulff and M. Davies (eds.) *Corpus-linguistic Applications: Current studies, new directions.* Rodopi: Amsterdam and New York, 1–6.

Glossary

affix   a morphological term which encompasses prefixes (morphemes added at the beginning of words) and suffixes (morphemes added at the end of words)

chunk   *see multiword unit*

colligation   the grammatical company of a word or phrase

collocation   the lexical company of a word or phrase

concordance line   a line of text taken from a corpus which presents a given search item together with its co-text

context   the parts of a text or situation that work together to convey meaning

corpus   a computerized collection of words

co-text   linguistic or textual surroundings of a given word which contribute to its meaning

data-driven learning (DDL)   direct use of corpus data in language teaching; originated by Tim Johns

discourse   a unit of language longer than a sentence

discourse marker   an item (a single word or phrase) which organizes texts and marks specific units of discourse

formulaic language   an umbrella term that is used to refer to different kinds of phraseological units found in natural language

formulaic sequence   *see multiword unit*

genre   a conventionalized form of language use that is associated with a specific discipline, institution or style

idiom principle   an idea which suggests that language users make extensive use of ready-made phrases or prefabricated chunks rather than creating them in a word-by-word manner; first proposed by John Sinclair (*see also open-choice principle*)

intertextuality   ways in which a given text or its fragments make references to other texts and elements of discourse

keyness   a kind of corpus analysis which explores the specificity of a given corpus by looking at its keywords; they are identified by comparing the frequency of words in a target vs. a reference corpus (usually a large general corpus)

key word in context (KWIC)   the most common format of presenting corpus data, in which the search word is displayed in the middle of short lines of text called concordances

lemma   a base form of a word together with its inflected forms

lexeme   an abstract term which underlies different grammatical variants of a word

lexical bundle   groups of words that tend to co-occur repeatedly in a specific type of discourse

lexical item   a unit consisting of multiple words which function as a whole; first proposed by John Sinclair

lexical priming   a psycholinguistic theory proposed by Michael Hoey which suggests that language experience determines language users' selection of words, phrases and patterns

lexical richness   a concept concerned with the quality and sophistication of vocabulary in a text or corpus; it is measured in several ways (e.g. via a type-token ratio)

lexico-grammar   a key notion in corpus linguistics which emphasizes the inseparability of grammar and lexis

lingua franca   a language that is used as a common means of communication by speakers representing different mother tongues

log-likelihood   a type of corpus statistic that is used to compare differences in word frequencies between corpora

morpheme   the smallest meaningful unit in language

multiword unit (MWU)   a lexical or lexico-grammatical unit which consists of two or more words but functions as a whole with a specific meaning

mutual information (MI)   a type of corpus statistic that is used to measure the strength of a partnership between words

n-gram   a contiguous sequence of n-words (e.g. 2-grams or 3-grams) found in a text or corpus

node   a search word or phrase that is presented in the center of a concordance line

open-choice principle   an idea which suggests that language users are unrestricted in their linguistic choices as long as they produce grammatical sentences; first proposed by John Sinclair (*see also idiom principle*)

parsing   the process of annotating a corpus for syntactic structures

pattern   a combination of language elements (both lexical and grammatical) which tend to repeatedly occur together

polysemy   the capacity of words and phrases which have multiple meanings

register   a specific type of language that is associated with a particular situation or context

rhetorical move   a pattern or fragment of a text which fulfills a specific communicative function; first introduced by John Swales

semantic preference   a typical semantic environment in which a word or phrase occurs

semantic prosody   pragmatic or discourse meanings of a word or phrase resulting from its phraseological patterning

span   the size of a search window that is used to find collocates of a word

speech act   an utterance that has a performative function in communications (e.g. apologizing or complimenting)

tagging   the process of adding codes with linguistic information to all words in a corpus

T-score   a type of corpus statistic which is used to identify collocations

T-test   a statistical test that is used to compare two groups to determine whether they are statistically different

token   each occurrence of a word or phrase in a corpus

type   all unique words in a corpus

type-token ratio   a type of corpus statistic which is a measure of lexical richness; this ratio is obtained by dividing the number of types by the number of tokens in a corpus word a sequence of letters surrounded by empty spaces or punctuation marks

word family   a base form of a word together with its inflected forms and transparent derivatives

word form   a term used to refer to different realizations of one lexeme

wordlist   a list of words ranked according to their frequency in a corpus

Commentary on tasks

There are over 11,000 occurrences of 'abroad' in COCA so your analysis of the patterning of the word 'abroad' will be limited to a selection of concordances (e.g. 100 lines). Examples of recurrent chunks that the word occurs in include: 'at home and abroad', 'from abroad', 'go abroad', 'live abroad', 'study abroad', 'travel abroad'.

Word	Frequency in COCA
wall	77,018
outlook	7,774
chimney	1,953
favorably	1,804
harmonize	424

Task 4.2: Using the chart option of the BYU-BNC interface, compare the frequency of 'you', 'right' and 'now' in the spoken and academic sections of the BNC.

	Spoken BNC	Academic BNC
you	268,290 (26,926.84 per mil)	10,512 (686.64 per mil)
right	34,891 (3,501.82 per mil)	7,204 (469.88 per mil)
now	30,134 (3,024.39 per mil)	9,712 (633.46 per mil)

We can clearly see that the three words have a higher frequency in the spoken section of the corpus.

Task 4.3: Check the frequency of 'you know' and 'I see' in COCA and compare it with the frequency of most commonly occurring words from the following list: http://www.wordfrequency.info/free.asp.

'You know' has 367,470 occurrences in COCA. This is similar to the frequency of the word 'back', which is the 104th most frequent word in the corpus.

'I see' has 27,457 occurrences in COCA. This is similar to the frequency of the word 'historical', which is 1480th most frequent word in the corpus.

Task 4.4: Using the BYU-BNC interface, check the frequency of the following items and decide whether they belong to basic- or advanced-level vocabulary. Which pedagogical criteria will you take into account?

	Type frequency in the BNC	Frequency band based on Nation's (2006) 1,000-word BNC lists	Type of vocabulary based on Schmitt and Schmitt's (2014) framework	Type of vocabulary based on O'Keeffe et al.'s (2007) pedagogical considerations
As well	30,107	1st 1,000	High-frequency	Basic vocabulary
Debate	7,945	2nd 1,000	High-frequency	Basic vocabulary
In spite of	2,692	4th 1,000	Mid-frequency	Basic vocabulary

(continued)

(continued)

	Type frequency in the BNC	Frequency band based on Nation's (2006) 1,000-word BNC lists	Type of vocabulary based on Schmitt and Schmitt's (2014) framework	Type of vocabulary based on O'Keeffe et al.'s (2007) pedagogical considerations
As usual	1,326	6th 1,000	Mid-frequency	Basic/advanced vocabulary
Motorway	1,372	6th 1,000	Mid-frequency	Basic/advanced vocabulary
Shuffle	593	10th 1,000	Low-frequency	Advanced vocabulary

> Task 5.1: Explore the most frequent collocations of the word 'back' in COCA. Treat 'back' as a node and try to find examples of upward or downward collocates. Do your results confirm Sinclair's (1991) findings?

The frequency of 'back' in COCA is 655,389.

> Examples of upward collocates: the (289,187), to (242,997), and (167,436), come (35,497)

> Examples of downward collocates: welcome (7,764), bring (7,557), put (7,543)

> Task 5.2: Use the BYU-BNC interface to compare the frequency of two colligational patterns around the verb 'hear': 'hear + pronoun + bare infinitive' and 'hear + pronoun + gerund'. Which pattern is more frequent? Is there a difference in the meaning that is conveyed depending on which colligation is chosen?

> [hear] + pronoun + bare infinitive occurs 761 times in the BNC
> [hear] + pronoun + verb-ing occurs 353 times

In traditional grammars it is often said that [hear] + verb-ing is used to emphasize that the action is not complete (it is in progress), while [hear] + bare infinitive indicates that the speaker experienced the whole event.

Task 5.3: Look at the sample of concordances from COCA displayed in Figure 5.7 and explore the colligational behavior of the phrase 'so far'. What grammatical tenses does it occur with?

'So far' tends to occur with the present perfect tense.

Task 5.4: Using the BYU-COCA interface, search for examples of colligations (verbs, nouns and adjectives) around the preposition 'for'.

The first ten most frequent verbal colligations with 'for': 'looking for', 'waiting for', 'pay for', 'look for', 'is for', 'used for', 'work for', 'known for', 'called for', 'wait for'.

The first ten most frequent adjectival colligations with 'for': 'responsible for', 'good for', 'ready for', 'important for', 'available for', 'difficult for', 'necessary for', 'hard for', 'sorry for', 'possible for'.

The first ten most frequent nominal colligations with 'for': 'time for', 'need for', 'center for', 'support for', 'thanks for', 'reason for', 'money for', 'room for', 'way for', 'responsibility for'.

Task 5.6: Using the academic section of the BYU-COCA corpus, check the frequency of the following ten lexical bundles taken from Durrant's (2015) study. Are there any interesting patterns in the way they are distributed across different academic disciplines?

Quite conveniently, the BYU interface allows you to view the frequency of words and phrases across a number of academic disciplines. First, use the 'Chart' option to see the frequency of a given lexical bundle in the different sections of the corpus. Next, click on 'academic' to check the occurrence of the bundles across different academic disciplines. As demonstrated in the table below, most of the items exhibit different frequency patterns depending on which discipline they are used in. Interestingly, out of the ten items, only 'the presence of the' exhibits differences in terms of its frequency. In COCA, this phrase occurs with the highest frequency in humanities, while in Durrant's (2015) study, which was based on the British Academic Written English Corpus (BAWE), its highest rate of occurrence was found in science and technology.

	Frequency in academic COCA	Discipline with the highest frequency
the presence of a	858	medicine
the presence of the	782	humanities
on the surface of	283	science/technology
the shape of the	362	medicine
at the bottom of	507	miscellaneous followed by science/technology
of the concept of	407	humanities
the existence of a	701	law/political science
the existence of the	416	law/political science
the fact that it	568	philosophy/religion followed by humanities
the form of the	519	humanities

Task 6.4: You prepare an English class and you want your students to study phrasal verbs that contain the prepositions 'up' and 'down'. Using the BYU-COCA interface, look for examples of such verbs in American English and select concordances that will serve as a basis for the class.

Some of the most frequent examples of phrasal verbs with the particle 'up' include: 'set up', 'come up', 'pick up', 'grow up', 'end up'. It is worth noting that 'come up' can also co-occur with the preposition 'with' to form a different phrasal verb: 'come up with'.

Some of the most frequent examples of phrasal verbs with the particle 'down' include: 'sit down', 'go down', 'shut down', 'come down', 'look down'. Note that 'look down' tends to be followed by the preposition 'at' to form a three-word verb 'look down at'.

Task 7.2: Using the ICNALE online interface (http://language.sakura.ne.jp/icnale/online.html), look for examples of collocations with the verb 'make'. Try to find some examples produced by different LI groups of Asian learners as well as native speakers of English.

Examples of the most frequent collocations of 'make' produced by Japanese EFL learners: make money, make friends

Examples of the most frequent collocations of 'make' produced by Korean EFL learners: make money, make sense

Examples of the most frequent collocations of 'make' produced by Taiwanese EFL learners: make money, make friends

Examples of the most frequent collocations of 'make' produced by native-speaker students: make money, make sure

> **Task 7.3:** Using the Asian Corpus of English (http://corpus.ied.edu.hk/ace/index.php?m=search&a=index), find examples of the use of two discourse markers: 'from my point of view' and 'so to speak'. Are these conventional or approximate forms of chunks?

The corpus contains two conventional forms of 'from my point of view' and six of 'so to speak' (the interface displays seven examples of 'so to speak' but one of them is duplicated).

> **Task 8.1:** Using the 'sections' option on the BYU-COCA interface, compare the most frequent verbs in two different registers of English: fiction vs. academic. Figure 8.1 shows how to conduct this search, with frequency as a sorting criterion. How much do the data from the two registers differ from each other? Once you have made some initial observations, carry out a similar analysis for other word classes (e.g. adjectives).

Corpus of Contemporary American English

SEC 1 (FICTION): 104,900,827 WORDS

	WORD/PHRASE	TOKENS 1	TOKENS 2	PM 1	PM 2	RATIO
1	SAID	445158	34882	4,243.6	337.3	12.6
2	KNOW	193097	32626	1,840.8	315.5	5.8
3	GET	153018	26939	1,458.7	260.5	5.6
4	SEE	151012	77831	1,439.6	752.6	1.9
5	GO	122022	21566	1,163.2	208.5	5.6
6	GOT	118623	7778	1,130.8	75.2	15.0
7	THINK	110739	26337	1,055.7	254.7	4.1
8	LOOKED	106536	5382	1,015.6	52.0	19.5
9	GOING	104836	15759	999.4	152.4	6.6
10	COME	102475	26139	976.9	252.7	3.9
11	SAY	99279	22674	946.4	219.2	4.3
12	MADE	98685	59770	940.7	577.9	1.6
13	WANT	97795	19940	932.3	192.8	4.8
14	THOUGHT	88960	12936	848.0	125.1	6.8
15	MAKE	64839	57606	808.8	557.0	1.5
16	ASKED	82665	22334	788.0	216.0	3.6
17	KNEW	82440	7804	785.9	75.5	10.4
18	TAKE	82177	38356	783.4	370.9	2.1
19	CAME	80755	18565	769.8	179.5	4.3
20	TELL	77963	9043	743.2	87.4	8.5

SEC 2 (ACADEMIC): 103,421,981 WORDS

	WORD/PHRASE	TOKENS 2	TOKENS 1	PM 2	PM 1	RATIO
1	USED	80325	17003	776.7	162.1	4.8
2	SEE	77831	151012	752.6	1,439.6	0.5
3	FOUND	63948	51435	618.3	490.3	1.3
4	MADE	59770	98685	577.9	940.7	0.6
5	MAKE	57606	84839	557.0	808.8	0.7
6	USING	56490	8879	546.2	84.6	6.5
7	PROVIDE	45067	2705	435.8	25.8	16.9
8	BASED	44429	2421	429.6	23.1	18.6
9	USE	42305	17381	409.1	165.7	2.5
10	BECOME	40535	19153	391.9	182.6	2.1
11	TAKE	38356	82177	370.9	783.4	0.5
12	REPORTED	35301	2201	341.3	21.0	16.3
13	SAID	34882	445158	337.3	4,243.6	0.1
14	GIVEN	32940	17196	318.5	163.9	1.9
15	KNOW	32626	193097	315.5	1,840.8	0.2
16	HELP	31635	31838	305.9	303.5	1.0
17	INCLUDE	31388	1579	303.5	15.1	20.2
18	NEED	30601	41980	295.9	400.2	0.7
19	INCLUDED	29993	2520	290.0	24.0	12.1
20	SAYS	29885	65156	289.0	621.1	0.5

Figure 8.1a Answer to Task 8.1

The results are color-coded, with green indicating words that are more frequent in the fiction section as compared to the academic section. In contrast, the pink color indicates words that have a distinctively low frequency in the academic section of the corpus relative to the fiction section (see the column called 'ratio'). For instance, the verbs 'said', 'know' and 'get' have a much higher frequency in fiction, while the verbs 'provide', 'based' or 'reported' are more academic as they are found more frequently in academic texts.

As far as adjectives are concerned, fiction texts exhibit a high occurrence of words such as 'little', 'big' or 'sure'. In turn, academic texts are characterized by words such as 'social', 'significant' or 'economic'. These are clear differences which demonstrate that the use of vocabulary is largely register-dependent.

Task 8.2: Use the classic version of the VocabProfile program (http://www.lextutor.ca/vp/comp/) to identify examples of academic words from Coxhead's AWL list in two different online articles: one about sport and the other about health. Which text contains more examples of academic vocabulary?

Figure 8.2a Answer to Task 8.2 academic words in a text about sport

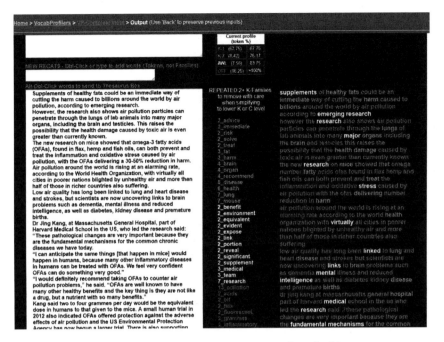

Figure 8.2b Answer to Task 8.2 academic words in a text about health

These vocabulary profiles (see the 'Current profile' tables at the top) demonstrate that the text about health appears to be more demanding lexically than the text about sport, if we take the frequency of general and academic vocabulary as an indicator of difficulty. More specifically, while the text about health contains many high-frequency words at the first and second 1,000 frequency level, it contains more academic (AWL) vocabulary.

Examples of academic words in a text about sport: 'assume', 'confirm', 'investigate'.

Examples of academic words in a text about health: 'benefit', 'environment', 'equivalent'.

Task 8.3: Table 8.1 displays the first twenty most frequent word families from the AWL and the AVL. What do these lists reveal about academic vocabulary? Are there any similarities between the two lists?

Most of the items on both lists are nouns but none of them are shared by both lists. This is likely to result from differences in the methodologies employed to create the AWL and AVL.

> Task 8.4: Use the Analyze text tool available at http://www.wordandphrase.info/academic/analyzeText.asp to explore the distribution of academic words in the text about health you selected for Task 8.2. Does it contain any examples of AVL words?

This screenshot presents examples of AVL words from the online article about health used in Task 8.2. The words are divided into two frequency ranges: Range 1 (1–500 most frequent words from the AVL, presented in yellow) and Range 2 (501–3,000 most frequent words from the AVL, presented in green). The words 'emerging' or 'research' belong to Range 1, while Range 2 includes examples such as 'according' or 'known'. All the words highlighted in red can be treated as technical vocabulary.

> Task 8.5: Compare the frequencies of the top five lexical bundles from the AFL in the academic vs. non-academic sections of COCA. Use Rayson's online corpus calculator (http://ucrel.lancs.ac.uk/llwizard.html) to check whether the frequency values differ in terms of statistical significance.

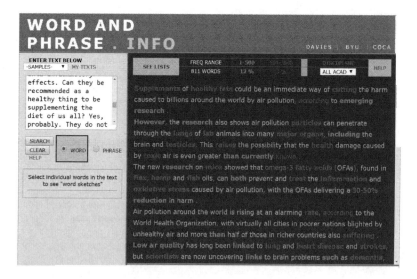

Figure 8.4a Answer to Task 8.4

	Frequency in academic COCA*	Frequency in academic COCA per million word	Frequency in non-academic COCA**	Frequency in non-academic COCA per million word	Log-likelihood
in terms of	15,306	148	25,236	58.6	+7363***
at the same time	9,196	88.9	24,901	57.9	+1155***
from the point of view	461	4.9	494	1.3	+403***
in order to	20,546	198.7	24,186	56.2	+16141***
as well as	38,612	373.3	52,620	122.3	+25088***

* the size of academic COCA is 103,421,981 words
** the size of non-academic COCA is 430,366,951 words
*** significant difference at p < .05

All the five lexical bundles occur with a higher frequency in the academic section of the corpus, which is confirmed by the significant values of the log-likelihood tests.

> **Task 9.1:** Using data from the academic section of COCA, find examples of concordances in which the word 'fact' contributes to lexical cohesion.

Sample concordances that demonstrate the textual role of the noun 'fact':

Year	Source text	Concordance
2015	ReadingImprovement	LeBlanca & Bearison, 2004). Questions from tutees may alert tutors to the **fact** that the tutors themselves do not fully understand aspects of the concept or task.
2015	ReadingImprovement	at Time 1 or 2. Because of these repeated measure ANOVA results and the **fact** that the mean for fluency accuracy and rate at Time 3 was greater for the
2015	PlasticSurgery	low response rate included the large number of undeliverable messages (>100) and the **fact** that all family physicians, regardless of whether they performed emergency work, were included
2015	PlasticSurgery	, 29). However, the impact of such findings is mitigated by the **fact** that the majority of these studies used nonvalidated aesthetic scoring scales and lacked

(continued)

(continued)

Year	Source text	Concordance
2015	ReadingImprovement	the present study, as well as the results of previous research, and the **fact** that the SMILA approach is based on well-established principles of effective reading instruction, we
2015	ReadingImprovement	and interventions must incorporate multiple domains to influence multiple early literacy skills. # The **fact** that Group 1 (SIMI) also showed the largest gains

---

Task 9.2: Figure 9.2 presents a short fragment of a conversation from the spoken section of COCA that represents the use of the word 'smashing'. The conversation took place during a TV show presented by Sean Hannity on Fox News. Can you identify any examples of lexical repetition and relexicalization?

Examples of repetition and relexicalization have been bolded.

ROVE: I think that now means that — again, I'm finding it difficult to find the right place here, but that would put McCain over 800, 826. And he would need — this number wrong here at the bottom. He now needs less than 270 votes in order to get the nomination.

WALLACE: So **he's really on his way?**

ROVE: **He's on his way.**

WALLACE: Let's talk about the Democratic side. I mean, we're talking about a **smashing Obama victory** in Virginia, a **very healthy victory** in Maryland. The fact that we're able to call it so quickly. Is Hillary Clinton in trouble?

ROVE: Absolutely. But, again, remember the proportionality of the Democratic contest rules means that tonight she came in **roughly**, according to the FOX News count, up 23 delegates. If he continues this tonight, basically two to one victories, he will come out — he'll pick up **roughly** 50 delegates.

Task 9.3: There are seventy-nine occurrences of the phrase 'further research' in the academic section of the BNC. Do any of them confirm the findings of Flowerdew and Forest?

Examples of concordances that demonstrate the signaling function of the phrase 'further research':

Type of language	Discipline	Concordance
written	medicine	The obligate activator apo-C II has been shown to result in poor activation of lipoprotein lipase in vitro when present in very low or excess amounts in VLDL. Excess of Apo-C III 2 has also been demonstrated in diabetic subjects with severe hypertriglyceridaemia (Holdsworth et al, 1982). Catabolism of VLDL by lipoprotein lipase is impaired in vitro with this C-apoprotein abnormality and may therefore produce a clearance defect in vivo. **Further research** is needed in this area and it is possible that important abnormalities in the' modulating' apoproteins may be found.
written	medicine	Such monitoring might help provide feedback to the service on its effectiveness. However, the main use would be to identify groups of patients to whom special attention should be paid because of changing patterns of self-poisoning and self-injury in the area. There are a number of other needs associated with the problem of attempted suicide. Apart from a general improvement in clinical services, **further research** is required to evaluate the effectiveness of different methods of managing patients after they have left hospital. In particular, more still needs to be known about the characteristics of patients most likely to benefit from treatment. We now know that special aftercare can benefit women, but male attempters appear more difficult to help. Further work is required to find new therapeutic methods for men. Child and adolescent attempters are a group with special requirements, and careful thought should be given to how best to meet their needs.
written	medicine	More comprehensive interventions than school health education alone will be needed to reduce teenage smoking. Other measures including further restrictions on access to cigarettes and on the promotion of tobacco products need to be considered. **Further research** will be needed to develop effective school based health education projects, which should be formally field tested under normal conditions before widespread dissemination.

Task 9.4: Compare the frequency of the following discourse markers in the spoken and written subsections of COCA.

	Frequency in spoken COCA*	Frequency in spoken COCA per million word	Frequency in written COCA**	Frequency in written COCA per million word	Log-likelihood
you know	296,608	2,711.4	70,862	167.0	+612438***
I mean	111,167	1,016.2	20,826	49.1	+246875***
actually	75,427	689.5	71,592	168.7	+68238***
right	295,214	2,698.7	293,234	690.9	+254606***
in other words	5,120	46.8	11,568	27.3	+959***
so to speak	1,279	11.7	1,602	3.8	+831***

* the size of spoken COCA is 109,391,643 words
** the size of written COCA is 424,397,289 words
*** significant difference at p < .05

All the six examples occur with a higher frequency in the spoken section of the corpus, which is confirmed by the significant values of the log-likelihood tests.

Task 9.5: Using data from the spoken part of COCA, analyze how the speech act of apologizing can be realized by means of different lexical units.

Examples of lexical forms that participate in the realization of the pragmatic function of apologizing:

We sincerely apologize
I apologize
I'd like to apologize
I want to apologize
I apologize for that
We want to apologize for
Sorry
Sorry about that
I'm sorry
I'm very sorry

Task 9.6: Figure 9.4 presents a selection of concordance lines for the phrase 'true feelings' taken from the BNC. Explore the semantic prosody of the phrase in terms of how it fulfills the discourse function of expressing reluctance or inability.

here are fifty-three occurrences of the phrase 'true feelings' in the BNC. Here is sample of some of them.

No of concordance	KWIC
1	problems, especially the er, he hasn't actually dealt with the **true feelings** that he had towards his father, and who instead chose to vent his rage
2	and Hari realized that he had used the laugh many times to conceal his **true feelings.'** I won't promise anything,' she said following him,'
3	I've dared set my will against his. And if they guess my **true feelings** – 'They'll say nothing. Not in public, at least, if you make
4	distracted. A refusal in such circumstances may well not reflect my employer's **true feelings** on the matter, but once having sustained such a dismissal, I could not
5	his safety was almost too much to bear. She tried to mask her **true feelings** from her mother and sister, but her throat ached with tension and she felt
6	Joan's seeming ill-humour was a ploy to conceal even from herself her **true feelings** – the quickening of her pulses at mention of the beloved, told a different
7	be ashamed of snobbishness – or perhaps I only taught him to keep his **true feelings** from me. But he remained – though I'm sure he honestly fought against
8	one of nature's radicals, someone to whom he could reveal his new **true feelings**. As for his own talk – that, once begun, had, as
9	Hope smiled to himself: the smile broadened, and to disguise his **true feelings** he turned the smile on Mr Crump; who was greatly encouraged as he had
10	before the Armistice was signed, she realised that she had been denying her **true feelings** for years. She had loved Connor from the day she set eyes on him
11	you do whatever you wish.' Stephen's controlled voice disguised his **true feelings**, but Christina sensed his jealousy and changed the subject.' Why don't
12	you're probably a very good husband, but you like to hide your **true feelings**." Oh, don't be so serious, Basil,' smiled
13	a statement of fact. Dexter was surprised that the TV presenter revealed her **true feelings** towards Nicola so quickly: most people in his experience,
14	'd ever seen, but which she always felt quite at odds with her **true feelings**. In fact, there were lots of things she'd like to change about
15	turned, looking at the girl, smiling at her reassuringly, keeping his **true feelings** from showing. Games. It was all one big game to DeVore.

By looking at the collocates of 'true feelings', we can see that it is precede
by many negative verbs such as 'disguise', 'without revealing', 'not admit their
'hiding your', 'conceal'. This confirms Sinclair's observations about the negativ
semantic prosody of 'true feelings' as a way of expressing speakers' reluctance to
reveal what they feel.

Index